AIR POWER'S LOST CAUSE

AIR POWER'S LOST CAUSE
The American Air Wars of Vietnam

Brian D. Laslie

ROWMAN & LITTLEFIELD
Lanham • Boulder • New York • London

Published by Rowman & Littlefield
An imprint of The Rowman & Littlefield Publishing Group, Inc.
4501 Forbes Boulevard, Suite 200, Lanham, Maryland 20706
www.rowman.com

86-90 Paul Street, London EC2A 4NE

British Library Cataloguing in Publication Information Available

Library of Congress Cataloging-in-Publication Data

Names: Laslie, Brian D., author.
Title: Air power's lost cause : the American air wars of Vietnam / Brian D. Laslie.
Other titles: American air wars of Vietnam
Description: Lanham : Rowman & Littlefield, [2021] | Series: War and society | Includes
    bibliographical references and index.
Identifiers: LCCN 2020049448 (print) | LCCN 2020049449 (ebook) | ISBN
    9781442274341 (cloth) | ISBN 9781442274358 (epub) | ISBN 9781538189207
    (paperback)
Subjects: LCSH: Vietnam War, 1961-1975—Aerial operations, American. | Air power—
    United States—History. | United States. Air Force—History—Vietnam War, 1961-
    1975. | United States. Navy—History—Vietnam War, 1961-1975. | Vietnam War,
    1961-1975—Naval operations, American.
Classification: LCC DS558.8 .L365 2021 (print) | LCC DS558.8 (ebook) | DDC
    959.704/3480973—dc23
LC record available at https://lccn.loc.gov/2020049448
LC ebook record available at https://lccn.loc.gov/2020049449

In the fall of 1997 I took my first class with Dr. Kyle Sinisi. Between 1997 and May of 2001, I took numerous classes with both "Captain" Kyle Sinisi and Colonel/Brigadier General Michael Barrett. In the spring of 2021 I published this book in their series. For pushing me to be a better historian for over twenty years and helping me every step of the way, I dedicate this book to them.

You have a row of dominoes set up; you knock over the first one, and what will happen to the last one is that it will go over very quickly.

—President Dwight D. Eisenhower

My solution to the problem would be to tell them frankly that they've got to draw in their horns and stop their aggression or we're going to bomb them back into the Stone Ages.

—General Curtis E. LeMay, *Mission with LeMay: My Story*

Contents

Acknowledgments

A LIST OF ACKNOWLEDGMENTS IS just like an acceptance speech at the Academy Awards, with two exceptions: having more time to get it right, and the lack of a gold statue to sit on my desk.

I would first like to thank Dr. Kyle Sinisi and Brigadier General Michael Barrett at The Citadel. They invited me into this project and were both professors of mine when I was an undergraduate there. Not only for this work, but for a lifetime of learning, I am in their debt.

Dr. Robert Thompson III helped get this project started and was always able to answer any questions I had about the "ground" war in Vietnam. Dr. Michael Hankins of the Smithsonian National Air and Space Museum spent many hours reading this manuscript and many more on the phone with me, discussing it. His talent and contributions toward helping me to coalesce ideas and concepts are immeasurable. Dr. John Terino also went through this manuscript with a fine-tooth comb, and I am forever grateful.

As with every other book I have written, special thanks goes to the Clark Special Collections Branch at the US Air Force Academy library. I would never have been able to do this work without the help of the director, Dr. Mary Ruwell. As the project came to a close, Dr. Judith Henchy, head of the Southeast Asia Center at the University of Washington, graciously helped to locate sources that spoke to the perspective of North Vietnamese participants.

The great team at the Air Force Historical Research Agency (AFHRA) under Dr. Charlie O'Connell and Dr. Dixie Dysart helped with primary source location, both with original documents and turning many of them into digital format. These stellar members included Sam Shearin, Leander Morris,

Tammy Horton, and Maranda Gilmore. I have to single out Sam Shearin, as his prowess in responding to random e-mails remains unmatched in the modern era. I would be remiss if I didn't mention a few others here, including Sheon Montgomery at the Vietnam Archive at Texas Tech, and Edwin E. Moïse and his superb Vietnam bibliography.

Many men were willing to share their histories and perspectives with me, including Mr. C. R. "Lucky" Anderegg; General Merrill McPeak, former chief of staff of the US Air Force; and Fred Smith, among others. At the Air Force Association, Mr. Chet Curtis aided in tracking down the Misty Fast-FAC Pilots Panel from 2011.

Finally, I would like to thank the terrific team at Rowman & Littlefield, including Katelyn Turner, Melissa Hayes, Janice Braunstein—and, especially—my editor, Susan McEachern, for sticking with this book to the end. As always, the greatest thanks and acknowledgments go to my wife, Heather, and my daughters, Savannah and Aspen.

Abbreviations

AAA	antiaircraft artillery
AAR	after-action report
ACM	air combat maneuvering
AD	air division
ADVON	Advanced Echelon
AGM	air guided missile
AIM	air intercept missile
Air Cav	air cavalry
Airmobile	infantry units arriving on the battlefield via helicopter, usually UH-1s
AOC	air operations center
APC	armored personnel carrier
ARVN	Army of the Republic of Vietnam
Bandit	confirmed enemy aircraft
BARCAP	Barrier Combat Air Patrol
BDA	bomb damage assessment
Bingo	minimum fuel call
Bird Dog	forward air controller in an O-1
B/N	bombardier/navigator
Bullseye	location used by pilots to denote position; typically Hanoi
BVR	beyond visual range
CAP	combat air patrol
CAS	close air support

CBU	cluster bomb unit
CHECO	Contemporary Historical Examination of Current Operations
CIA	Central Intelligence Agency
CINC	Commander in Chief
CINCPAC	Commander in Chief, Pacific
CINCPACAF	Commander in Chief, United States Air Force, Pacific
CINCPACFLT	Commander in Chief, Pacific Fleet
CJCS	Chairman, Joint Chiefs of Staff
CMC	Commandant of the Marine Corps
CNO	Chief of Naval Operations
College Eye	EC-121 airborne command-and-control aircraft
CORDS	civil operations and revolutionary development support
COSVN	Central Office for South Vietnam
CRP	control and reporting station
CSAF	Chief of Staff of the Air Force
DACT	Dissimilar Air Combat Training
DCS	Deputy Chief of Staff
DIA	Defense Intelligence Agency
Disco	EC-121 airborne command-and-control aircraft
DMZ	Demilitarized Zone
Dust-off	medical evacuation via helicopter
ECM	electronic countermeasure
FAC	forward air controller
GCI	ground control intercept
GIB	guy in back; weapons system operator; also RIO or WSO
GPES	ground parachute (or proximity) extraction system
GVN	Government of (South) Vietnam
HARM	high-speed anti-radiation missile
HOTAS	hands-on throttle and stick
HUD	heads-up display
IADS	Integrated Air Defense System
IFF	identify friend or foe
JCS	Joint Chiefs of Staff
JCSM	Joint Chiefs of Staff Memorandum
JFACC	joint force air component commander
LAPES	low-altitude parachute-extraction system
LGB	laser-guided bomb
LOC	lines of communication

LORAN	long-range navigation
LZ	landing zone
MACV	Military Assistance Command, Vietnam
MiG	Mikoyan and Gurevich (МиГ) Design Bureau aircraft
MiGCAP	MiG combat air patrol
NLF	National Liberation Front
NFO	naval flight officer (*see* RIO)
NVAF	North Vietnam Air Force
NVN	North Vietnam
PAVN	People's Army of North Vietnam
PDJ	Plaine des Jarres (Plain of Jars)
PGM	precision-guided munitions
PIRAZ	positive identification radar advisory zone
PLAAF	People's Liberation Army Air Force (China)
POW	prisoner of war
RESCAP	rescue combat air patrol
RHAW	radar homing and warning
RIO	US Navy "GIB"; the radar intercept officer
RP	route package
RVN	Republic of Vietnam
RVNAF	Republic of Vietnam Armed Forces
SA-2	Soviet-made surface-to-air missile
SAC	Strategic Air Command
SACLO	Strategic Air Command Liaison Officer
SAM	surface-to-air missile
SAR	search and rescue
SEA	Southeast Asia
SEAD	suppression of enemy air defense
SNIE	Special National Intelligence Estimate
SVN	South Vietnam
TAC	Tactical Air Command
TACAN	Tactical Air Navigation System
TFR	terrain following radar
TRADOC	US Army Training and Doctrine Command
TTP	tactics, techniques, and procedures
USG	United States Government
USIA	United States Information Agency
USSR	Union of the Soviet Socialist Republics/Soviet Union
VC	Viet Cong

VM	Viet Minh
VN	Vietnam
VNAF	South Vietnamese Air Force
WEZ	weapons employment zone
WSO	USAF GIB; weapons system operator
YGBSM	you gotta be shitting me

Introduction

A T THE VIETNAM MILITARY HISTORY MUSEUM, located in the middle of Vietnam's capital city of Hanoi, stands a monument formed from collected and assembled parts and pieces of American military aircraft lost during what Americans commonly refer to as the Vietnam War. It is composed of siding from the giant B-52 Stratofortress bombers; the wings, engines, tails, and fuselages from tactical fighter aircraft; and the hulls of helicopters. At its summit stands the back end of an aircraft, where the fuselage meets the horizontal stabilizers like some kind of macabre cross. Clearly visible in the wreckage are an American roundel of a white star on a blue field, as well as the emblem of the Tactical Air Command, the US Air Force command responsible for the training and equipping of fighter pilots in the 1960s. The monument represents North Vietnamese victory as much as it demonstrates American losses, if not outright defeat.

R. W. Komer said in the introduction to Thomas Thayer's groundbreaking *War Without Fronts* that Vietnam "was so different as hardly to be explicable in conventional military terms. . . . It was a multi-dimensional politico-military conflict encompassing not only out-of-country bombing and a 'main force' war of more or less conventional forces, but a guerrilla struggle, a clandestine terror campaign, and the like." Into this morass I decided to explain the air wars that took place in Southeast Asia from 1961 to 1975.

When I expressed concern to a colleague over the complexity of air power in Vietnam, himself a scholar of pacification in the conflict, he replied, "If Vietnam has taught me anything, it is that the more complex the problem, the better the story." His response reminded me of the 1986 comedy film

Back to School, where Professor Terguson, played by stand-up comedian Sam Kinison, said at the introduction to his history course, "So why don't we dive right in by interpreting one of the easiest events in the last twenty years of American history. Now can someone tell me why in 1975, we pulled our troops out of Vietnam?" A student in the front row answered the question, saying, "The failure of Vietnamization to win popular support caused an ongoing erosion of confidence in the various American but illegal Saigon regimes." I asked myself, was she, the student, correct? Was that all there was to it? If so, how was air power used, or ill-used, in an attempt to reach that goal?[1]

Air power—the use of military aircraft to achieve an effect—was just one of the many political tools used against America's enemies during this conflict (obligatory tip of the hat to Carl von Clausewitz). In a way, air power represented the most iconic aspect of the Vietnam War: F-4 Phantoms and F-105 Thunderchiefs, napalm exploding in dense jungles, and the ubiquitous UH-1 Huey helicopters disgorging soldiers into rice paddies or on top of mud-covered hills. When an American hears the word *Vietnam*, these are likely as not the images that come to mind even for the generations born after—including the author—the conflict ended.

Historian Wayne Thompson said the war in Vietnam is the "tale of air power badly used." It seems obvious with the virtue of hindsight that the reason for this was the disjointed nature of *how* American political and military leaders decided to use air power. During the US involvement in Southeast Asia, what is traditionally referred to by Americans as the "Vietnam War," rather than the Second Indochina War, and to the people of Vietnam as the *Khang chien chong My* (the American War), there were no less than *six* different air wars. At least, the military services acted as if there were six separate air wars rather than a cohesive air war. These were 1) the air-to-ground war in North Vietnam (strategic air campaigns), including major operations Rolling Thunder, Linebacker I, and Linebacker II (taken together, these are typically known as the "out-country war"); 2) the air-to-air war in North Vietnam, itself an outgrowth of the strategic bombing war against the North; 3) the air-to-ground war in South Vietnam (the in-country war); 4) the US Navy's air-to-air and air-to-ground war in North Vietnam/South Vietnam (fundamentally different enough from the USAF's that it deserves separate treatment, and interservice rivalry was so fierce that it may as well have been a totally separate war); 5) the "secret" air wars in Laos and Cambodia; and 6) the US Army's air mobile war.

Instead of a combined aerial effort, the services treated each of the above air wars as separate entities. Military leaders even divided North Vietnam into sections, called Route Packages, and fought the war as individual contests, many times in a battle against each other instead of the enemy. It was nothing short of disjointed and ineffective.[2]

The natural question arises, was this disjointed and ineffective use of air power preventable? If the answer is yes, what should control of air power have looked like during Vietnam, and would a different command-and-control structure have made any difference to the eventual outcome of the conflict? The first question is certainly easier to answer than the second or third, and the reply is a resounding *Yes!* Less than two decades after the Vietnam War ended, the United States and other allies fought an air and ground war against the country of Iraq after its invasion of Kuwait, which provides us with one possible and successful example of what command and control of the air war might have looked like.

The overall commander of the campaign, General Norman Schwarzkopf, led the combined air, land, and sea forces. His joint force air component commander (JFACC; pronounced *jay-fack*) was US Air Force Lieutenant General Charles Horner. Horner commanded not only the air force assets in the region, but also navy and marine aircraft as well. As the overall air commander he had control of each service's aircraft and was able to apportion and allocate them as needed to conduct a unified air operation against the enemy. His ability to do so was a direct result of the failures of command and control in Vietnam and the fundamental changes made to doctrine in the wake of that war.

As to my third question, would a combined effort of air assets have made the air wars of Vietnam turn out any differently? That is a significantly more difficult question to answer, and as one colleague pointed out, counterfactuals are not a job for a historian. After all, there were ground and naval forces engaged in large numbers in the conflict, as well, and their role was far from negligible.

This book is about the air war in Vietnam, or what might better be called *the air wars of Southeast Asia*. The aim of this book is to tell the complete history of these air wars from the beginning of American involvement until final withdrawal. It is about the strategic, operational, and tactical levels of war. Although it is impossible to divorce war from politics, especially in the case of American air power used during Vietnam, this work seeks to keep political discussions in their own arena, knowing the success of that effort is difficult given the proclivity of senior administration officials to pick tactical targets over a lunchtime meeting. This book will also look at the air war from the perspective of the North Vietnamese Air Force, as well—at least as much as possible, given the paucity of sources.

No overarching air campaign or cohesive air strategy existed for the duration of American participation in the conflict in Vietnam (including South

Vietnam, North Vietnam, Laos, and Cambodia), which thus undermined employment of air power. Although air power used differently might not have changed the ultimate outcome of the war, it would have provided—for those who fought the war—a more-cohesive understanding of how air power was being employed. That being said, the air wars that occurred during what Americans call the Vietnam War were ultimately unwinnable, and the way in which the war has been remembered represents a "Lost Cause" of air power.

Air Power's Lost Cause will look at how American air forces (army, navy, air force, and marines) approached and conducted the air war in Vietnam, but time will also be given to examining the day-to-day lives of the American fliers living on bases in South Vietnam and Thailand, and aboard ships in the Gulf of Tonkin. For North Vietnam, a nation that mobilized the entire resources of the state, it was a war of unification and survival. For the United States, the war was quite different, but nevertheless fought on a grand scale. Although not a "total" war as the US military and policymakers understood the term, the country still expended massive amounts of national treasure to fight the conflict as part of the global struggle of the Cold War. Furthermore, it fell to the same assets used to prosecute the supposed and expected total war with the Soviet Union to fight the war in Southeast Asia. The same aircraft and munitions designed for a war with the Soviets had to be modified to fight the very unconventional wars in and around Vietnam.

The point of this book is to add something new to the discussion of air power and the war in Southeast Asia. To be sure it is an uphill battle, considering the many great books already in existence, but through a comprehensive approach perhaps something new will present itself when linking the different air wars together into an operational whole. Despite the many different air wars going on at any one time, they were all part of the single—albeit perhaps not cohesive—air portion of the overall war to save South Vietnam. Hopefully, this single volume will provide a useful starting place for those hoping to understand how air power was used throughout the conflict.

As Stanley Karnow so eloquently said in *Vietnam: A History*, "So American soldiers went into action in Vietnam with the gigantic weight of American industry behind them. Never before in history was so much strength amassed in such a small corner of the globe against an opponent apparently so inconsequential." This American might proved inadequate to defeat the enemy it was called upon to beat. An online textbook used by both the US Military Academy and the US Air Force Academy called the first major bombing campaign against North Vietnam, Operation Rolling Thunder, "a frightening display of American technological and air superiority." I often read this quote aloud and then ask my students, *So what? To what end?* The textbook goes on to say, "Throughout the war, airpower would disappoint the expectations of its advocates." In the set-piece battles, air power performed admirably, but as a coercive tool to make North Vietnam change its outlook, it failed.[3]

What was Vietnam? The contours of the conflict are easy enough to discern. It was a contest for control of a divided country between one half, South Vietnam—aligned with the United States—and the other half, North Vietnam—aligned with the communist powers of the Soviet Union and China. The war, at least in the beginning, was irregular: a struggle between one nation-state and one non-nation-state. As more American troops moved into the south and as North Vietnam moved more regular forces down the Ho Chi Minh Trail system, aspects of regular warfare emerged. Here it is important to note that the American military establishment—and the air force, in particular—had a preference for regular war: a war between two nation-states. The United States began the war in hopes of bolstering South Vietnam and, in doing so, expelling a relatively small number of guerrilla forces from the country.

The principal enemy of the United States, North Vietnam, received the overwhelming majority of its supplies from outside the country. Both the Soviet Union and China provided resources to North Vietnam. The United States could not touch these resources until they were set up inside North Vietnam, and even then, many of these targets remained "off-limits." In order to protect equipment and resources, including marshaling yards, storage areas, airfields, and ports, North Vietnam, with the aid of the Soviet Union, set up a proliferating and deadly Integrated Air Defense System (IADS) network. Once inside North Vietnam, many of these supplies followed a primitive delivery system into Laos and Cambodia, and finally, into South Vietnam; here is where air power was plied against these supply routes.

The war in Vietnam was never meant to become a "major war." American military and political leaders, especially in the early years of American involvement, viewed it as a lower-level conflict, and yet, the United States ended up using massive amounts of men, machines, and materiel—assets meant for a total war in Western Europe—against the North Vietnamese. While Vietnam was not a total war for the United States, it was still fought using the same assets of total war. The US military ended up using everything in its conventional tool kit to defeat the communist forces. This, I believe, is an important point. The American military had enough land, air, and maritime assets conducting operations in Vietnam to blunt a Soviet attack through a part of Western Europe. The forces being used in South Vietnam could have gone force on force against a Soviet strength of similar size, but this mass of materiel seemed incapable of holding off the inevitable unification of the country under the Yellow Star of North Vietnam.

A renewed interest in the Vietnam War has been heralded by the fiftieth-anniversary commemorations and the release of the PBS documentary series

The Vietnam War in 2018 by master documentarian Ken Burns. In the history of the war in print, much has been written on American involvement during the Vietnam conflict. Total books number in the thousands, with works focusing on every aspect, from tactical to strategic, from the rice paddies of Vietnam to the comforts of the Oval Office. However, when focusing exclusively on the air war, the literature becomes sparser, but by no means insignificant.[4]

There are still hundreds of popular and public histories on the air war and what air combat was like during the Vietnam War. Popular books that focus on the air war are generally split between the USAF and the US Navy, and most of these tend to come from the perspective of fighter pilots in the war. Less has been written or published on the bomber pilots, and even less still on transport, cargo, and tanker operations.[5]

Recent studies have claimed to turn attention to the North Vietnamese side of the air war, but this highlights a problem in the study of aerial combat during Vietnam that continues to plague scholarship. Official sources inside Vietnam today remain difficult to access, and the inability to delve into Vietnamese archives is a central problem in this field, perhaps *the* central problem for Americans studying the air war.[6]

Inside Vietnam today, the People's Army Publishing House has several books on the air portion of the "American War," but few of these have English translations. There are two notable exceptions. The first is *The Christmas Bombing: Dien Bien Phu in the Air: A Triumph of Vietnamese Will and Intelligence.* The second, and significantly easier to locate, is Merle L. Pribbenow's translation, *Victory in Vietnam: The Official History of the People's Army of Vietnam, 1954–1975.* However, only one chapter in the latter volume deals specifically with the air war. Pribbenow notes that "very little on the war was written from anything other than the American perspective," and while the original work contained much communist rhetoric, he found that "many of the accepted 'truths' contained in some of our most notable histories were, quite simply, wrong." Until a scholar of air power undertakes a study that includes the sources in the State Records and Archives Department of Vietnam, as well as the books from the People's Army Publishing House, a hole will remain in the historiography, ensuring an incomplete picture of the war from the Western perspective.[7]

Finally, there is another underlying theme explored in this work, and it is the one which I use in the book's title. Following the Vietnam War, scholars re-created and maintained certain aspects of the "Lost Cause" ideology used in the study of the US Civil War and Reconstruction era. Today's proponents employ the trope of the Lost Cause to explain the complex reaction Southerners had to their defeat. These Lost Cause narratives sought to justify the antebellum South through misleading and bad-faith arguments. Although most often used by scholars to help explain the South's reaction to losing the Civil War, nowhere were these arguments more apparent than in Margaret Mitchell's *Gone with the Wind*.

Some of the tenets of the Lost Cause include: states' rights and not slavery as the ultimate cause of the war, with most Confederate soldiers fighting for their states—not the preservation of the institution of slavery; slavery as a cause and factor throughout the war was unimportant, and many of the enslaved were, in fact, happy with their station. Likewise, books on air power in Vietnam often have similar tropes and false narratives. Civil War historian and scholar David Blight said, "[T]he Lost Cause was born of grief, but just as importantly, it formed the desire to contend for control of the nation's memory." Blight went on to say, "The Lost Cause took root in a Southern culture awash in an admixture of physical destruction, the psychological trauma of defeat." The same is true for the history and memory of American air power after the Vietnam War. There are aspects of Lost Cause ideology present in the interpretation of the American experience in the Vietnam War.[8]

American Civil War historian Gary W. Gallagher wrote in his book, *The Myth of the Lost Cause and Civil War History*, "The architects of the Lost Cause acted from various motives. They collectively sought to justify their own actions and allow themselves and other former Confederates to find something positive in all-encompassing failure. They also wanted to provide their children and future generations of white Southerners with a 'correct' narrative of the war." Lost Cause ideology was planted in the fertile soil of defeat and grew in the verdant environment of a conquered people struggling for answers. The same could be said for air power in Vietnam.[9]

When the might of American air power failed to break the will of the communist forces, and once the last American aircraft had left the region, air power advocates and the US Air Force in particular developed their own Lost Cause ideology about its results. Much like Southern apologists in the early twentieth century, proponents of this theory created a myth about what US air power could have accomplished. This ideology is represented by two principal ideas: The first is that "more bombing or heavier air attacks conducted earlier" in the war would have changed the outcome; and the second, that when heavier bombing did occur during Operation Linebacker II, this forced North Vietnam to end the conflict. Neither of these assertions is true.

US Air Force officials noted and fervently believed that Linebacker II "ended" the war, and that if more air power had been applied against North Vietnam sooner, the North Vietnamese would surely have surrendered any claim on South Vietnam, perhaps as early as the mid-1960s. Noted air power historian Marshall L. Michel III stated in his work on the final air campaign of the war, *The 11 Days of Christmas*, that after the war ended, it became "an article of faith among many former U.S. military officers that the Vietnam War was lost because the U.S. political leadership used half measures until late in 1972." But the USAF and air power proponents never acknowledged that 1965 or 1966 was not 1972, and that any comparison between the two demonstrates the fallacy of this argument. The context of the time matters.[10]

It seems that some who flew and fought in Vietnam did not recognize, as historian Mark Clodfelter called it, "the limits of air power." The air force's Lost Cause ideology developed around three core tenets: Air power in Southeast Asia was used in an incorrect manner (gradualism); the role of technology in this conflict was never exploited against the "Third World" nation of North Vietnam; and the actions or inactions of senior leaders, both inside and outside the military establishment, demonstrated their lack of understanding of what air power could accomplish if only it was used in the "correct manner." American military planners and senior presidential administration officials perceived that the bombers and fighters that would be used to beat the Soviet Union were perfectly capable of defeating a smaller force. As the old saying went, "The dog we keep to lick the cat can lick the kittens too."[11]

1

Getting Involved

THE AMERICAN MILITARY BECAME INVOLVED in Vietnam and the surrounding countries because it fit into the larger Cold War policy of the containment of communism, even though in the late 1950s, many Americans could not locate the country of Vietnam on a map—not unlike Americans in the twenty-first century trying to locate Afghanistan on September 10, 2001. This is not to say the American people were somehow oblivious to geography, or that because your average American could not locate Vietnam, it was somehow not important to a larger military or diplomatic issue. This is simply to indicate that Vietnam was a far-off country on the other side of the world that had nothing to do with the daily lives of the American people. This, of course, would change during the ensuing decade.

Over the course of the next eleven years, from 1961 to 1972, the country that one day would simply be Vietnam etched itself into the American psyche. It did so in a way that was much more powerful and more traumatic than the later wars in Afghanistan or Iraq. The simple reason for this seems to be that due in no small part to the draft, the divide between civilian and military was that much closer during Vietnam than it was in the post-Vietnam and present-day all-volunteer force. America's involvement—or rather, the series of unfortunate events that slowly pulled the United States into a conflict in Southeast Asia—began long before American forces arrived "in-country."

A starting date of October 24, 1954, is as good a date as any to begin. During the Geneva Conference that ran from April until July of that year, participating diplomats—including representatives from the countries to be created out of French Indochina, USA, United Kingdom, USSR, the People's

Republic of China, and France—decided to partition the State of Vietnam at the 17th parallel and to create a three-mile-wide demilitarized zone. On this date in October 1954, the United States moved to support forces in the South. The United States air arms, particularly the USAF, became involved in South Vietnam a few years later, in 1961.

This inauspicious entry into South Vietnam began with the Farm Gate operation—the training of South Vietnam's Air Force (VNAF) pilots.[1] The training mission was clearly not a total war. One could argue that initially it was not even a limited or small war. Vietnam did not begin for the American military as a conflict that needed its latest, most technologically advanced assets; in fact, the Geneva Accords specifically prohibited those types of weapons when conducting operations in Vietnam. Article 17, section (a) stated, "With effect from the date of entry into force of the present Agreement, the introduction into Viet-Nam of any reinforcements in the form of all types of arms, munitions and other war materiel, such as combat aircraft, naval craft, pieces of ordnance, jet engines and jet weapons and armored vehicles, is prohibited." Thus, in line with the Accords, American leadership initially prohibited jet aircraft from operating in the theater. Rather, early in the conflict the USAF conducted operations exclusively with vintage, low-technology, propeller-driven aircraft, including A-1 Skyraiders and B-26 Invaders. These were used because they were the easiest aircraft with which to train South Vietnam pilots and also as a means to ensure that the US military was not in violation of the aforementioned agreement.[2]

The Threat

Initially, United States advisors in South Vietnam faced the National Liberation Front (NLF), more commonly called the Viet Cong, or "VC" for short. In the military phonetic alphabet, the enemy thus became "Victor Charlie," or just "Charlie" for short. As glibly stated in the 1987 film *Good Morning, Vietnam*, the purpose of the American service member in Vietnam became to locate Charlie: "Well, we ask people, 'Are you the enemy?' And whoever says yes, we shoot them."[3]

The National Liberation Front was composed of both regular forces (not to be confused with the regular forces of the Army of North Vietnam) and guerrillas. Much later in the war, the People's Army of Vietnam (PAVN), emerged as the primary opponent as the war escalated throughout the 1960s, and as America became more deeply involved. Soviet support ensured that the North Vietnamese were equipped with the latest in Soviet air defense weapons. Throughout the duration of the war, the terms "VC" and "PAVN" were used interchangeably, sometimes confusingly.

When the US Air Force started operations in South Vietnam, according to a contemporary report, it faced somewhere in the neighborhood of 12,000 to 25,000 "hard-core" Viet Cong guerrillas operating in the South, although depending on the method of counting—and the organization doing the counting—these numbers varied wildly. These figures remain largely unreliable today. The same report cited above—part of an official US Air Force history series—indicated that between 1962 and 1963, US forces killed or wounded nearly 49,700 VC despite their overall number remaining static. In four months, one unit reported more than 4,000 dead Viet Cong. Lieutenant Colonel John Paul Vann divided this number by 50 percent, but still counted as many as 2,000 dead, a number that should have seriously hindered Viet Cong in the area, much less their expansion, but expand they did. If the low estimate of 12,000 and the high estimate of 25,000 are added to the claimed 49,700 casualties, it gives an unreliable number of VC operating in South Vietnam somewhere between 61,700 and 74,700 between 1961 and 1963. Again, all of these numbers are highly unreliable.[4]

It was clear from the beginning that no one had a good idea of how many VC were in South Vietnam or who exactly was a VC. No matter how many Viet Cong members were killed, wounded, or captured, the organization had no problem replacing those they had lost, for several reasons. These included a ready cadre of replacements in North Vietnam that were prepared to move south and fill gaps in the ranks; a well-organized replacement system to mobilize and utilize these troops; a large portion of the Republic of Vietnam (South Vietnam) that was sympathetic to their cause; and the fact that the more VC that were killed by the Americans or South Vietnam forces, the more members of the South were driven into the arms of the North.

The report noted above was part of an Air Force operation to document the history of the conflict in Vietnam as it occurred, aptly named "The Contemporary Historical Examination of Current Operations," or CHECO for short. Members of the program collected, analyzed, and published periodic reports detailing the air campaign in South Vietnam. When the war expanded, the CHECO reports also expanded, and these publications continued throughout the conflict. An introduction in the reports noted that "the value of collecting and documenting our SEA [Southeast Asia] experiences was recognized at an early date" and provided "timely and analytical studies of USAF combat operations." Although classified at the Secret and Top Secret levels, their distribution to units both in-theater and back in the United States ranged from the Office of the Secretary of the Air Force down to the wing level, and even the history department at the US Air Force Academy, and provided ongoing commentary about the state of air force operations during the war. In total, the USAF produced some 250 separate CHECO reports throughout the war.[5]

A CHECO summary report produced in 1964 noted that "the VC had developed a highly effective replacement system whereby higher level [*sic*] military units placed a levy against lower level units." This is to say nothing of the replacements flowing south from the Democratic Republic of Vietnam (North Vietnam), but also through Laos and Cambodia. The states bordering South Vietnam—Laos, Cambodia, and North Vietnam—all provided some manner of sanctuary or logistical support to the VC. What eventually became known as the Ho Chi Minh Trail—noted as the "Laos Artery" and "Cambodian Artery" in earlier contemporary reports—stretched from North Vietnam into Laos, south into Cambodia, and ran the length of South Vietnam's border as far south as slightly northwest of Saigon, meaning that the artery pumping the lifeblood of supplies into South Vietnam had numerous capillaries extending into the country. Nevertheless, compared to the US military in the 1960s, it was still a very rudimentary force, but one that had no intention of attacking the United States as a peer competitor. To win the war, they simply had to not be defeated.[6]

Jungle Jim and Farm Gate

October 11, 1961, marked the date that the US military began an air war against the Viet Cong in South Vietnam. On this date, the 4400th Combat Crew Training Squadron—nicknamed "Jungle Jim"—deployed to Bien Hoa Air Base and was the first USAF unit to conduct combat operations. The code name for this operation was Farm Gate. Farm Gate followed the mandate that no jets would be used, only propeller-driven airframes. Farm Gate also demonstrated the importance of the air–ground cooperation between the army and air force, as the latter provided close air support (CAS), the support to troops in contact, one of the USAF's fundamental missions and, historically speaking, one of the most contentious and contested mission sets.[7]

The simple fact was that the American Department of Defense had no intention of large-scale aerial operations occurring in South Vietnam; the ground element was going to be enough to subdue VC forces in the region. In December of 1961, Secretary of Defense Robert McNamara stated that Vietnam was going to be a ground war. He went on to state that while "naval and air support operations are desirable, they won't be too effective."[8]

Jungle Jim crews served two purposes: Ostensibly, they were there to train the South Vietnamese aircrews. Initial Farm Gate missions mandated that a

South Vietnamese aircrew member had to be in the cockpit and these strikes flown against "known" Viet Cong villages and marshaling areas. However, the Americans were also there to fight. Unsurprisingly, the South Vietnamese pilots of the Vietnamese National Air Force (VNAF) bristled at being told to climb into the backseat while the American pilot flew the strike, and it became a constant struggle to find qualified South Vietnamese pilots willing to fly with their American counterparts.[9]

On October 1, 1961, the Pacific Air Forces (PACAF) deployed a control and reporting post (CRP) to South Vietnam. The CRP opened operations at Tan Son Nhut Air Base outside of Saigon. The CRP provided radar coverage for South Vietnam and trained South Vietnamese personnel on Air Traffic Control procedures. The reporting post eventually expanded into the tactical air control system. Along with the CRP, other assets necessary for the command and control of aircraft became established throughout South Vietnam. First, a "heavy radar" became active in January of 1962, followed by "gap filler" radars (to complement the coverage of the Da Nang radar), which began operating in the spring.[10]

On November 16, 1961, President Kennedy announced that the United States planned to further aid South Vietnam. Farm Gate operations began the following month, and the name "Jungle Jim" faded from common usage. The last month of 1961 saw American presence in Vietnam larger than earlier in the year, and continuing to grow. It immediately became a slippery slope for greater US involvement. Although American crews were there to train the South Vietnamese aircrews and act only as instructors, they had the leeway to conduct missions if the South Vietnamese forces "did not have the capability," a vague phrase that left the decision up to the subjective judgment of the American pilots, who would prefer to sit in the front seat and command the mission anyway. This policy lasted for more than a year, and a Military Assistance Command, Vietnam (MACV) directive reiterated it the following November.[11]

By March of 1962 an air operations center (AOC) had been established at Tan Son Nhut outside of Saigon, again, established to train personnel of South Vietnam's Air Force to oversee and conduct the war in the air, but as American involvement became more pronounced, the training mission was slowly subsumed into the US-run air war. Along with the opening of the AOC came an increase in American technology into the country, namely increases in radar coverage. At Tan Son Nhut and then in Saigon and Pleiku, the air force installed their own large radars to monitor air traffic.[12]

Another problem early in the conflict involved the ability of South Vietnam ground units in the Army of the Republic of Vietnam (ARVN) to call in air strikes. Although these units often had American personnel who could speak to the AOC, President Diem insisted that any request for assistance come from a South Vietnamese officer on the ground with the army units. However, not unlike conflict between the US Army and US Air Force, there was distrust between ARVN ground commanders and their South Vietnam Air Force observers. This was further complicated by the unwillingness of ground commanders to learn the proper procedures to call in air strikes. As one US Air Force report stated, "Not only were ARVN commanders unfamiliar with tactical air power, they were afraid of it."

It was bad enough that there was trouble in the coordination between ARVN troops in the field with their American advisors and the air force airmen inside the AOC, but the air forces of America and South Vietnam were not the only aircraft operating in South Vietnam. As one report noted, "The AOC exercised operational control over all tactical air operations conducted by the USAF and VNAF, but did not have such control over light aviation activities of the US Army and the USMC." In other words, the USAF might detail an aircraft to support army ground operations, but have no prior knowledge that other US Army air assets might also be operating in the vicinity.[13]

Conflict between the US Army and the USAF over command and control of air power continued in the opening stages of the conflict, one of the main problems being who maintained operational control over aircraft performing missions in-theater. Already confusion reigned in South Vietnam. According to one Project CHECO report, "[T]here were aircraft operating within the Republic of Vietnam which had VNAF markings and Vietnamese crews; VNAF markings and U.S.-Vietnamese crews; U.S. markings and U.S.-Vietnamese crews; and U.S. markings with U.S. crews." However, at this point, even with aircraft being flown by US crews, the belief remained that the United States could train the South Vietnam Air Force to stand on their own and provide for the security and safety of their own troops on the ground. From a larger perspective, the entirety of America's actions in South Vietnam in the early 1960s rested on the belief that South Vietnam could and would defeat the communist insurgency on its own. However, not everyone in the Kennedy administration felt these were reasonable assumptions.[14]

Chief of staff of the USAF, General Curtis LeMay, had this to say on the role of American pilots "training" and flying with the South Vietnamese pilots:

And we put our own people in there flying those airplanes. They went to the greatest subterfuge. Supposedly we were supposed to be there training them. They weren't in combat. Actually they were in combat, I don't know how many missions, just by dumping the Vietnamese in the back seat of the airplane—not that he was going to do any good back there—but supposedly training him. But we weren't training him; we were in combat and had to have somebody along. That was the subterfuge that was required.[15]

LeMay's remembrances differ from that of his successor, General John P. McConnell, who stated that

> there wasn't any air power in Vietnam except the Vietnamese Air Force, which was actually in a training status more than anything else and was fighting under the advisory group of which there were several Americans. At first, the Americans were not allowed to participate in combat with the Vietnamese. Later on, they were allowed to participate in combat with a Vietnamese pilot as an adviser but not actually in command of the aircraft until the Gulf of Tonkin incident.[16]

LeMay's comments are undoubtedly the more accurate. The early CHECO reports bear out that Americans were indeed performing combat operations and also often commanded the aircraft on any given mission, rather than trusting their VNAF counterparts. There is the very real possibility that McConnell in 1969 was not going to admit this fact in an interview, even for a presidential library.

Early air power in Vietnam provided support to Vietnamese ground units, but this support was not used appropriately for the enemy faced at the time. Rather than maneuver around hamlets, South Vietnamese combat leaders often preferred to call in artillery strikes or air assaults. Even if an ARVN unit received sniper fire from a single combatant, it was not uncommon to call in an air strike against the entire hamlet. Even as the United States was becoming involved in Vietnam, its operations with the South Vietnamese were already alienating the very people they were there to protect. However, this was disputed at the time. A memorandum provided to the RAND Corporation disagreed with the assessment that the bombing drove the population into the hands of the VC.[17]

The author, having recently returned from a fact-finding mission in South Vietnam, noted that there was "evidence suggesting that civilians in Vietnam are less prone to adverse behavior on account of air strikes than is generally supposed." The same memo went on to state that air power hindered all aspects of the Viet Cong's ability to wage war. This was based on interrogations of captured VC personnel, although it is difficult to ascertain the truth in these statements. It seems probable that the RAND interpreted what it wanted to interpret from this study, which was that air power as a tool was working.[18] Other studies agreed with this assessment, and when considered in the context of the high body counts mentioned earlier, senior American leaders, both military and civilian, had reason to believe their overall program in South Vietnam was working as well.

Particularly helpful as a unit of measurement was body count. The idea of using body counts as a measure of success appeared early in the conflict. With no front lines to move on a map, no territory to be gained and held, and no country to invade as an indication of success, American military leaders sought other ways to indicate progress was being made against an ephemeral enemy. As one officer in Saigon said early in the war, "In a war without battle lines, perhaps the best overall index of progress is that of casualties," but as previously mentioned, this made little difference when the National Liberation Front was capable of simply replacing the casualties they suffered with new troops. Looking for ways to quantify the war, the US Air Force began experimenting with new uses of air power against the insurgency.[19]

Other, more questionable, methods of air power began to be used in 1961 as well. Under the code name Operation Ranch Hand, and with approval from the president of the United States, the USAF began conducting aerial-spraying operations using specially designed herbicides, with the explicit goal of crop destruction and denying the Viet Cong a source of food. Although the most infamous of these was undoubtedly Agent Orange, the United States used numerous color-coded "Rainbow Herbicides" against North Vietnam throughout the war; these included pink, green, purple, and blue, each with its own chemical makeup, but most often a butyl ester derivative. In total the military used ten different compounds for the Ranch Hand missions.

The operations moved from crop destruction to deforestation and defoliation, and eventually even included airdrops inside of Laos. Early uses of Ranch Hand herbicides inside South Vietnam saw more than 281,000 "gallons of formulation" used. By month, each use of the various agents covered somewhere between 1,080 to more than 9,500 acres coated in the chemical compounds. This probably did not deny the VC any food supplies, as the Laos and Cambodian arteries were more than enough to keep the soldiers in the field supplied, but it undoubtedly denied the people of North and South Vietnam their own crops, and led to a generation of disease and birth defects in the unified country of Vietnam. Ranch Hand provided another way for the American military to quantify what was being accomplished by counting the amount of formulation dropped, crops destroyed, and acres coated.[20]

In addition to herbicides, the US military also introduced the use of napalm into the conflict. As one report stated, "The VNAF had observed the results which could be obtained from Napalm and had arrived at the conclusion that it was an effective weapon." The US State Department in Saigon urged "discretion" in its use, noting that "political considerations would suggest limiting use [of] napalm to high-priority targets which [are] clearly Viet Cong installations." Nonetheless, the use of napalm as an attack munition became nearly as common as general purpose bombs, and remained a lasting visual legacy of the war in Vietnam.[21]

The Situation Changes

The American presence in Southeast Asia continued to expand throughout early 1962. By July of 1962, the Military Assistance Command Vietnam (MACV) was established under the Commander in Chief, Pacific Command (CINCPACOM). This created a "theater within a theater" scenario where the command headquarters in Hawaii was senior to the one operating in Vietnam, but was often overlooked in favor of going directly to the MACV commander. The air force organizations in the region included both 13th and (eventually) 7th Air Force. These air force organizations had subordinate wings and squadrons responsible for conducting day-to-day air operations. These command and control arrangements remained contentious throughout American involvement in Vietnam.[22]

By the end of 1963, the situation around the world—but especially in Southeast Asia—had fundamentally changed. In South Vietnam, President Ngo Dinh Diem was killed on November 2 after a coup d'état removed him from power. The United States had promised not to interfere with the removal of Diem, although it is clear the Kennedy administration believed the coup would end in the exile of Diem, and not in his death. Three weeks later, President John F. Kennedy also died by an assassin's bullet, killed just twenty days after Diem, and replaced by Lyndon Baines Johnson.[23]

The incident in the Gulf of Tonkin (covered more fully in chapter 5) with the USS *Maddox* that occurred in August of 1964, whether actual, embellished, or conspiratorial, brought the United States deeper into conflict with North Vietnam. In a meeting of the National Security Council that occurred after the incident, Secretary of State Dean Rusk stated, "An immediate and direct reaction by us is necessary. The unprovoked attack on the high seas is an act of war for all practical purposes." A decision was reached to strike back at North Vietnam, and a list of "major U.S. reinforcements," including "ships, men and planes," was approved.[24]

In October of 1964, the chairman of the Joint Chiefs of Staff (CJCS), General Earle Wheeler, sent a memorandum to the secretary of defense outlining the service chiefs' belief that further action against North Vietnam was required in order to "prevent the collapse of the US position in Southeast Asia." Wheeler's letter further pointed out that both the commandant of the US Marine Corps and the chief of staff of the Air Force believed "that, if indeed, time has not run out, it is fast doing so. Unless we move now to alter the present evolution of events, there is great likelihood of a VC victory. They see no useful alternative to initiating action against the DR [Democratic Republic of Vietnam] now through a planned and selective program of air strikes."[25]

Less than a month later—on the eve of Election Day in the United States—a telegram from Maxwell Taylor at the embassy in South Vietnam announced an attack on the air base at Bien Hoa. The attack damaged or destroyed twenty-seven aircraft and killed four service members. Taylor believed retaliation was the only option, recommending the MiG air base at Phuc Yen, northwest of Hanoi, as the most attractive target. Rusk responded that while he understood Taylor's desire, this attack had to be viewed as part of the wider escalation of events.[26]

On February 8, 1965, the USAF introduced jet aircraft into the fight in South Vietnam for "in-country" operations. Less than one month later, on March 2, 1965, the USAF flew its first combat missions against targets in North Vietnam. The strike, composed of eighty-four F-100s, F-105s, and B-57 bombers, hit targets north of the 17th parallel. This widening of the war necessitated an increase in personnel into the region, as well, and meant that the USAF needed to keep track of just what these widening operations hoped to accomplish. In addition, they needed to start keeping a historical record of the growing conflict.[27]

In March of 1965, General Hunter Harris, commander in chief of Pacific Air Forces, wrote a letter to the USAF chief of staff, General John P. McConnell, to introduce the senior air force commander to the aforementioned Project CHECO.[28] Project CHECO began in 1962, when then air force chief of staff General Curtis LeMay instructed the Pacific Air Forces to collect and document air force operations in Southeast Asia. The first report was attached to Harris's letter to McConnell. In the letter Harris stated, "I have been concerned about the eventual end of hostilities in RVN and the inevitable and protracted post-mortem which will follow. Of particular concern is how the role of air power will emerge."[29] Harris noted that in Vietnam, air power now had its chance to prove its decisiveness once and for all, and turn "defeat into victory." However, if air power failed to be the decisive element, then the advantage turned to the "communists and the pacifists." Harris, by no means a Nostradamus, concluded his letter by saying, "It troubles me . . . that for all our military superiority we have been out-maneuvered by a third-class power."[30]

A report titled "Punitive Air Strikes, Expository Paper #1" named a different enemy than North Vietnam:

> One may state . . . that the net result of our air attacks on Laos and North Vietnam, whether good or bad, will greatly influence the future composition and force structure of US airpower, its utility in the pursuit of political objectives, the willingness of the executive to employ it, and public understanding and acceptance of aerospace power.[31]

It seemed to indicate that it was more important to defend air power theories than it was to defend aircrews against the enemy.

The following CHECO report, "Punitive Air Strikes, Possible Communist Counters, Expository Paper #2," seemed to take a different position. Here, in a report titled "Possible Communist Counter to Punitive Air Strikes," existed at least one example where the US Air Force recommended that, rather than increasing air pressure against North Vietnam through the the introduction of more-modern aircraft, the service should take a reverse approach.

A second CHECO report covering these air strikes indicated that at least some members of the air force wanted to "go low." Since "[t]here is nothing inherent in the doctrine of guerrilla warfare which makes it capable of exploitation by only the communists," and since "we have yet to find successful means to defend against insurgency," the report recommended the possible use of punitive and guerrilla warfare inside North Vietnam. The report further stated that "it seems possible that controlled insurgency operations within the DRV would provide the opportunity to capitalize on the very aspects of guerrilla warfare which have proven so successful for the insurgents in South Vietnam."[32]

Life on American Bases

Historians tend to focus on the combat operations of not only the Vietnam War, but all aerial conflict. There is a certain *in medias res* aspect to this, in which the story begins once a flight of aircraft is wheels up and headed to the target. This view tends to obfuscate the day-to-day combat rituals: the waking up and donning of the flight suit, a truck ride or walk to the squadron, the morning brief, a walk to the locker room to strap on the G suit and survival equipment, the van ride or step to the aircraft, walk-around, ladder up and into the "office" (all while weighted down with twenty or more pounds of gear), strapping into—most pilots would say strapping *on*—the aircraft, helmet on, oxygen mask on, preflight, taxi, and takeoff.

However, there is—and always has been—an element of truth to the fact that those who flew aerial combat had it better than the troops on the ground out in the field. American airmen had rooms, sheets, and a bed to sleep in at night.

What was life like for the American aircrews and enlisted personnel in Southeast Asia?

It varied greatly depending on rank and location—again, not unlike the American military experience in the first part of the twenty-first century in southwest and central Asia. There was certainly a great juxtaposition between those selecting targets in DC and the men living in SEA executing these selections, but the pilots of Vietnam made do with what they had, or what they could scrounge.

In South Vietnam, American fliers could find themselves at one of a dozen bases that ran the gamut from rural bases like Pleiku to bases collocated in major cities like Da Nang or Bien Hoa and Tan Son Nhut outside of Saigon. Da Nang was the farthest north, but still well south of the DMZ. Farther south was Chu Lai, primarily a base used by the US Marine Corps flying F-4s. Following the coast south, the next major instillation was Phu Cat. Farthest south, in the Mekong Delta, was Binh Thuy sitting astride the Bassac River. Life and entertainment on these bases ranged from urban nightlife to significantly more rural settings. However, most day-to-day activities centered on the squadron. Pilots could expect to fly anywhere between three to five missions a week. Between the actual missions, briefings, prep, and paperwork kept most pilots busy enough, not unlike fliers today. When there was free time, it was used in one of a few pursuits: blowing off steam at the officers' club, reading, or attempting to stay in touch with those back home.

In January of 1969, at Phan Rang in the south, one American bomber pilot, Lieutenant Colonel Dallas K. Stephens, dictated a letter to a friend back home on a Panasonic tape recorder. While waiting to be picked up for a night mission "up towards the north," he listened to Rolf Harris's "Tie Me Kangaroo Down, Sport" and talked into the tape recorder. He noted the sounds of an average night at the base, saying, "As the evening progresses we hear a little firing out on the perimeter and some aircraft coming in, returning from missions. These are the noises that interrupt our evening solitude and quiet." Stephens noted that the tape recorders were in high demand as the televisions were "very meager here," and the one local station "wasn't worth a nickel." Consequently, service members who could afford it bought recorders, made tapes "like mad," and passed them around as a form of entertainment.[33]

The other sounds of the evening also included the takeoffs and landings of the F-100s, what Stephens called the "mini-bombers," a "term of humorous disparagement" from the pilots of the B-57s—which Stephens flew—stationed at Phan Rang. Since the F-100s were capable of carrying four M-117 750-pound bombs and the B-57, a much larger complement of eight, the bomber pilots thought of the F-100 as something of a lackluster bomber. The B-57 fliers also felt that what the F-100 pilots were good for was to "put out noise." Stephens dictated in his recording for his friend back home, "If you could harness the noise the F-100 puts out on takeoff, you could win the war with it as a secret weapon."[34]

During the course of the taped letter, Stephens told his friend:

If you heard a thump that was the Korean artillery that guards the perimeter. Every night they use H&I [Harassment and Interdiction]; even when they don't sight anything, they know where the trails normally used by VC in the area are and at irregular intervals they open up in these areas and send a few rounds out there just to harass anything that might be moving in that area.

Stephens added, "You may get the impression that the night isn't entirely quiet around here . . . which is absolutely true! It takes us a few weeks after arrival to get accustomed to the fact that you're living in a boiler factory." Stephens also discussed other topics ranging from how he (like so many others on base) was handling being separated from family to the social issues facing the country in his absence.[35]

It is interesting to note that on the tape, Stephens mentions receiving a phone call from his friend Norm Eaton at the wing headquarters building, inquiring as to whether Stephens wanted to leave the squadron and take over the wing plans office. While Stephens would return home six months later, Eaton would not. Only a few days after making this recording, on January 13, 1969, Eaton was shot down and killed during a nighttime attack in Laos.[36]

South Vietnam was not home to all American airmen fighting in the Vietnam conflict. Seven bases in Thailand housed American air force or other service pilots: Udorn, Nakhon Phanom, Ubon, Korat, Takhli, Don Muang, and U-Tapao. Between the bases in South Vietnam and the Royal Thailand Air Bases, the Americans held Cambodia and Southern Laos in a bracket of American air power.

At Udorn Royal Thai Air Force Base life was generally not that bad, if one could become accustomed to visits from rats, rice bugs, and Krait snakes. American personnel could travel off the base to Udorn's restaurants—favorites among air force personnel included the Three Sisters and the King Star Nightclub—where Americans could have Thai food in its original state or "American hot," which cut down on the spiciness. American personnel in Thailand had the ability to take annual leave, something unique to the American experience in that region.

C. R. Anderegg, a young F-4 back-seater to Captain John Jumper, described his accommodations this way many years later:[37]

We lived in hooches that were wooden one-story [buildings] with a corrugated tin roof with a window air-conditioning unit. There were 2 to 3 to a room (15x10). We used black curtains for privacy. There was a TV in the room, but [it] only worked half my tour because a damaged aircraft crashed into the local base TV station. Base had a pool (rarely used) and the squadron had a "beach" that [was] really just lawn chairs out front of the hooches. For entertainment there were outdoor movies, but generally I spent a lot of time reading.[38]

Anderegg's idea of entertainment was somewhat removed from others' remembrances. Most officers at bases throughout South Vietnam and Thailand enjoyed their off-time at the O Club. Many clubs started out as a converted hooch, but later a stand-alone building was procured and a full bar established. Traditional fighter-pilot games like dead-bug and MiG sweep were favorites, along with songs like "Sammy Small" and "Mary Ann Burns"—all providing ways to release the tension from the deadly business of flying. The clubs also served as ad hoc tactics and analysis rooms where the day's events could be relived. One marine officer recalled, "The conversations at the club ran the gamut, with nothing off limits. The brass garnered their share of negative commentary and there were no repercussions. What were they going to do, make us lieutenants and send us to Vietnam?"[39]

Fight or Flight

The year 1964 was one of the major turning points in the war. The US government had a clear choice: either extricate from Vietnam or expand the war. In 1964, the president, secretary of defense, and the Joint Chiefs of Staff approved the use of jet aircraft for operations in-theater. The introduction of dozens of fighter and bomber squadrons indicated a new and more involved commitment from America's air forces, as it represented a fundamental shift in how the war would be fought. Instead of a low-level advisory mission, America now committed weapons designed for major combat operations. By 1965, a sustained bombing campaign was under way against North Vietnam.

For better or for worse, with a growing American presence in Thailand and South Vietnam, the American military sat down at the table to play a hand of asymmetric poker. It seemed on the surface a game the American military could easily win. North Vietnam did not enjoy some of the asymmetric advantages the United States did, but North Vietnam did have an ace up its sleeve, and that was the backing of China and the Soviet Union. This allowed the relatively non-industrialized nation of North Vietnam to level the playing field against the United States in the growing conflict.

The Soviet Union provided North Vietnam with air defense systems including the deadly SA-2 Guideline and its associated Fan Song radar system. The Soviets and Chinese also provided the air force of North Vietnam with MiG-17, MiG-19, and MiG-21 fighters. In the coming years, these aircraft and North Vietnam's fighter pilots' ability and willingness to change tactics proved to be a match against the US military's air arms in the sky over North Vietnam. Although the United States held a slightly better kill ratio in air-to-air combat against the North, the United States was never able to gain complete air superiority.

In July of 1965, Undersecretary of State George Ball wrote a memo to President Johnson calling for the United States to cut its losses in Vietnam and attempt to negotiate an end to hostilities. The same day, Secretary of Defense Robert McNamara in his daily presidential memo called for "intensifying the air war through the mining of Haiphong and other ports, destruction of rail and road bridges from China, and destruction of MiG airfields and SAM sites." The next day the Joint Chiefs of Staff concurred with McNamara's assessment and called for an increase in total sorties being flown against targets in North Vietnam. In short order, McNamara backtracked from these heavier tactics, but it proved that senior administration officials still could not come to decisive conclusions or agreement on the conflict in Vietnam, even as the American presence in the region continued to escalate.[40]

By September of 1965, there was outright discord inside the Department of Defense. JCS memo 670-65, dated September 2, called for attacking "lucrative" targets in North Vietnam, including petroleum, oil, and lubricant (POL) facilities and power plants. On September 15, McNamara responded to his chiefs, calling the memo a "dangerous escalatory step."[41]

After 1965, the asymmetric fight the United States hoped to enjoy evaporated. The war moved to a new stage at this juncture. The US air arms now operated not World War II–era propeller-driven aircraft, but the latest models of fighter and fighter-bomber aircraft available to them. That being said, the US Air Force, the dominant air arm in SEA, focused its attention on multiple enemies, and sometimes not the correct ones. In one CHECO report from 1965, the staff from PACAF noted,

> Regardless of how the conflict in SEA is finally concluded . . . the USAF should now—if it isn't already—be deeply involved in plans to defend airpower against deliberate, unjustified derogation of its military value; and efforts to exploit that which exemplifies the powerful, discriminate, versatile, and potentially decisive role of airpower in the air attacks against Laos and North Vietnam.[42]

It seemed that defending air power theory against naysayers was just as important as killing the enemy.

Conclusion

What started as an advise-and-train mission transitioned into something else entirely. The fear that the US position in Southeast Asia might collapse led to an insidious increase in the number of men and materiel into South

Vietnam and Thailand. By 1965, the United States had decided to stand and fight in Vietnam, and in doing so, largely shouldered South Vietnam into a supporting role in the war. The increase in American forces and the decisions made inside the White House and the Pentagon moved the air war in South Vietnam beyond the borders of that country. The United States hoped to use air power to "bring the enemy to the conference table or cause the insurgency to wither from lack of support." [43]

Neither of these desires proved easy to achieve. Instead, the air war in Vietnam fractured along country, service, and inter-service lines. Rather than one air portion of an overall campaign to defeat communism and protect South Vietnam, numerous aerial operations began to occur, and not all of them were cohesively linked together. Air wars and portions of air wars took place in South Vietnam, in North Vietnam, in Laos, and in Cambodia. The US Air Force and the air arm of the US Navy fought the enemy and carried on a conflict with each other. Even where inter-service rivalry was not present, lines drawn over Vietnam prevented any form of true cooperation between the services.

The only way to truly understand these air operations is to look at them individually, beginning with the expanding air war in South Vietnam.

2

The War in the South

Buildup

B Y 1965, THE US MILITARY WAS FULLY COMMITTED to a war in Southeast Asia, and it brought to bear much of its combat force. Johnson's massive electoral victory in November 1964, along with large public and political support, gave him the leeway to expand the war in Vietnam. This was the same combat force, in theory, that would blunt a Soviet move through the Fulda Gap in Europe, but now found itself in the jungles, mountains, and deltas of North and South Vietnam. At nearly the same time, North Vietnam positioned its forces for an expansion into South Vietnam.

After Johnson's reelection, the United States placed an additional 120,000 troops in the country, bringing the total number of American service members to more than 200,000 by the end of 1965. America was committed. Operating in South Vietnam, there were over 170,000 men serving with the Viet Cong. Regular soldiers from the Army of North Vietnam also began flowing south along an expanded Ho Chi Minh Trail. If the United States was about to magnify its actions throughout the country, it was going to have to do so against an enemy better prepared to face them than the 12,000 to 25,000 "hard-core" Viet Cong guerrillas at the beginning of the decade. One of the main advantages the United States had was its asymmetric ownership of air power in the South.[1] Commanding American forces in South Vietnam—as of June 1964—was General William Westmoreland. His deputy, Lieutenant General John L. Throckmorton, was also an army officer. Inside the Pentagon, two air force chiefs of staff, generals Curtis LeMay and his successor, John P. McConnell, both lobbied to have the MACV deputy position converted to an air force officer.

After being denied on multiple occasions by the other members of the Joint Chiefs, senior USAF leaders finally accepted the creation of a new deputy position for air operations. This USAF officer would be "dual-hatted" as both an MACV deputy and as the commanding officer of the senior air force organization operating in South Vietnam, the 7th Air Force. The first commander of the 7th, Lieutenant General Joseph H. Moore, had already been in-country for two years, and his time in Vietnam was at an end. It would take a new officer, serving simultaneously as MACV deputy for air operations and commander of the 7th Air Force, to attempt to bring order to air operations in Vietnam. This proved easier said than done.[2]

At this point, and lasting throughout the conflict, a confusing wire diagram existed. Under the Pacific Air Forces fell two numbered Air Forces, the 7th and the 13th, both of which also reported to the MACV commander. While 13th Air Force held responsibility for flowing forces into Southeast Asia, 7th maintained responsibility for the conduct of combat operations. The 7th Air Force eventually commanded a total of fifteen wings, both in South Vietnam and Thailand.

Again, it is important to note that the MACV commander had four fighting forces under his command: an army force, navy forces, air force forces, and a marine amphibious force. The trouble was, the navy operations from Dixie and Yankee Stations, and the USAF operations from South Vietnam and Thailand, were all air operations, but they were not directed by a senior air commander. This was a failure of what military professionals commonly call "unity of effort."[3]

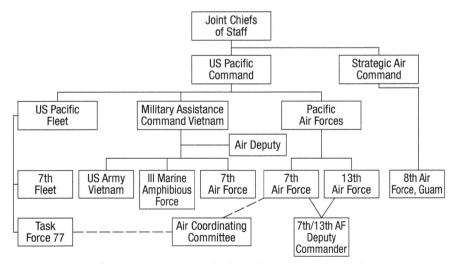

The complicated command-and-control relationships present during the Vietnam War

Into this command-and-control morass in South Vietnam walked General William Wallace Momyer. In July 1966, Momyer transferred to Vietnam to serve as deputy commander for air operations, Military Assistance Command, Vietnam, and at the same time as commander, 7th Air Force. By the time Momyer arrived in-theater he had done it all. Momyer knew air power. He was an official "ace," with eight kills during World War II. He instructed students at the Air War College and had commanded a wing in Japan. He had also been in command of an air division; had served on the staff at Tactical Air Command (TAC) and the Air Staff inside the Pentagon; and finally, he had commanded Air Training Command—all before arriving in Vietnam. He was considered tough and hard-nosed—his call sign "Spike" was well earned—but he was also an airman's airman, equally comfortable discussing tactics as he was discussing greater esoteric matters, such as what air power could provide.[4]

As Momyer took in his surroundings, he quickly realized he was not the overall commander for air operations in Vietnam, despite having a title that said he was. Momyer served two bosses: Westmoreland, for operations in Laos and South Vietnam, but also the commander of the Pacific Air Forces, General Hunter Harris. Momyer controlled none of the US Navy assets belonging to Task Force 77, nor did he control the B-52s—even when these bombers operated in South Vietnam. This was because the Strategic Air Command (SAC) refused to relinquish control of their "strategic assets," even though they conducted very tactical missions. Momyer's immediate boss, Westmoreland, admitted that his "interest in the air war was somewhat incidental," and only due to the fact that the air war was related to the ground war.[5]

For all of his experience, beginning with World War II, through Korea, and now into Vietnam, Momyer's concepts and belief in air power led him to some predetermined conclusions about its use that were not helpful in his current position. For starters, Vietnam was not World War II, and the use of air power could not be executed as such. Despite the many comparisons made over the years, Vietnam also had little in common with Korea. Historian Don Mrozek noted that Momyer approached Vietnam believing it was "essentially simple conventional conflict masquerading as a subtle and complicated counterinsurgency." Here again was the desire to see Vietnam as something it was not, the need to visualize the conflict as something more understandable and easier to combat—something air power could be applied to in a conventional manner.[6]

Even with this brief assessment of command relationships, it is painfully clear that senior American military leaders spent as much time fighting each other as they did the North Vietnamese forces. One historian noted:

> During their participation in the war in South Vietnam, the armed forces of the United States were afflicted by serious interservice disputes over airpower issues.

Broadly, the main areas of disagreement concerned the command and control of airpower assets, close air support of ground forces and the application of the new concept of air mobility to military operations.[7]

General Westmoreland as MACV held a ground-centric view of the overall conflict and viewed air power as a supporting function. Momyer, as the deputy for air and the 7th Air Force, viewed air power as an independent and co-equal contributor to overall success, but also viewed air power holistically regardless of service. The Commander in Chief Pacific Fleet (CINCPACFLT), Admiral Ulysses Simpson Grant Sharp Jr., viewed naval air power as organic to the fleet even when it operated in North Vietnam. Only when navy assets flowed into South Vietnam did the 7th Air Force gain control of them for planning and execution purposes. As previously mentioned, the SAC continued to hoard the B-52s even when these aircraft performed close air support.[8]

Another problem for Momyer was marine air. Falling under the "single manager" school of thought, Momyer believed that marine aircraft stationed in South Vietnam should fall under his control and then be apportioned out to wherever it was needed most. US Marine Corps (USMC) doctrine has never aligned with the USAF's perception of how to control air power. Larger than just a problem in Vietnam, major conflicts have often seen when senior USAF and USMC leaders try to come together over the apportionment of air power assets. Perhaps author Peter Mersky summed it up best when he stated, "As in every military action involving Marine aircraft, the subject of who controlled them in Vietnam came up early. And, as usually occurred, the Air Force laid claim to that responsibility. The Marines were understandably leery of letting their aircraft come under the junior service's control once again. . . . Marine air for Marines, first!"[9]

Throughout all of these discussions about how air power was supposed to be used, the senior commanders at least agreed on one thing: Most rotary-wing airmobile assets belonged to the US Army, and since they belonged to the army and supported the movements of combat troops on the ground, they were not "air power." This made for an odd distinction. If a UH-1 belonged to the army, it supported the ground war, but the USAF also used UH-1s for search-and-rescue and special operations. In either case, the use of helicopters represented a new and innovative use of air power in Vietnam.[10]

The Army's Own Air Way of War: The Air Mobile Mission

The army developed its own conception of air power through the Air Cav/Air Mobile units. These could rapidly deploy rifle squads into battle in the

UH-1A Iroquois, nicknamed (and forever to be known) as the Huey.[11] Other UH-1s could be configured with guns and rockets to provide support to the troops already on the ground. Historians and those who served in Vietnam generally consider these assets to be more closely linked to the ground war, an understandable concept given their mission of maneuvering soldiers onto and off of the field of battle, but they are included here for fitting the concept of air power as defined by Brigadier General Billy Mitchell, who said, "Air power may be defined as the ability to do something in the air. It consists of transporting all sorts of things by aircraft from one place to another."[12]

At the end of the conflict, more than five thousand helicopters were lost and more than two thousand soldiers killed in action as a result of this new use of air power. Service rivalries also played a part in the development of the Air Cav/Air Mobile units, as the army still did not have full confidence in the air force's ability to provide close air support.

The Air Mobile concepts executed during the conflict in Vietnam represented a unique use of air power that is often—erroneously, in the opinion of the author—not considered as part of aerial warfare. However, if Billy Mitchell believed that air power was the "ability to do something in the air," then air mobility should certainly fall under the air power rubric and not be solely considered as part of land operations simply because it falls across arbitrary service lines and interpretations of what *is* and *is not* air power.

US Army rotary-wing assets were some of the first aircraft to arrive in Vietnam, being introduced into theater in December of 1961. The air mobility concept, developed during contentious arguments between the US Army and the US Air Force, fit well into the environment in which the military found itself during Vietnam. Army planners felt that "increased airmobility for most Army units would be useful for the major contingencies that could be forecast." As it turned out, air mobility proved useful for unplanned contingencies as well. Some senior USAF officers disagreed with the sentiment that the army could be responsible for airmobile maneuver using indigenous helicopters, with General Curtis LeMay quoted as saying it was the US Air Force that should own "everything that flies, down to the last puddle jumper."[13]

In 1962, at the urging of Secretary of Defense Robert McNamara, the US Army issued a report as part of the Tactical Mobility Requirements Board, more commonly called the Howze Board, named for board chairman General Hamilton H. Howze. The findings of the board were succinct. According to Howze, "Adoption by the Army of the airmobile concept—however imperfectly it may be described and justified in this report—is necessary and desirable. In some respects the transition is inevitable, just as was that from animal mobility to motor." Howze indicated that, as a technological innovation, airmobile was unavoidable and the army needed to embrace it.[14]

The air mobility concept of operations foresaw taking a standard US Army division and stripping it of one-third of its ground vehicles and increasing its rotary-wing aircraft by a factor of four. The first Air Mobile Division, US 1st Cavalry Division (Airmobile), arrived in Vietnam in the summer of 1965 and entered combat that fall. Discussed later, the first major use of the air mobile concept proved successful during Operation Silver Bayonet and the Battle of Ia Drang in November, but was used to little effect in the overall war effort. Although the airmobile units represented another asymmetric advantage of the United States, they did not deliver a decisive punch. As US Army historian George L. MacGarrigle noted, "There would be no climactic battles or quick victories; the Americans were too strong and the insurgents too elusive."[15]

Employment of helicopters began long before the 1st Cavalry Division arrived in-theater. Use of helicopters by both the US Army and South Vietnamese forces was as old as American involvement. By late 1962, National Liberation Front forces had recognized that helicopter tactics to move even moderate forces around the battlefield was something of a game-changer. A history of air mobility operations quoted a portion of an instruction pamphlet that was found on a captured VC prisoner:

> It can be said that all the recent augmentations of forces that the USA has sent to the Diem government were primarily intended to strengthen the Diem rear area forces, increase their ability to pass information rapidly, and [to provide] the wide employment of helicopters in the movement of troops. Therefore, if we can destroy or greatly reduce the enemy's heliborne capability, we will, in essence, have destroyed the mobility necessary to the US raid tactics. Although we have succeeded in inflicting some loss on the enemy in his heliborne operations, the enemy has in some places caused us fairly heavy losses. We must therefore find means of coping with the enemy's helicopter tactics. Widespread efforts must be directed to combatting heliborne landings and shooting at helicopters.[16]

The Viet Cong recognized that their ability to down a helicopter could exponentially increase their ability to inflict casualties.

The role of rotary-wing assets continued to expand on pace with the US Army's expansion into the wider war, culminating with the introduction of the 1st Cavalry Division in-theater in 1965. The use of Hueys as gunships was something of an ad hoc adaptation in this early period, but the concept of helicopter gunships matured with the introduction of AH-1 Cobras in 1967. This provided the air mobile division with both transportation and increased firepower.

Lieutenant General John T. Tolson, author of a US Army history of air mobility, asked in the conclusion of his work, "What does it all mean?" How did air mobility fit into the overall concept of air power in SEA? As mentioned, the USAF has traditionally been loath to view army rotary-wing assets as air power, despite having its own fleet of the same. More pointedly, the USAF, at least unofficially, viewed air power as air assets belonging to the senior air forces commander in-theater. Tolson noted, however, that "[t]he one inescapable conclusion is that the Airmobility concept is irreversible. The thousands of officers who have learned to think and fight and live in three dimensions will never allow themselves to be restricted to two dimensions in the future. Airmobility will change and grow, but it is here to stay."

Tolson's focus on the three dimensions harkened back directly to the principles and teachings of Billy Mitchell, Alexander de Seversky, and other early air power theorists who often invoked or noted that only those who possessed an "air-mindedness," those who had operated in the third dimension, were capable of truly understanding and employing air power. The fact remained that although indigenous to the army, rotary-wing assets remain an important component of air power.

The US Army was not the only service to maintain control of its own air power assets.[17] A note on US Marine Corps aviation is worth reiterating here. While each service retained control of their own organic air units, nowhere was this truer than the USMC. Throughout the war, USMC air remained organic to that service. The USMC doctrine has always viewed marine air through a unique lens: "The primary mission of the Marine Corps air element is to provide close-air combat support for our advancing infantry." This meant there were always two tactical air forces at work in South Vietnam—those controlled by the commander of the 7th Air Force and those controlled by the USMC. Again, the disjointed nature of commanding, controlling, and employing four different services' collections of air power assets indicated that none of them would inherently work well in an integrated fashion. Major reforms after the war ended eventually saw to it that all air assets fell under a single air commander, and the same was true of the other domains: land, sea, and, eventually, Special Forces troops as well.

What Type of Air Force Is Needed? Bringing Aircraft to the Fight

Like everywhere in Southeast Asia, the war in the South was divided among participants and lacked a cohesive command-and-control element to oversee the conflict in a meaningful way. USAF fighters fell under the command of the 7th Air Force; USAF strategic bombers (B-52s) reported through Strategic Air Command (SAC) to the Joint Chiefs of Staff (JCS) and the president, and later, to Pacific Command/Military Assistance Command Vietnam (PACOM/MAC-V). Into South Vietnam in 1965 poured the very best of air

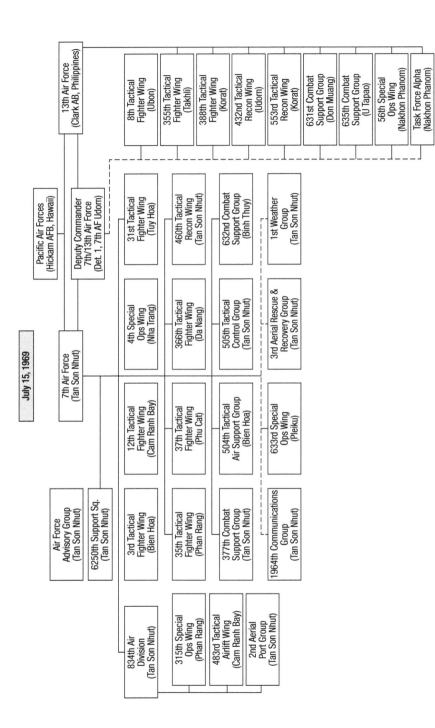

7th Air Force and 13th Air Force Wings and base locations

force fighters and fighter bombers, into places like Da Nang, Chu Lai, Phu Cat, Tuy Hoa, and Cam Ranh Bay along the coasts, as well as farther south, surrounding Saigon, at Bien Hoa and Tan Son Nhut. Twelve bases in all bedded down the bulk of the air force assets in-country. Often, these bases also found themselves home to USMC F-4 units or aircraft belonging to the Republic of Vietnam Air Force.

At Bien Hoa Air Base, the F-100 Super Sabres of the 3rd Tactical Fighter Wing began arriving in October, and by November 25, 1965, they were prepared for operations. Nearly simultaneously, the 12th Tactical Fighter Wing from MacDill AFB, Florida, began arriving at Cam Ranh Bay with their F-4C Phantom aircraft. Both units and aircraft would see long service in the conflict to come. Each wing brought between three and four squadrons of aircraft with them, and each squadron could include between twelve and twenty-four aircraft. By the end of 1965, the USAF had more than five hundred combat aircraft supported by more than twenty-one thousand airmen scattered at the bases throughout South Vietnam. For an organization whose mission just a few years before had been aiding, training, and equipping the VNAF, the USAF in South Vietnam now looked prepared to execute a major campaign against a peer competitor.[18]

In addition to the F-100s the USAF also deployed many of the other "Century Series" aircraft in the early rotations into South Vietnam. This included the F-102s, F-104s, and F-105s. The 102s and 104s were principally used as interceptors for the stateside Air Defense Command (ADC), where they fell under the North American Air Defense Command (NORAD) for the purpose of intercepting Soviet bombers as part of that organization's Cold War structure. Doctrine for these interceptors dictated that the aircraft would take off, be vectored toward their targets (a stream of Soviet bombers), fire their missiles, and return to base. It was never envisioned that these aircraft would be used as traditional "fighter" aircraft.

The F-105 Thunderchief, originally created to be an aircraft capable of low-altitude, high-speed penetration and nuclear delivery, demonstrated the most utility throughout the war in Vietnam. More commonly called the Thud—the origins of the nickname are murky—its contributions are noted throughout the literature, both academic and more popular publications, but its reach even stretched to features of North Vietnam's geography. A mountainous region that moved from the northwest to the southeast became known as "Thud Ridge." The Thud features prominently in the pages that follow throughout the engagements of Southeast Asia.[19]

In South Vietnam, the F-102s served much the same purpose that they did in the United States: as an air defense force. Beginning in 1962 and lasting until December of 1969, F-102s sat alert at Bien Hoa and Da Nang in South

Vietnam and Udorn and Don Muang in Thailand. Although principally used as an air defense fighter, the F-102s saw limited use on combat air patrols protecting the high-flying B-52s on Arc Light missions. Throughout its employment in Vietnam only fifteen F-102s were lost: three to antiaircraft artillery (AAA), one to an air-to-air loss, and four to mortar attacks on the ground. The rest were lost to accidents.[20]

The USAF was never particularly satisfied with the F-104; it only accepted 170 out of a programmed buy of 610 F-104As and 26 out of a programmed 112 of the F-104Bs. It was a number of the 77 F-104Cs that saw service in Vietnam, flying out of Da Nang and Udorn. Its operational use was anything but stellar, and an official air force history noted that enemy ground fire rapidly took its toll on the aircraft. By 1967, all F-104s had been replaced by "more efficient" F-4Ds. During 1965, the USAF was going through something akin to "trial and error" in building up its forces.[21]

With the sole exception of the F-105, all of the other Century Series aircraft proved to be of limited use during the Vietnam War. This is not to call their contributions unimportant; rather, the USAF found the F-4 and F-105 better suited to the type of combat faced in both the North and the South. The USAF as an organization also treated the early Century Series aircraft as an "also-ran" during the war, but especially in official histories of the conflict. One history produced by the Air Force Association does not even mention the F-102 or F-104, but it does call the F-4 the "[b]est fighter of the Vietnam War and most versatile," and the F-105 the "[s]ignature airplane of the Rolling Thunder campaign from 1965 to 1968." It is no wonder that the F-105 and F-4 became emblematic of air force operations in Vietnam, and that these two aircraft feature prominently at hundreds of museums around the United States today, most notably on the cadet terrazzo at the US Air Force Academy. Beyond the "fighters" labeled above—the F-105s and F-4s provided air-to-ground operations—there was also a need for the aircraft that could place heavier amounts of "iron" onto the battlefield: bombers.[22]

Arc Light

Operation Arc Light deployed B-52s (initially to the island of Guam and later to U Tapao, Thailand) for the purpose of using the "strategic" bombers in a more "tactical" close air support and interdiction role. SAC's primary nuclear delivery aircraft instead dropped conventional loads of general purpose bombs. Although gone were the days of World War II and Korea, where hundreds of American strategic bombers laid waste to industrial towns, American technology had evolved to the point where one American single-seat F-4 carried more bomb tonnage (18,000 pounds) than a fully loaded B-17 (8,000 pounds), and a B-52 could carry more than four times what the F-4 carried (up to 70,000 pounds). The heavy bombers were outfitted with an increased weapons load making them capable of carrying eighty-four 500- or 750-pound bombs internally, plus an additional twenty-four bombs carried on external wing racks.

The Arc Light missions began on June 28, 1965. A recent survey by historian Mark Clodfelter found that many of the pilots on these missions felt they were flying "milk runs." One pilot recalled, "The job had all the excitement of being a long-haul truck driver without being able to stop for coffee." Another said, "We weren't much different than the truck drivers that drove the bombs from the port to the base; we were just the last leg of delivering the bombs to where they were needed on the ground."[23]

However, one of the main purposes in using the heavy bomber in an interdiction and close air support (CAS) role was that it freed up fighters and fighter-bombers for other missions. Historian John Schlight noted that "the bombers could release large numbers of fighters for close air support and battlefield interdiction missions, which was what led to using the strategic bombers in a tactical role in the first place." Rudimentary math shows that a single B-52 freed up at least four F-4s for other missions.

However, not all participants were thrilled with using B-52s in this manner, namely the Strategic Air Command. B-52s, whether they were in the United States or sitting on airfields in Guam or Thailand, were still, principally, nuclear bomb–delivering aircraft, and SAC worried that their conventional use in Vietnam came at the detriment of their primary role. Thus, to ensure that the B-52s would continue to be capable of filling the role of nuclear delivery, SAC maintained operational control of the B-52s throughout their deployments. Inside of 7th Air Force's headquarters, SAC kept a liaison officer (SACLO) and later an advanced echelon of officers (SAC ADVON), whose purpose was to maintain control of the bombers and coordinate activities between 7th Air Force, Strategic Air Command in Omaha, and the 3rd Air Division on Guam.[24]

Calling this command-and-control system inefficient would be generous. American forces on the ground in contact with the enemy could reach back to 7th Air Force headquarters and request support for ground operations, but 7th AF then had to ask the SACLO or SAC ADVON for use of the B-52s. At weekly meetings, the 7th AF commander asked for a number of strikes from the B-52s, but the MACV commander had final say. The 7th AF commander, General Momyer, and the commanders that followed him, continually asked for operational control of the B-52s, but this never worked out. The chief of staff of the air force, the commander of Strategic Air Command, and the lower-ranking 7th AF commander never came to an understanding or a solution to satisfy all members. Momyer later wrote, "We airmen couldn't agree."[25]

Momyer's opinion and preference to have operational control of the B-52s' striking targets in South Vietnam made the most sense. As the on-scene commander in charge of day-to-day operations, he, and other 7th Air Force commanders, were best positioned to allocate air strikes in the correct manner. Having to ask for sorties from a liaison officer working for another headquarters fragmented his ability to properly use the forces available to him in-theater. Since the B-52s conducting operations in South Vietnam were used in the same manner as any other fighter or bomber in-theater, it made sense for the 7th Air Force commander to use these forces as he saw necessary. Simply put, from the perspective of the 7th AF commander in South Vietnam, there was no difference in an F-105 dropping bombs, a B-57 dropping bombs, or a B-52 dropping bombs. The only difference was in the number of aircraft being used or the number of bombs being dropped against any one target.

On the first Arc Light mission, weather proved to be as much of an enemy as the enemy inside Vietnam. Strong winds from a typhoon provided an unexpected tailwind that pushed the first cell of bombers ahead of schedule. In order to rendezvous with the tankers, the first cell circled around, which brought their flight path directly into the cell of three aircraft behind them, which was now approaching the refueling area early, as well. Two of the B-52s collided, resulting in the deaths of eight of the twelve crew members.[26]

The overwhelming majority of B-52 strikes during the war in Vietnam fell under the auspices of the Arc Light missions. Of the total number of B-52 missions throughout the conflict, 92 percent came in South Vietnam, Laos, and Cambodia; only 6 percent were against targets in North Vietnam. The B-52s used against troop concentrations in the South had another advantage not enjoyed by fighter or light bomber aircraft. B-52s traveled in cells of three and cruised in the lower portions of the stratosphere, meaning they could not be heard by anyone on the ground, which meant these cells of bombers were capable of placing as many as 324 individual bombs onto a target with no warning.[27]

The men who flew the Arc Light missions feared their own aircraft much more than they did the enemy. The lack of air defense systems in the South did not mean the men who flew the heavy bombers were immune to the fear of going down. Rather, it seems that it transferred the fear to their own aircraft, which some worried would simply fall apart due to age and fatigue. It was not an unfounded fear. From 1965 through 1972, the air force lost twelve bombers to accidents.[28]

SAC was still SAC, whether it was preparing to drop nuclear payloads or conventional ones. Strict checklists existed for how to conduct the bombardment mission, and no deviation was allowed. One survey found that 74 percent of B-52 crews believed they had minimal to no flexibility in choosing or changing the tactics used on a mission. This would prove disastrous during Operation Linebacker II later in the war. When prodded about this lack of flexibility decades later, one crew member responded rhetorically, "We were SAC, remember?"[29]

The B-52 crews believed that SAC's priority was the aircraft's well-being and not their own. One veteran remembered, "If there was any risk to the goddamn airplane, don't do it. We could replace the crews but not the airplane." Fighter pilots (operating in both the North and the South) coming from the Tactical Air Command (TAC) believed something similar. Fighter pilots felt there was absolutely more emphasis placed on their aircraft than on the crews. Refusal to make changes at the Fighter Weapons School and a belief that aircraft production was "sufficient to cover current loss rates," without mentioning loss of the crews themselves, made fighter pilots believe they were viewed as expendable, since the air force could always produce another jet. Either way it was viewed, pilots had a very cynical impression of how higher headquarters felt about their welfare.[30]

Conclusion

Thus, inside of South Vietnam, the US Air Force brought F-4 Phantoms, F-100 Super Sabres, F-105 Thunderchiefs, and B-52 Stratofortresses as their principal combat aircraft. The USMC also stationed squadrons of their fighters in South Vietnam as well. Joining these were some of the Century Series fighters—the B-57 Canberra light/medium bomber; Forward Air Controllers in the form of O-1 Bird Dogs, O-2 Skymasters, and the OV-10 Bronco, AC-119 and AC-47 gunships; and rescue helicopters, including the HH-3E Jolly Green Giant. Also needed were command-and-control aircraft to direct all of the above aircraft, and this fell to the crews of the EC-121 Super Constellation flying under the "College Eye" program. Finally, all manner of air-to-air refueler (KC-135) and cargo aircraft (C-130, C-141, and C-124) kept the air war moving forward.

In 1964, there were 460 aircraft of all types in-theater; by 1965 that number had nearly doubled to 889; and two years later, it doubled again, with 1,768 aircraft present. This did not include the fighter and attack squadrons serving on the navy carriers in Dixie and Yankee Stations. The United States was now prepared to wage a full-scale air war against the insurgent, guerrilla, and soon-to-be-regular People's Army forces in South Vietnam.[31]

3

The War in the South

Close Air Support

THE AIR WAR IN SOUTH VIETNAM was primarily a close air support mission. Pilots flying out of bases in South Vietnam and Thailand provided support to troops on the ground throughout the country. In total, the US Army and the Army of South Vietnam (ARVN) conducted hundreds of operations of various sizes, intensity, and duration throughout the conflict. The US Air Force, US Navy, and US Marine Corps were there to provide support to the US forces on the ground. Furthermore, this traditional use of air assets in a supporting role fit nicely with General Westmoreland's preconceived notions about the use of air power, somewhat to the chagrin of his air chief, Lieutenant General Momyer. Westmoreland's view was ground-centric; Momyer's was not.

When looking at a map of South Vietnam in the mid- to late 1960s, the American military units occupied the country in four separate corps areas (I–IV) running north to south. Army units set up bases along the borders with Laos and Cambodia in an attempt to stem the flow of men and materiel into South Vietnam. A series of regular army, USMC, and Special Forces camps stretched up the western edge of South Vietnam and acted as blocking positions for the resources that exited the Ho Chi Minh Trail from Laos and into South Vietnam.

The year 1965 was not entirely about the buildup of US forces in the country; it was also about intermittent contact between American and South Vietnam forces on one side and probing attacks and ambushes by Viet Cong forces on the other side. In the early-morning hours of February 7, 1965, the 409th Battalion of the Viet Cong launched an attack against Camp Holloway outside of Pleiku, a city located nearly in the center of the country. Viet Cong forces infiltrated the camp and placed satchel charges on and around aircraft and helicopters parked on the ramp. The explosions from these devices destroyed five UH-1s and one CV-2B Caribou reconnaissance aircraft and damaged another twenty aircraft. Eight US service members died, in addition to more than one hundred wounded. Simultaneous attacks also took place near the coastal towns of Tuy Hoa and Nha Trang. Further mortar attacks occurred at other USAF and South VNAF bases.[1]

These assaults led President Johnson to order reprisal attacks—under the name of Operation Flaming Dart—against targets in North Vietnam, namely the base at Dong Hoi. In a tit-for-tat response, North Vietnamese forces killed twenty-three Americans in a mortar attack at Qui Nhon, to which Johnson again responded, this time with Flaming Dart II. Air power scholar Mark Clodfelter quoted Johnson as saying: "I thought perhaps a sudden and effective air strike would convince the leaders in Hanoi that we were serious in our purpose, and also that the North could not count on continued immunity if they persisted in aggression in the South."[2]

The Flaming Dart attacks were the precursor to a sustained bombing campaign ordered against North Vietnam a few weeks later: Operation Rolling Thunder. Attacks on US bases in the South expanded the war into a new and sustained phase—the bombing of targets in North Vietnam, a different and more dangerous air war than the one occurring in South Vietnam. The probing and sabotage attacks drew the ire of the president, but these were still smaller tactics used as harassment and not emblematic of the overarching plans of the regular forces of North Vietnam, which used the Ho Chi Minh Trail systems to move forces into position for large-scale confrontations with American forces.

A more-traditional force-on-force phase of the war was about to begin.

Ia Drang, Air Mobility, and Close Air Support

The Battle of Ia Drang remains important for several reasons. First, it marked a shift from guerrilla warfare to the use of more-conventional tactics by the PAVN. It was the first large-scale combat operation for the United States during the war, as well as the first large-scale use of the air mobile mission with the 1st Cavalry Division. In addition, it is perhaps the best remembered battle of the entire war, thanks in large part to the 2002 film *We Were Soldiers*, based on the eponymous book by Lieutenant General Hal Moore, the on-scene commander during the battle. Along with Khe Sanh and the Tet Offensive, this battle remains stuck in the consciousness of American society as representative of the entire war in Vietnam, although Ia Drang was but one battle in a larger overall campaign—Silver Bayonet—that took place in the wake of the Viet Cong attack against Plei Me.

In a manner of speaking, Ia Drang "had it all." Every remembered aspect of the Vietnam War could be found in this valley: olive drab–clad soldiers moving through fields in battle gear, incoming Hueys dropping off soldiers, and USAF aircraft providing close air support (CAS). A modern-day (2020) Internet image search shows various scenes from the battle, including American soldiers looking out toward the enemy as a UH-1 departs close by and soldiers loading wounded comrades into helicopters.[3]

Beginning on November 14, 1965, and ending four days later, the Battle of Ia Drang, part of the PAVN's overall Pleiku campaign and the American Operation Silver Bayonet, found American troops bogged down in a fight for survival. At landing zone (LZ) X-Ray members of the 1st Cavalry Division landed at the base of the Chu Pong Massif in a valley with units of the PAVN encamped above them and prepared for battle.Lieutenant Colonel Hal Moore's soldiers became surrounded by the PAVN, with one company becoming separated from the main group shortly after the infiltration began. Historian William Head noted that the battle contracted to the point that it might have resulted in a defeat akin to "Little Big Horn in 1876 or the British annihilation at Isandlwana in 1879."[4]

The US Army's G3 General Staff of the US I Field Force, stationed in Nha Trang, kept a meticulous daily journal and closely followed the unfolding battle. On the evening of November 14, discussions between the 1st Cavalry Division's commanding general, Major General Harry Kinnard, and I Field Force's Lieutenant General Stanley Larsen, included the idea of using B-52s to support the ongoing battle. This was the first time the giant strategic bombers were specifically used in a CAS role to aid troops in contact on the ground, but rather than being a one-off emergency measure, the B-52 strikes proved useful in destroying troop concentrations behind the front lines. Since there were no surface-to-air missile (SAM) systems being operated by the PAVN in South Vietnam, MACV decided that the B-52, much to the chagrin of SAC, could be used in this role in future operations.[5]

One source from Vietnam, a website dedicated to the memory of Major General Nguyen Van Hieu, who served on the I Field Force G3, noted that "the Ia Drang campaign (alias Pleiku campaign, alias Plei Me campaign) was an air war conducted by SAC B-52 strike, supported by a ground force operated by the 1st Air Cavalry Division." It is doubtful that the entire campaign was developed simply in order to bring the B-52 into the role of close air support, but rather it provided a useful opportunity to use the B-52 in a new way.[6]

After the battle, Westmoreland wrote the following in his diary:

> I told the J-2 and J-3 to get together to develop a more responsive arrangement with SAC in striking targets picked up by intelligence. We have made real progress with the 3d Air Division and SAC in recent weeks and I want to keep the pressure on them and gain further improvements. I would like to be able to bring a B-52 strike down within seven hours after acquiring suitable intelligence.[7]

It seems obvious that rather than any subterfuge on Westmoreland's part, he used the B-52s available to him as MACV commander. Since Arc Light missions had begun in the summer of 1965, there was no reason not to use them to strike PAVN troop concentrations to the rear of the Ia Drang battle.

By November 15, the situation on the ground had become desperate. Moore's forces were in danger of being overrun. Early that morning Moore discussed this with his air force liaison, Lieutenant Charles Hastings, and made the decision to make the radio call "Broken Arrow." This directed every available aircraft in the region to come to Moore's support, much like ships respond to a distress call of SOS. The platoon cut off from the rest of Moore's men was in specific danger of being destroyed—"One platoon of this company [Bravo Company] was cut off from the battalion, practically in the shadow of the Chu Phong slopes. . . . An AC-47, requested after nightfall, expended 12,000 rounds against the high ground to the west of the platoon's position"—but this did not stop the PAVN from their attempt to overrun the separated platoon's location. Further air strikes were called in at dawn on November 15, with a pair of propeller-driven A-1 Skyraiders, call signs Hobo 1 and 2, dropping general purpose munitions, napalm, and white phosphorus. Only American air power kept the soldiers' position from being overrun.[8]

The final PAVN assault came on November 16, and air support aided greatly in holding off the attack as well as attacking the PAVN forces once they were in retreat. Participating in action that day were three F-100s (Falcon flight), which dropped napalm and general purpose bombs followed by strafing runs within a football-field length of the American forces. Later in the day, F-4Cs also strafed the area, but by far the most munitions came from the aforementioned B-52 strikes. Eighteen B-52s dropped 344 tons of munitions on the slopes of the Chu Pong Massif above LZ X-Ray. B-52s followed up this first bombing run by dropping propaganda leaflets and safe-conduct passes.[9]

On November 19 the PAVN attacked again and "drove a wedge" between American forces on the ground. The situation rapidly devolved into hand-to-hand combat, and air support was called in. The forward air controller liaison on the ground, Captain Joe Pirie, "called for the target to be marked with 20mm cannon fire from the fighter since WP [white phosphorous] markers were considered too dangerous to the closely engaged friendly forces." Using their cannon fire, the F-4s slowly but surely separated the PAVN from the American units. Once the strafing F-4s forced enough distance between the two warring factions, the Phantoms then dropped napalm. This was done at such close range that some American forces in the battle "were singed."[10]

The following days saw the PAVN less inclined to mass and engage the Americans in direct combat. On the slopes of the Massif, the PAVN forces held on to their positions with "a dedication bordering on fanatic." The battle came at a heavy cost to both sides: 240 killed in action and another 247 wounded for the Americans, and over 1,200 PAVN and VC forces killed. Without air power, it is likely American KIAs would have been significantly higher, if not catastrophic. An air force report later noted, "Without air-power in its entirety; the close air support and interdiction, the B-52 strategic bombers-turned-tactical, the FACs, and the overall coordination and response within the Tactical Air Control System, the cost would have been much higher."[11]

In the immediate aftermath, both sides had reason to see the fruits of victory in the battle, but also much to correct. The PAVN had stood toe-to-toe against ARVN and the Americans, but could not stem attacks from the air. The Americans could point to a high body count of enemy KIA, but the PAVN remained in control of the highlands along the Cambodian border. Over fifty years later, both sides continue to claim the Battle of Ia Drang as a victory. In 2005, on the fortieth anniversary of the battle, Colonel General Nguyen Nam Khanh wrote in the People's Army newspaper that when placed together,

> everyone finally unanimously agreed that in the Plei Me Campaign in general and the Battle of the Ia Drang in particular we had won a strategically significant and political important victory. This was because the Battle of the Ia Drang Valley was the key, decisive battle of the entire Plei Me Campaign. For the American army, the Battle of the Ia Drang Valley had become a terrifying defeat, something that General Westmoreland admitted in his memoirs, when he wrote that the US 1st Air Cavalry Division had suffered "serious losses" in its first battle in the Central Highlands. The fighting in the Ia Drang Valley had exceeded the bounds of a tactical engagement and had become a campaign-level battle.[12]

In the immediate aftermath of the battle Westmoreland was much more prosaic about the battle, calling it an "unprecedented victory" for US forces, adding that it was "unprecedented in intensity of action, magnitude of troops involved (in South Viet Nam), and the degree of success by friendly forces." Furthermore, bolstered by what he viewed as success at Ia Drang, Westmoreland committed American ground forces to further search-and-destroy missions based upon the lessons he had learned from this battle. American ground troops used similar-style missions for the next three years. William Head noted that Westmoreland "decided the employment of air mobility, artillery fire and CAS could and would obtain all future battlefield objectives."[13]

A Shau

If 1965 was primarily about getting forces and equipment into the country, then 1966 saw the rise of the use of these aircraft in support of increased ground operations. If CAS proved exceptional at Ia Drang, this was not always the case. The A Shau Special Forces camp sat astride the border between South Vietnam and Laos. At the camp, Special Forces units maintained tabs on the movement of NVA troops into South Vietnam. Throughout the war A Shau remained a tightly and hotly contested environment. A marine F-4 radar intercept officer (RIO) remembered the difficulty in providing support around the valley: "The A Shau was always a hotbed of enemy activity for a variety of reasons. It was near the Ho Chi Minh Trail and Laos. The valley was thickly wooded with a high canopy, and enemy forces were difficult to track and fight." In March of 1966, roughly 17 American personnel, 149 Chinese Nung (ethnic Chinese living in South Vietnam) troops, and 210 South Vietnamese "Civilian Irregular Defense Group" troops manned the A Shau fort and its 2,300-foot airstrip.[14]

The attack on the A Shau camp began in the early-morning hours of March 9, 1966, with mortar and sniper attacks against the triangular-shaped fort. Heavy fog and cloud cover not only hindered American air strikes, but also made it difficult to observe these explosions on the ground as well. A forward air controller (FAC) inside the compound was forced to adjust fire using only the sound of the explosions. An AC-47 Spooky—a converted troop carrier turned gunship—arrived on scene around 1300, but was shot down shortly thereafter. Further CAS sorties that afternoon had to be called off due to weather.

By the next morning, the situation at the camp had become desperate. According to an after-action report, "At 1000 hours the 'A' detachment commander requested the entire camp, except for the communications bunker and north wall, be bombed and strafed." As the afternoon wore on, the "situation of the defenders deteriorated gravely." After the loss of an A1-E Skyraider and the difficulty of continuing to provide CAS, MACV headquarters made the decision to abandon the camp and committed III MAF headquarters to send in helicopters for the evacuation. Personnel moved to a helicopter landing zone, but confusion and panic ensued. According to the report, South Vietnam forces mobbed American helicopters. American Special Forces troops attempted to escape and evade, but this ultimately failed, and 172 personnel previously at the camp were eventually listed as "MIA, believed KIA."[15]

The fall of the A Shau camp seemed to be another example of an isolated location falling under isolated attack that did not seem to fit meaningfully into the larger construct of the war. However, for the North Vietnamese it proved to be a major victory that helped to further open the valve of troops and supplies flowing into South Vietnam. The fall of A Shau demonstrated there was a lot air power could do, but also proved in equal measure how much geography and weather affected air operations of all services.

Operation Cedar Falls

Beginning on January 8, 1967, the United States launched their largest ground operation to date code-named Cedar Falls. Two full army divisions plus additional brigades and regiments headed into the "Iron Triangle" outside of Saigon. In this case, the North Vietnamese chose not to engage directly with the US Army, and either escaped into Cambodia or into an elaborate series of cave complexes. The ground forces meticulously walked the terrain, clearing it of any vestiges of armed resistance.

Air support during Cedar Falls provides a window into the difficulty of ascertaining what air power accomplished overall. In total, one CHECO report noted, "Air support of CEDAR FALLS comprised some 1,113 tactical and 102 ARC LIGHT sorties. Total munitions thus expended amounted to more than 3,900 tons. In support of the operation, the 308 C-123 and C-130 sorties hauled 1,456 tons of cargo and 2,710 passengers."

This proved a relatively light load for air power when compared against Ia Drang or later operations, but it is the follow-on sentences that showed the cognitive dissonance of American action in Vietnam: "Confirmed enemy killed by air [KBA] were relatively insignificant in number, but verification was greatly hampered by the nature of the terrain and type of target. Air support was particularly important, however, in keeping the communists fragmented and incapable of concerted action against the friendly ground forces."

This seems difficult to hold as truth since most Vietnam forces escaped into safe havens in Cambodia and did not want to engage with the American forces in set-piece battle. It was impossible for air support to keep enemy units fragmented, since those units chose not to engage the fielded forces in the first place. This represented a *post hoc ergo propter hoc*. It seems the report wanted to indicate that because bombing occurred, then the fielded forces remained fragmented. The same report also noted that "air softened and opened up the meticulously fortified complexes and rendered them indefensible in many instances." In other words, air support for Cedar Falls blew holes in the ground revealing the location of the evacuated and empty cave complexes.[16]

The same CHECO report also noted, "To deprive the enemy of any population control and qualify the area for a free-fire zone, its 6,000 civilian inhabitants were evacuated for resettlement elsewhere and their villages and crops were totally destroyed." In retrospect, this seems an odd way to bolster support for the government in South Vietnam, especially when it is noted that the air force bombed roads to the north of a local village in order to "dissuade the inhabitants from escaping." These inhabitants were then informed by loudspeaker that their village was to be evacuated, and all residents "were to assemble immediately with their belongings at the village school" in preparation for relocation. Cedar Falls saw air power used against an enemy already removed from the battlefield.[17]

Operation Junction City

In early 1967 the US Army along with ARVN forces launched Operation Junction City, another multi-division search-and-destroy operation which included the largest airborne drop operation since the Korean conflict. Some 845 paratroopers of the 173rd Airborne Brigade jumped out of sixteen C-130s in the only mass airborne operation of the war. The operation used a "hammer and anvil" approach, with the paratroopers sealing off any routes into Cambodia and the 1st and 25th Infantry Divisions sweeping northwest in search of the Central Office for South Vietnam (COSVN).

As ground forces moved forward, "the USAF waged a constant war of harassment and interdiction within the zone." The importance of air support in the South can probably not be overstated. The air force believed that close air support and interdiction in the South was indispensable, saying that "tactical air was one of the major factors responsible for turning a potential disaster into an allied victory." On the first day of the operation the USAF provided 111 F-100 strikes, 53 F-4 strikes, and 18 sorties by the B-52s. F-5s and B-57s also provided support. Each day of the operation saw diminished use of air support, with strikes dropping from over 200 the first day to less than 100 by D+3.[18]

On February 28, the PAVN and VC forces engaged the Americans in what became a series of battles: Prek Klok I, Prek Klok II, Ap Bau Bang, Ap Gu, and Suei Tre. In the initial battle (Prek Klok I), B Company of the 1/16th Infantry using the radio call sign "Devour" was ambushed by Viet Cong forces and overrun in a matter of minutes. The rest of the company was forced into hasty defensive positions as a VC regiment surrounded them. Overhead FACs called in air support in the form of F-100s. The Super Sabres dropped 500-pound bombs and strafed the enemy positions. B-57s provided heavier attack runs and later F-100 flights brought in napalm. These continuous CAS missions provided time for B Company, 2/18th Infantry, to reach their beleaguered comrades. B Company of the 1/16th Infantry suffered nearly 50 percent casualties during the day's combat.[19]

The air liaison officer on the ground, Major Clay Jackson, reported:

> The air was absolutely effective in this incident. . . . There were several napalm drops by Yellowjacket Flight (the three divert F-l00s) which broke the back of the attack and from that point on, pressure on the company was relieved and we started winning instead of having the issue in doubt as to whether the company was going to survive at all.[20]

Prek Klok I was followed by a respite as the ground forces continued to clear the area. Although there was near-daily contact, larger Viet Cong forces continued to eschew contact with the American forces. However, on March 10, 1967, the situation changed with an attack shortly before midnight. A battalion-sized force attacked under cover of darkness and indicated that Viet Cong forces were willing to engage in combat with the Americans.

A similar attack occurred on the night of March 19–20 near the hamlet of Bau Bang at Firebase 14. Led by a herd of fifteen cattle to aid in probing the parameters' defenses, the Viet Cong dropped mortars and grenades into the base. Air mobility units flew into the base and F-4s and F-100s caught the attacking forces out in the open. A combined-arms approach overwhelmed the Viet Cong forces. Army historian George MacGarrigle noted: "Twenty-nine tons of air-delivered ordnance, 3,000 artillery rounds, and large quantities of tank and automatic-weapons fire had proved too much for the Viet Cong."[21]

Junction City continued through March and April, with the army and air force working effectively together. The USAF provided over 5,000 tactical fighter sorties as well as 126 Arc Light missions, but perhaps the greatest contribution made by the USAF during this operation was its logistics effort and use of C-130s to air-drop supplies. At the end of the day, the "victory" of Junction City proved ephemeral. Although 5,000 structures were destroyed and 2,728 enemy counted as killed, the operation did not meet Westmoreland's expectations. Central Office for South Vietnam (COSVN) escaped and the Viet Cong adapted new tactics to counter American supremacy.

Junction City, perhaps more than any other operation of the war, clearly represented the war in South Vietnam—a decisive American victory, but with little to show for it strategically. After the war, there was an oft-heard refrain that the American military won every battle in which it engaged with the enemy. Although a debatable point, especially when one throws the various aerial operations into the conversation, it became emblematic of American perceptions of the war.

The Battle of Khe Sanh and the Tet Offensive

Next to Ia Drang and the Tet Offensive, no other engagement is as familiar fifty years later as the US Marine Corps stand at Khe Sanh. On the hill that gave the base its name, six thousand members of the III Marine Amphibious Force, ARVN, US Army, and USAF were surrounded by the PAVN. From January of 1968 to July of that year, the USMC along with members of the army, air force, and ARVN remained encircled in the combat base which overlooked the Rao Quan River and sat just south of the DMZ. The area had seen numerous combat operations dating back to 1964 with the arrival of American Special Forces. Sitting at a strategic crossroads, south of the Demilitarized Zone, Khe Sanh provided access to Laos, along Highway 9. This afforded the USMC a base of operations from which to monitor and interdict materiel flowing into South Vietnam along the Ho Chi Minh Trail. It proved to be a hill that Westmoreland was willing to metaphorically die on.

One air force report noted, "From the time the decision was made to hold Khe Sanh, its tenability became almost solely dependent upon airpower." Historian Donald Mrozek noted that the "defense of Khe Sanh could not be freed from memories of the French defeat at Dien Bien Phu in 1954," and the French garrison was certainly on the minds of base defenders as well as senior leaders who chose to hold the base at all costs. The singular difference between the two was the ability of the American forces to leverage air power for the dual purpose of attacking the PAVN and resupplying the marines at the garrison, or what historian Bernard Nalty called "firepower and logistic support." The French military had fewer than two hundred planes, most of an archaic nature. By 1968, the US military was operating more than two thousand aircraft—not to mention thousands more rotary-wing assets capable of supporting the marine garrison.[22]

Air power at Khe Sanh was given the operational name of Niagara because of the virtual waterfall of bombs dropped around the base—98,721 tons in total. Air power joined the battle on January 22 and ended in March, which meant that the air power support at Khe Sanh began before and continued concurrently with the Tet Offensive, which began on January 30. Westmoreland became obsessed with the defense of the garrison, going so far as to designate Lieutenant General Momyer as the "single manager for control of tactical air resources throughout South Vietnam and the extended battle area." This was a departure from previous command-and-control arrangements in which Momyer only held control of a portion of the air power operating in South Vietnam; namely, he lacked direct control over USMC aircraft, viewed by the Corps as indigenous flying artillery. Momyer also gained command and control over fighters and fighter-bombers stationed in Thailand. Previously, these aircraft only attacked targets in North Vietnam and along the Ho Chi Minh Trail.[23]

Westmoreland recognized the ongoing buildup of PAVN forces in Laos and informed the commanding general of III Marine Amphibious Force, General Robert E. Cushman, that this buildup in his area provided an opportunity to ply air power against massed formations of troops: "We should be prepared to surprise and disrupt enemy plans for an offensive against Khe Sanh with heavy bombing attacks on a sustained basis."[24]

Both Westmoreland and Momyer knew that the PAVN were building up their forces for an attack that could occur at Khe Sanh, but also saw that a more-general attack could fall anywhere in South Vietnam. Momyer seemed to recognize that there was a possibility of a general offensive throughout the country, informing his staff: "[T]he build-up of forces and materiel seems to indicate a much broader objective than Khe Sanh. He may be in the midst of a major build-up to wrest the initiative from us throughout the country. He may be after much bigger game than Khe Sanh." Momyer also directed his staff to keep up the interdiction campaign in Laos until the enemy tipped his hand.[25]

Air power, combining the forces of all services, provided the primary defense of the Khe Sanh base. Since the PAVN had to mass their forces to attack the base, there "was no shortage of lucrative targets."[26] This included the continued use of B-52s as a close air support platform. An enemy notebook captured after the battle of Khe Sanh ended noted the effects of the B-52 attacks:

From the beginning until the 60th day [of the siege at Khe Sanh] B-52 bombers continually dropped their bombs in this area with ever growing intensity and at any moment of the day. If someone came to visit this place, he might say that this was a storm of bombs and ammunition which eradicated all living creatures and vegetation whatsoever, even those located in caves or in deep underground shelters.[27]

From January 22 through March 31, 1968, the combined air forces of the USAF, USN, and USMC continually increased the number of CAS sorties around the Khe Sanh base. In January, the combined air arms completed 5,000 sorties, 3,334 of which were B-52 strikes. In February there were 8,708 sorties (1,057 B-52 strikes), and in March, 10,228 sorties (1,176 B-52 strikes).

This added up to nearly 100,000 tons of munitions deposited around the base itself, 59,542 of which came from the B-52s.[28]

Other than securing the continued occupation of the camp and the marines, soldiers, and airmen stationed there—which it assuredly did—it is difficult to quantify what this bombing accomplished. Air force reports listed trucks, gun positions, and bunkers destroyed as well as secondary fires started. One report indicated that as many as ten thousand PAVN soldiers died as a result of the bombing, and that other enemy troops were "demoralized" by the attacks.[29]

Exactly how dire was the situation at Khe Sanh? USAF historian Jacob Van Staaveren authored a top-secret report in 1970 that noted:

> General Westmoreland had warned that if the situation near the DMZ and at Khe Sanh worsened drastically, nuclear or chemical weapons might have to be used. This prompted General McConnell to press, although unsuccessfully, for JCS authority to request Pacific Command (PACOM) to prepare a plan for using low-yield nuclear weapons to prevent a catastrophic loss of the Marine base.[30]

As mentioned, there were two primary ways Khe Sanh differed from Dien Bien Phu. The first was firepower, and the second was the ability of the American forces to keep the base resupplied. While the B-52s and tactical fighters attacked mass troop formations, the USAF and USMC tactical airlift in the form of C-123 and C-130 aircraft, as well as rotary-wing assets, air-dropped and air-landed supplies into the garrison. Air drops were done in the form of 576 separate missions, 15 of which were ground proximity extraction system (GPES), and an additional 58 by the low-altitude parachute extraction system (LAPES). In addition to the 12,340 tons of resupply brought into the camp, the USAF also evacuated all casualties and reinforced the marines with additional forces through the cargo aircraft. Jacob Van Staaveren compared the resupply efforts to another famous air mobility mission, saying that the effort at Khe Sanh was "[s]urpassed perhaps only by the Berlin airlift, [and] was the dramatic demonstration of aerial resupply for the surrounded garrison."[31]

The ability of the USMC to hold on to Khe Sanh—with the aid of tactical air support that included not only aerial attack, but also aerial resupply—has to be viewed alongside the dichotomous fact that the USMC was ordered to abandon the base in the summer of 1968. Perhaps no other battle of the entire war demonstrated that even when American forces decisively defeated the enemy on the ground or through the air, it mattered little in a theater where fronts were as ephemeral as the enemy.

Three weeks after the siege at Khe Sanh began, the NVA and Viet Cong launched the Tet Offensive. Khe Sanh was only one part of ongoing NVA operations that dragged American forces out of the more-populated garrisons and cities toward the Laos and Cambodian borders in preparation for the Viet Cong offensive. Battles in late 1967—including Dak To, Loc Ninh, and Khe Sanh in early 1968—pulled American forces away from major cities and lulled them into a false sense of confidence that the regular NVA were pinned against the border country. As previously mentioned, both Westmoreland and Momyer had intelligence that indicated a general offensive was possible, but they, along with most others, missed the nature of the offensive. Rather than trapping the NVA on the border, it was the Americans who found themselves pinned away from the main event. The NVA chose the night of January 30 and the early-morning hours of January 31, the Vietnamese New Year, to launch their offensive.[32]

From Quang Tri and Hue in the North to Saigon in the South, large portions of cities rapidly fell to the Viet Cong forces. The VC struck at American air bases, breeching the perimeters and destroying aircraft where they sat parked on the ramps. Bases that sat farther outside the larger cities "emerged unscathed" according to one USAF history, and this included the bases of Cam Ranh Bay, Phu Cat, Phan Rang, and Tuy Hoa. On the ground the offensive "cost the Air Force millions of dollars in destroyed and damaged property," but this proved to be a lopsided tally when compared to what air power was able to do in helping to blunt the offensive throughout South Vietnam. During the intense fighting throughout the country, Westmoreland finally made Momyer the single manager for all air power assets conducting operations in South Vietnam. Momyer remembered later, "The flexibility of centralized control was never more dramatically demonstrated than when fighters and airlift forces were shifted from area to area to meet the enemy." For the first time in the war, all of the fixed-wing aircraft came under the control of the air component commander, making it feasible for him to respond with air power anywhere in the theater and to whatever priority COMUSMACV [Commander, US Military Assistance Command Vietnam] established.[33]

For the NVA and the VC, the problem for any offensive operation was that it forced them into, according to one report, a position where "he [the NVA/VC], concentrated his ground troops for attack," and this allowed American air power lucrative targets. Westmoreland then "sought to defeat the enemy country-wide, systematically using air power to support counterattacks designed to regain total control of Saigon, Hue, and the other cities."[34]

Although the Tet Offensive played out across South Vietnam, nowhere was the struggle greater than the city of Hue, what one US Marine Corps history called "some of the most intensive and bloody battles of the entire war." For the most part, the Tet Offensive was effectively blunted and then repelled. This was true everywhere, "except at the northern city of Hue, where fighting continued until the first week in March." The city of Hue was an important religious and cultural centerpiece to all Vietnamese people. Historian Bernard Nalty noted that the Imperial City of Hue was "a city that symbolized past greatness." The significance of the landmarks inside the city, including The Citadel, the heart of the old Imperial City, was so profound that in the immediate aftermath of the offensive, no artillery or air-to-ground munitions could be used. This mattered little, as even once restrictions were lifted, the reduced visibility and bad weather precluded close support sorties. One report noted the "morning and evening fog, intermittent rain, and almost constant overcast curtailed the employment of fighter and reconnaissance aircraft."[35]

As Nalty noted, on the ground, "Hue more closely resembled the urban combat of World War II in terms of duration, ferocity, and numbers involved." Fighting went from street to street and house to house, with the ARVN forces and US Marines engaged in urban combat that was quite different from the type commonly associated with Vietnam. The weather forced the USAF and USMC flying the CAS sorties to attack at night. One way both the USAF and USMC were able to strike targets in and around the city of Hue was through Combat Skyspot, which used ground-directed bombing and provided an all-weather and night-bombing capability.[36]

The ending of the hostilities in Hue "revealed the mass graves of local inhabitants murdered by the communist forces in acts of revenge or calculated terrorism that won no converts to their cause." Between punishment at the hands of the Viet Cong and collateral damage and deaths caused by the American and ARVN forces, the people of the city of Hue were sometimes caught between the proverbial rock and a hard place, or perhaps an unstoppable force and an immovable object.[37]

One official history noted that even as Momyer conducted Operation Niagara in defense of Khe Sanh, "the Seventh Air Force was still able to provide enough firepower to be a major factor in the defeat of the enemy offensive." Across South Vietnam, air power proved pivotal, both in terms of firepower and logistics support. However, the success for the South Vietnamese forces and their American allies proved ephemeral.[38]

There were downsides for the American forces in the wake of Tet. Even though air power had had a profound effect on the battlefield, there was widespread urban damage and civilian casualties. According to one air liaison officer serving with the 25th Infantry Division, the town of Tan Hoa "no longer existed. It's just a big scar on the earth now." Air force historian John Schlight noted that "Air Force fighter-bombers launched carefully controlled strikes, but in crowded urban areas, collateral damage proved unavoidable, resulting in civilian casualties and perhaps 600,000 new refugees that strained the resources of the Saigon government."

Tet also revealed that there was "doubt that the VNAF could have met its responsibilities in the first few days." There was a silver lining to this final statement, though. An analysis of VNAF actions throughout the Tet Offensive indicated that the organization "gained confidence in their ability to operate as a fighting unit. Specifically noted was an increase in morale and efficiency attributed to the shared hardships and success."[39]

The most significant effect of the Tet Offensive occurred not in Vietnam, but back in the United States. Again, an official air force history described the reaction to Tet by the American people: "The extent and nature of the 1968 Communist Tet Offensive proved to be a political disaster to the Johnson administration. The American people—who had only recently been assured the allies were winning the war—were shocked by the enemy's ability to strike throughout South Vietnam, even to the gates of the US Embassy in Saigon."[40]

Battle of Kham Duc

Kham Duc was an isolated Special Forces camp in the Quang Ting province, located west of Da Nang, south of Khe Sanh, and just east of the Laotian boarder. The camp sat astride a 6,000-foot paved runway with mountains surrounding the site, thus giving incoming aircraft the perception of flying into a bowl. Three miles southwest of Kham Duc, 33 US Marines, 8 Special Forces personnel, and 173 South Vietnamese troops occupied an old French fort at Ngoc Tavak, using it to identify enemy forces moving into the area.

In the early part of 1968, the NVA began extending Route 165 across Laos and into South Vietnam. The two camps monitored this expansion and coordinated with higher headquarters for interdiction against known enemy positions. These included fighter and B-52 strikes against the expanding route. More than 1,700 personnel were present at the two camps, and of these 272 were Vietnamese dependents. Whether because of its strategically vulnerable position or because of its mission monitoring NVA forces, it became apparent in early April 1968 that the North Vietnamese were taking a keen interest in Kham Duc, with an eye toward eliminating it.[41]

The enemy attack began on May 10, 1968. A situation report indicated that "enemy force is reported extremely determined." At Ngoc Tavak, a heavy artillery and mortar bombardment was followed by a grenade and satchel bomb attack. The camp was initially believed to be completely overrun, but it was later determined that it was evacuated in an orderly fashion, albeit with heavy casualties as the USMC, US Army Special Forces, and two Australians pulled back toward Kham Duc.[42]

At Kham Duc, the army artillerymen fired the last of their ammunition and then destroyed their 105mm howitzers. Overhead an AC-47 Spooky gunship provided close air support to deadly effect, even going so far as to fire on portions of the actual camp overrun by NVA, which forced them to retreat. An official air force history later said that survival on the ground depended greatly upon the AC-47 and later tactical air support.[43]

On the afternoon of May 11, Operation Golden Valley commenced to reinforce the base. This included insertion of an infantry company and an artillery battery into the camp throughout the day. Reinforcement concluded by nightfall and accounted for an additional 612 troops at the camp. On the second day of the attack it seemed MACV intended to hold the camp, but their calculations changed throughout the next several hours, as it became increasingly apparent that air power was proving only a temporary solution and not something 7th Air Force had the ability to keep up indefinitely. Holding the base became untenable. Even the use of B-52s, flying close air support as they had at Khe Sanh, did not stem or halt the attack against the base.[44]

By the morning of May 12, a decision needed to be made. MACV decided that Kham Duc no longer "had military or political significance," and sent word to Momyer at 7th Air Force to evacuate the base. Kham Duc was completely surrounded, all of the observation posts in enemy hands as their previous occupants attempted to evade back toward the relative safety of the main camp. As dawn broke, the Kham Duc camp was under continuous rocket and mortar attack. Despite being under a constant barrage, the tactical air support overhead became a "key factor in stopping the enemy assault," but it was clear that air power could only hold the enemy at bay for so long.[45]

However, a veritable umbrella of tactical fighter and attack aircraft circled overhead, controlled by at least three forward air controllers and one EC-130 Airborne Battlefield Command and Control Center (ABCCC). Momyer ordered the ABCCC—call sign Hillsboro—into the battle to coordinate all of the tactical air assets and pass them off to the appropriate FACs. USMC A-4 Skyhawks, US Navy fighters, and USAF A-1E Skyraiders, F-4 Phantoms, F-100 Huns, and F-105 Thuds all provided support on the morning of May 12. By 0830 that morning all B-52 strikes in Vietnam were rerouted in support of Kham Duc.[46]

Despite the overall effort given to the rescue, or perhaps because of it, chaos reigned in the air. First, MACV supported a rescue effort, but then due to enemy fire that blanketed the runway from every direction, decided it was too dangerous to land heavy aircraft. Hillsboro coordinated with the FACs and tactical aircraft to create a corridor around the runway down which the C-130s or C-123s could land. Somewhere along the way conflicting orders came down to the ABCCC that an extraction of ground forces would not take place, despite the fact that a rescue effort was already under way.[47]

Despite orders to the contrary, and whether these were ignored or lost in the fog and friction of the battle, another C-123 aircraft flew into Kham Duc at 1100. Three minutes later it was in the air carrying 44 American personnel and an unknown number of Vietnamese civilians. The next C-130 didn't land until 1530 that afternoon. As this aircraft, mission 603, began evacuating the base, tragedy struck. After taking off with roughly 150 people it was hit by ground fire and exploded.[48]

More C-130s followed mission 603 into the impossible situation that was Kham Duc. The next C-130 already on approach saw 603 explode, but the pilot was more concerned about the enemy fighters on the ground taking aim at his aircraft. After an abortive attempt to land, he approached Kham Duc for a second time. On approach, enemy rounds opened up holes in the floor of the cockpit, and the landing was so hard the hydraulic system ceased functioning. The C-130 careened into a crashed CH-47 and the pilot pushed his aircraft over into a ditch to avoid permanently blocking the runway. By the time it rolled to a stop in a ditch, a front tire had blown and the fuel tanks had been punctured. With the sole exception of the first C-123 no other aircraft had landed and successfully removed personnel from the base. This included two C-130s.[49]

Things finally improved in rapid succession when two C-130s landed and successfully took off with full loads. All this time tactical assets blanketed the surrounding areas with bombs and napalm. The final C-130 landed, but in the chaos and confusion a three-man combat control team disembarked, thinking they were supposed to get off the aircraft and aid unit leaders on the ground who, unbeknownst to the combat controllers, had taken off on the previous C-130. Luckily, a member of the crew of the C-130 they had just hopped off of saw them as they pulled away and the call went out that three Americans remained on the ground in what was essentially now enemy territory. One final act in this drama remained to be played out.[50]

Circling overhead was C-123 pilot Major Joe Jackson and his crew. USAF First Lieutenant Fred Smith was flying his fifth combat mission in support of the evacuation efforts that day:

> I was flying out of Cam Ranh Bay as a back-seater in an F-4C. The evening before we had been watching a movie when it was turned off and everyone was ordered to bed. The next morning we flew in support of the efforts to get everyone out of the Special Forces camp at Kham Duc. That mission we were flying with CBUs on the center-line station and 500-lb. bombs on the outboard. We didn't have a gun pod. The forward air controller told us a C-123 [Joe Jackson's

aircraft] was headed in to pick up the last guys. He wanted us to simulate a strafing run to keep the enemy's heads down. We did just that.[51]

Jackson dropped his aircraft out of the sky and onto the runway. Prior to touching down he ordered his loadmaster to have the rear cargo door open and ready to receive the three airmen. Landing, he dodged his aircraft as best he could around the shattered remains of the C-130 and MH-47, stopping directly next to the crew who were already making a beeline toward the waiting aircraft. Receiving heavy fire the entire time, no sooner had the three airmen clambered aboard than Jackson was pushing the throttles forward. He spent less than a minute on the ground. For his actions that day he would later receive the Medal of Honor.

Kham Duc was officially closed for business. Besides, without American Special Forces troops in the area, it provided "more freedom to apply tac air [tactical air attacks] and B-52 attacks against the enemy in the area."[52]

The CHECO report published two months after the evacuation stated:

> Kham Duc, in one sense, was a microcosm of the whole air war in Vietnam compressed into the time span of a single day. It brought practically every element of US air operations into play, and perhaps most important, it drew on resources from throughout Southeast Asia. Despite various problems which were encountered . . . integrated Air Forces accomplished a remarkably successful evacuation operation at Kham Duc while making it costly for the enemy attackers.[53]

Kham Duc saw it all. Fighters, bombers, attack aircraft, jets, propeller-driven, rotary-wing, airlift. If it functioned at some point during the Vietnam conflict, it probably played a hand in the rescue efforts at Kham Duc. Although the materiel cost was high—a CH-47, an A-1E, a CH-46, an O-2, a UH-1C, and two C-130s—the loss of life was significantly less thanks to the aerial evacuation, which successfully rescued 1,500 of the 1,760 people at Kham Duc.[54]

By the summer of 1968, both William Westmoreland and William Momyer's time in Vietnam had come to an end. Westmoreland departed in June of 1968 to become the twenty-fifth chief of staff of the US Army. Replacing Westmoreland was General Creighton W. Abrams. In August, Momyer departed to take command of the air force's Tactical Air Command, and Lieutenant General George S. Brown took command of the 7th Air Force. Abrams and Brown entered into a situation in which they did not enjoy a public or a press that were willing to accept their pronouncements of success as willingly as Westmoreland's. The war had taken a turn in the hearts and minds of the American people.

In 1968 Richard Nixon was elected to the White House, and after his in-auguration in 1969, the shift toward "Vietnamization" began. In the mean-time, the American commanders in Vietnam needed to continue to keep the PVAN out of the South. For his part, and to ensure another Tet did not occur, Abrams continued to make use of B-52s, which afforded him "the punching power of several ground divisions." Obviously, SAC continued to be opposed to what they viewed as a misuse of the strategic bombers, but with the war in Vietnam showing no signs of abating, and with the enthusiastic support of these bombing missions coming from MACV as well as the Nixon adminis-tration, they lost the argument. Upon taking office Nixon would also see the use of the big bombers expanded further to missions inside Cambodia.[55]

The 7th Air Force sorties in South Vietnam were aimed principally at sup-porting the ground effort. The American air forces also continued to train the South Vietnamese Air Force, but given Soviet support to the North, it was clearly apparent that South Vietnam would not be able to stand unaided once American materiel left the region. South Vietnam was not going to be flying the latest technologically advanced fighters or bombers. Flying CH-47s, UH-1s, F-5s, and A-37s (the latter adapted from an American training aircraft, the T-37), there was no way the RVNAF could sustain operations against a determined and coordinated attack against their country, short of massive American support.

Easter Offensive

Beginning on March 30, 1972, North Vietnam launched a massive and very conventional invasion into South Vietnam across three separate routes origi-nating in North Vietnam, Laos, and Cambodia. Americans remember it as the Easter Offensive, but in Vietnam it is known as the Nguyen Hue Offen-sive, or the *Chiến dịch Xuân hè* 1972. The offensive served as North Vietnam's attempt to set conditions for the negotiations at the Paris Peace Accords. By this point American troop presence and associated air power in-theater had been drawn down to an almost negligible amount—certainly not enough to blunt the North's offensive. In addition, the forces of South Vietnam could not hope to stand against the North despite the years spent preparing them to do so. Nixon refused to send in more troops; in fact, he continued the Vietnamization process of withdrawing American troops while the offensive occurred. While the idea of re-deploying American troops into South Viet-nam was not possible, the ability to do the same with American air power was possible. To that end, American air power across the services was bolstered.

The USAF executed Operation Constant Guard, which saw the deployment of 174 F-4s from the United States under TAC. SAC executed Operation Bullet Shot, sending B-52s to Guam. Associated tankers for aerial refueling also supported the two SAC and TAC deployments. Between May and July, the air force nearly tripled available strikers in the region. The US Navy also more than doubled the amount of carriers in the region, going from two to six by the end of April.[56]

Weather initially hindered the American counteroffensive. Only USN and USMC A-6 intruders and the USAF's new F/B-111 Aardvark were capable of providing an all-weather attack platform. Historian Bernard C. Nalty noted that weather problems in particular drew the ire of Henry Kissinger, who was quoted as saying, "It seemed to me that our entire Air Force consisted of delicate machines capable of flying only in a war in the desert in July. I suggested that if they could not fly, maybe they could taxi north for twenty-five miles."[57]

During the Easter Offensive, air power proved decisive in stopping the PAVN and forcing North Vietnam back to the peace table in Paris, even more so than the Linebacker Operations conducted against the North. Using the aircraft rushed into the breech, the USAF and USN pulverized PAVN units and moved to interdict their transportation system by destroying bridges, cutting roads, and blunting the North Vietnam's Army move toward the city of Hue in the North. This was done in conjunction with the bombing of targets in the North as part of the Linebacker Operations.

In the South, the use of B-52 strikes under Arc Light, tac air fighter-bombers, and the use of AC-47 gunships crippled the PAVN. Roughly 100,000 North Vietnam soldiers were killed or missing, a significant portion of the overall fighting force available. The use of B-52s, long questioned by the Strategic Air Command, proved especially valuable during the Easter Offensive. That being said, North Vietnam had reason to believe the offensive had been successful. They now controlled portions of South Vietnam, and these troops remained there after the signing of the Paris Peace Accords. It seemed, despite the success of the counteroffensive, the Americans were as ready to end the war as were the North Vietnamese. Only South Vietnam saw their own bargaining position weakened.

Conclusion

The air war in South Vietnam was characterized primarily as a CAS mission, with the interdiction of supplies being a second important component. The war in the North, covered in the next chapter, was both a strategic bombing mission and an air-to-air war. The war in North Vietnam saw the use of surface-to-air missiles and MiG fighters. In Laos and Cambodia, the air war was primarily comprised of search-and-destroy interdiction missions. It was only the air war in South Vietnam where CAS support represented the primary way of war.

The US military dropped more than four million tons of bombs on South Vietnam during the course of the conflict, to very little effect—at least the effect the American military was looking for, which was removing Viet Cong and PAVN forces from the conflict. Body count became the name of the game; even if these numbers became wildly inflated over the years, there is no doubt that American air power did indeed kill thousands of regular and irregular troops.

The bombing in the South fundamentally altered life for the South Vietnamese farmers living in the villages of the country. Historian Gregory Daddis noted in his book *Westmoreland's War* that villagers began working at night because they feared the air strikes that came during the day. Rather than reinforce solidarity with the people they were trying to defend, American air power drove a wedge between them due to what Daddis called the "disruptive force of American strikes across Vietnam." American air power proved to be a decisive asset, but certainly not in the way it was intended. Rather than demonstrating resolve and technological superiority, and reinforcing the South's desire for stability and independence, it did exactly the opposite, driving much of the populace against the American intervention, the South Vietnamese government, and into the hands of the Viet Cong and the NLF.[58]

The bombing in the South was not a total loss. At least the American military coordination between the army and air force worked well during the conflict. Air force historian Richard Hallion said, "The success of battlefield support did much to solidify bonds between soldiers and airmen." In South Vietnam, the USAF and the US Army had relatively good working relationships. Air power did what the army and the USMC wanted it to do: It provided support to troops on the ground. During the named operations— Junction City, Cedar Falls, Silver Bayonet, and hundreds of others—the USAF provided overhead and on-call CAS, and most ground commanders indicated they were pleased with the support they received. There is no doubt that at Khe Sanh, Ia Drang, and elsewhere, air power was not only instrumental, but decisive.

It was only after the war, during the debates about the procurement of a new attack aircraft for the US Air Force, that the question of whether the air force cared about or wanted to provide CAS reared its head, leading USAF chief of staff General John Ryan to inform the TAC commander, then General Momyer, "We will never be able to satisfy the Army on close air support no matter what we build to do the job."[59]

Although significant rivalry and competition existed during the war in South Vietnam, the lessons learned by both services forced them to work together in the aftermath of that conflict. Perhaps one of the greatest accomplishments between the services in the aftermath of Vietnam was the close coordination that developed between the USAF's Tactical Air Command and the US Army's Training and Doctrine Command (TRADOC), and the resultant "31 Initiatives." These initiatives led directly to the doctrine of AirLand Battle, the importance of the suppression of enemy air defenses, the development of Identification of Friend or Foe (IFF) systems, and dozens of other concepts that became hallmarks of military cooperation, evidenced in the combat successes during Operation Desert Storm. The friction that existed in the 1960s between the two services has never entirely dissipated, but it did lead to an understanding of the importance of successful joint operations.

Even during the Vietnamization period, the VNAF never came close to the level of air operations that the United States did. They were simply not trained or equipped to fight a war on the scale the United States was capable of operating from. America brought the very best of post–World War II industrial might to Southeast Asia. The aircraft designed for general war with the Soviets, missile employment, dropping nuclear weapons, or intercepting Soviet bombers all went through various changes to participate in a war very few could have found on a map.

The war inside of South Vietnam was marked by contact with enemy forces, the development and implantation of Air Cav/Air Mobile operations, and close air support to troops on the ground. Assets used in this theater included US Army helicopters and later gunships, USAF fighters under the command of 7th Air Force, and SAC bombers. In South Vietnam, the president of the United States and secretary of defense had less to say about target selection than they did in the North. Even though the air campaigns against North Vietnam were obviously part of the wider conflict, the war in the South for the American airmen was vastly different than when they had to fly north. In reality, they were essentially two completely different air wars.

During the entirety of the events covered in this chapter, a very different kind of air war occurred north of the demilitarized zone and the 17th parallel.

4

"To Deter Hanoi . . ."

The War in the North

T HE AIR WAR AGAINST NORTH VIETNAM, by the air forces of the United States, remains the most remembered, most discussed, and most controversial aspect of the various air wars of the Vietnam conflict. It was, primarily, an air-to-ground war. An offshoot of these campaigns was the air-to-air war, discussed in chapter 7.

The air arms of the US military took the war into the North in August of 1964. An official air force history described initial resistance in this manner: "[The strikers] encountered only a rudimentary air defense system which did not severely impede the attack. North Vietnam possessed no jet aircraft or surface-to-air missiles and had only a crude radar system. These deficiencies were soon corrected." Back in Washington, DC, debate about how to conduct a war against North Vietnam was fierce. The Joint Chiefs of Staff advocated heavier attacks, but Secretary of Defense McNamara argued against an all-out attack in North Vietnam for fear of drawing China or the Soviet Union into the war. This back-and-forth had implications for the line pilots flying in Vietnam.[1]

As attention—and aerial attacks—turned toward North Vietnam, a new phase of the war began. Initially, the strikes fell under Operation Flaming Dart, which hit targets in North Vietnam and escalated American involvement in the war. Shortly thereafter, beginning in March 1965 and lasting through October 1968, the primary mission became Operation Rolling Thunder. These operations used both navy and air force assets, but the services still did not coordinate their actions, leading to continued disjointed air operations thanks to the divided route packages (RPs).

Navy fighters and attack aircraft flew from the aircraft carriers in the Gulf of Tonkin and the South China Sea. USAF aircraft that attacked North Vietnam departed from one of seven Royal Thai Air Force Bases (RTAFB) or Royal Thai Navy Airfields. Four of these bases had fighters: Udorn in the north, Ubon in the southeast, and Korat and Takhli in the west. U-Tapao Royal Thai Navy Airfield housed KC-135s and SAC's B-52s. Don Muang north of Bangkok was principally a combat support base and saw a continued decreasing US presence throughout the war. Finally, Nakhon Phanom was a special operations base and also contained search-and-rescue assets.

This chapter dually explores the rapidly expanding air war in the North as well as the burgeoning SAM threat and arrival of MiG aircraft of the North Vietnam Air Force (NVAF) into the theater to counter the growing American bombing missions. By 1965, there was no doubt that American involvement had gone beyond any advisory and training missions and had developed into a full-scale military operation, conducting strikes around the clock. Operations including Iron Hand—the first attempts at Suppression of Enemy Air Defenses (SEAD)—began as commanders in-theater desperately tried to adapt and overcome what was recognized as tactical and training deficiencies aircrews received prior to arriving in-country. There was a singular primary goal to increase aerial attacks against North Vietnam. This was to "put pressure on Hanoi leadership to terminate the war" through the use of what one air force study called the "measured escalation of force."[2]

It is important to note that weather had a major impact on operations for both sides of the conflict. The monsoon season in North Vietnam ran from November to April, and in Laos it ran from April to November. This weather pattern shifted attention between the two countries. Not only did the cloud cover and rain hinder air operations, it also hindered movement on the ground as well. No amount of technology in the air or on the ground was capable of stopping Mother Nature's operations, and thus the weight of effort for both sides was somewhat dictated by the weather in North Vietnam and Laos.

The Physics of Flying in North Vietnam

The differences between flying combat missions in South Vietnam versus in North Vietnam were immense. For starters, pilots in South Vietnam flew "in-country" for one year and then rotated back to the United States. In North Vietnam, due to the higher loss rate and exposure to the greater risk of the North Vietnamese air defenses, pilots could expect to return home after "only" flying one hundred missions. The single best summation of the differences between missions in North and South Vietnam came from F-105 and F-4 Vietnam flier Ed Rasimus in his work *When Thunder Rolled*:

> In South Vietnam, the mission was close air support, the employment of tactical aircraft near friendly troops. The threat was small arms fire and bad weather. . . . There were no heavy anti-aircraft guns. There were no SAMs. There were no MiGs. . . . North Vietnam was a different mission. It was interdiction. It was going a long way into enemy territory against targets like bridges and railroads, factories and power plants. It meant barrages of triple-A and radar-guided SAMs and encounters with MiGs. It meant capture and torture, beatings and death. Bail out in the north and you were a long way from friendly forces.[3]

Public perceptions of flying fighters have been heavily influenced by air-to-air battles seen in movies: close-in flying where the enemy is nearly canopy to canopy, gun kills, missile shots that leave the rails and seconds later kill the enemy with laser-like precision. Movie dogfights—*Top Gun* being the most representative here—that occur over the course of five to ten minutes have soured the reality of what it was like for fighters or bombers in the jet age.

Flying at 10,000 feet, a Vietnam War pilot's horizon was 122 miles away, distance to horizon increasing correspondingly as altitude increased. If an American fighter pilot knew where to look and his view was unobscured by haze or other environmental factors, an enemy plane might be spotted visually as far away as ten miles, but of course, two combatants flying head-on to merge was rare, and MiGs more often than not were not seen before they attacked. Americans flying over the familiar landmarks of Thud Ridge or the MiG airfield at Phuc Yen could easily have seen the off-limits city of Hanoi. Naval aviators going "feet dry" into RP VI-B could pick up the also off-limits harbor city of Haiphong.

Pilots relied not only on their own internal radar, controlled by the WSO or NFO in the two-seat aircraft, but also the combined airborne and sea-based command-and-control systems: EC-121 Warning Stars and the US Navy's Positive Identification Radar Advisory Zone (PIRAZ). More than knights riding at each other in a jousting bout, intercepting an enemy, or locating your target on the ground, was about radar and radio discipline and geometric principles. It was about strict adherence to rules of engagement and following prescribed "standardization and evaluation." But this could only be accomplished after briefing, suiting up in a G suit, helmet, parachute, and survival gear, and strapping into the nearly 62,000-pound aircraft. Each and every mission began from either the ready room of an aircraft carrier or the confines of an air base in South Vietnam and Thailand—although no aircraft flying from a Thai air base could provide air support to troops in South Vietnam, another quirk of the diplomatic alliances and rules of engagement.[4]

North Vietnam was bracketed on three sides by American fighter and at-tack aircraft flying out of Yankee Station and South Vietnam and Royal Thai air bases. To cut down on confusion and to ensure that all aircrews were able to easily identify where other fighters were coming from (and thus, the type of aircraft being flown), "Each base had common call signs: The F-4s out of Ubon were wild animals—Lion, Tiger, Wolf, etc. The F-105s from Takhli were cars—Buick, Ford, Chevy, etc. The F-105s of Korat were trees—Oak, Fir, Elm, etc. Consequently, once on strike frequency, you had a good idea who was where and what was going on."[5]

After takeoff and forming up with your flight—typically of four—and the other flights from your base, it was almost invariably a necessity to find an or-biting air-to-air refueling KC-135. Aircraft laden with a full load of munitions needed fuel before and after missions. More than a dozen of these race-track-shaped tanker orbits provided fuel to the hundreds of fighter, fighter-bomber, bomber, and reconnaissance aircraft on a daily basis. Often overlooked, the aerial tankers provided the air bridge that allowed the air war over North Vietnam to occur. The USAF KC-135 flew over 200,000 missions during the Vietnam War and delivered 1.4 billion gallons of fuel in 8 million indi-vidual refueling actions. These numbers do not include the navy's indigenous carrier-based refuelers, including the A-3 Skywarrior and the A-4 Skyhawk. The USAF's Air Mobility Command Office of History dubbed Vietnam the "first Tanker War."[6]

Briefing, takeoff, formation, and refueling accomplished, pilots could then "push" to the "difficult" portion of their mission, their targets in North Viet-nam, found in one of seven different route package areas. The USAF and US Navy decided to divide North Vietnam up rather than work jointly together. From the 17th parallel and moving north, in consecutive order, were RPs 1 through 4; number 1 belonged to both the USAF and the USN, and numbers 2 through 4, the navy. RP-5 was the largest area, containing the northwest portion of North Vietnam, and belonged to the air force. RP-6 was divided into two sub-portions, A and B. RP-6A was the USAF and RP-6B, the USN. Inside RP-6 were the major industrialized cities, including Hanoi and the port city of Haiphong. For much of the war, these cities were off limits, and a buf-fer or no-fly area extended ten miles from the center of Hanoi and five miles around Haiphong. Finally another no-fly zone extended for twenty miles south from North Vietnam's border with China. Since the border with China was not a straight line, neither was the no-fly zone. Throughout the war, this provided problems for American aircraft operating in RP-5 and RP-6. If this seems confusing, it was. American pilot Ed Rasimus called the entire system "extensive, ridiculous, and illogical."[7]

Once a pilot found himself inside a North Vietnam RP, he now had to contend with the enemy's defensive countermeasures. On a bad day, this included the triumvirate of AAA, SAMs, and swarming enemy MiGs. Imagine taking an exit off of the highway and braking into the turn while a fellow traveler continues along the original route at 80 miles per hour. In under a minute the traveler continuing on the highway will be more than a mile down the road. Now, instead of a highway exit, the turn is conducted by a MiG-21, and instead of 80 miles an hour, the speed increases to 300 to 400 miles per hour, while the powerful F-4 continues forward, or the F-4 powers into a rolling climb, demonstrating just how quickly two aircraft could gain separation of miles in the aerial arena. This applied to aircraft in the same flight as well. Seconds—rolling into or out of a bombing run—caused a separation of several thousand feet, and it was easy to lose sight of flight leads.

Flaming Dart and Rolling Thunder (March 1965–October 1968)

An attack on the American base at Pleiku on February 6, 1965, directly led to President Johnson calling for retaliatory strikes against the country of North Vietnam. After learning of the attack that killed eight Americans, wounded more than one hundred, and saw ten aircraft destroyed, Johnson reportedly said, "I've had enough of this." On February 7, 1965, the first Flaming Dart mission was flown, targeting North Vietnamese army bases, logistics outposts, and communication centers. At the time of the attacks the chairman of the Council of Ministers of the Soviet Union, Alexei Kosygin, was in Hanoi. Kosygin hoped to convince the leaders in North Vietnam to open negotiations with the United States. When the bombing began, Kosygin's mission became the first casualty.

Flaming Dart missions were soon followed by a full-scale bombing campaign named Rolling Thunder. This operation was a graduated and controlled use of fighter-bombers for air-to-ground attack missions that, at its heart, attempted to get North Vietnam to stop aiding the counterinsurgency in South Vietnam. This never happened. *The Pentagon Papers* called the operation "a comparatively risky and politically sensitive component of U.S. strategy." There continued to be a great fear of widening the war beyond the boundaries of Southeast Asia. Thus, much of the operation was controlled very strictly from inside Washington, DC, with the Defense and State Departments weighing in heavily on target selection and approval, and in many cases, the president himself giving final approval. Senior leaders discouraged "the preparation of extended campaign plans which might permit any great latitude in the field."[8]

Thus was born the initial list of ninety-four targets. Contrary to popular belief, this was not a strategic air campaign document meant to cripple North Vietnam's industrial capability. Rather, the initial target list was more operational and tactical. The JCS divided the targets into three categories: Category A "included those targets the destruction of which was expected to bring an immediate reduction of DRV support to the PL [Pathet Lao] and VC forces." Category B "included targets the destruction of which would reduce the DRV military capability." Only Category C focused on industrial targets, and only eight of these were listed. Each of these target sets and the overall air campaign was explored in a "Top Secret/NOFORN (No Foreign Access)/Air Force Eyes Only 1968 Air War College Report."[9]

Category A targets included airfields (five total), road lines of communication (four), military barracks (six), ammunition dumps (two), military headquarters (eight), and supply dumps (five), for a total of thirty targets in the first category. Category B went on to list a further sixty-one targets, all of which can be considered tactical and operational targets focused more on hindering North Vietnam's transportation system, with attacks on ports, storage depots, railroads, rail yards, and storage areas. Only Category C targets included specific industrial targets: the Viet Tri chemical plant, Thai Nguyen Iron and Steel Combine, Haiphong Radio Station, Hanoi International Radio/Receiver Station, and a thermal power plant/machine tool factory. This demonstrates that air planners plying their trade during Vietnam were not wedded to a World War II industrial warfare model. Although LeMay is remembered for wanting to bomb North Vietnam "back into the stone age," the JCS target list actually reflects an emphasis on strategic paralysis and interdiction more than on industrial targets.[10]

In January of 1965, Maxwell Taylor, ambassador to South Vietnam, sent a message to President Johnson requesting, as soon as possible, an "extension of air strikes against the DRV in accordance with the Phase II concept. In the meantime, I would hope that, regardless of GVN performance in respect to the criteria, the USG would be ready at any time to approve reprisal strikes to respond as appropriate to major VC terrorism." Taylor got his wish with the onset of Rolling Thunder. However, there were indications almost immediately that the attacks against North Vietnam were not having the desired effects.[11]

In May, and not long into the Rolling Thunder operation, the chairman of the JCS, General Earle Wheeler, sent a memorandum to Secretary McNamara in which he stated, "[O]ur air strikes have not reduced in any major way the capability of the DRV armed forces to perform their mission of defense of the homeland, to train their own and infiltration forces for South Vietnam and Laos, and to provide logistic support at present levels of activity." As to whether or not the air strikes against the North were having any type of morale effects among the people, Wheeler was forced to conclude that Western journalists in the North "see no signs that the people are pressing the regime for a settlement of the conflict. Rather, the popular reaction to the strikes seems to be that of 'grim determination to continue the fight.'" Wheeler noted that even though air attacks hindered to an unknown degree North Vietnam's logistics capabilities, there seemed to be no doubt that the attacks "have not reduced their over-all military capabilities in any major sense. Neither have we seriously hurt the North Vietnamese economy." A separate Special National Intelligence Estimate, dated June 2, 1965, stated with regard to ongoing and gradually escalating operations, that "as long as the Communists think they are winning in South Vietnam, bombing of North Vietnam is unlikely to lead them to make conciliatory gestures."[12]

President Johnson requested that Secretary McNamara provide an official evaluation of the Rolling Thunder operation in July of 1965. McNamara responded on the thirtieth of that month, and the assessment was not good. The secretary of defense pointed out that Flaming Dart and Rolling Thunder had both been initiated as reprisal operations for the Gulf of Tonkin incident, the attack on the Bien Hoa airfield, and the Christmas Eve 1964 bombing of the Brinks Hotel in Saigon that killed two Americans and wounded dozens more. From these incidents the United States had initiated bombing missions to both force a settlement to the conflict and to interdict supplies flowing south.[13]

Selecting Targets in North Vietnam

Many of the intelligence photos used to select targets inside North Vietnam came from air power of a different sort. President Johnson's national security advisor, Walt Rostow, noted that SR-71 reconnaissance flights "were invaluable to the president. We learned precisely the locations of missile and antiaircraft batteries, what ships were in the harbor unloading, and obtained up-to-date targeting intelligence for our bombing missions." Rostow went on to state that without the SR-71 flights and the photographs they provided, "Johnson would never have allowed any tactical air operations in the North."[14]

President Johnson kept strict control of target selection for the Rolling Thunder campaign and all targets in North Vietnam. The official history of the Joint Chiefs of Staff noted that

> President Johnson kept the Joint Chiefs of Staff on the margin of his policymaking for the Vietnam War. The President attempted to oversee every detail of

military operations, at the cost of increasing physical and emotional strain. He relied for advice primarily upon a small group of trusted officials—McNamara, Secretary of State Dean Rusk, and successive presidential national security advisers, McGeorge Bundy and Walt Rostow. Johnson used his regular Tuesday luncheons with these principals as his main venue for managing the war; for example, the luncheon attendees picked the targets for ROLLING THUNDER.[15]

The picking of targets by policymakers in Washington, DC, particularly by the president of the United States and a small cabal of trusted advisors, should not be overlooked. It has been noted in multiple sources that President Johnson once quipped, "[T]hey can't even bomb an outhouse without my approval." The officers at MACV and 7th Air Force did not have the leeway to select their own targets. A former chief of naval operations and Vietnam veteran, Admiral James K. Holloway III, noted:

> The targeting, in terms of general policy, broad guidelines, and sometimes even specific objectives, came from Washington to CINCPAC. A specificity of the Washington targeting directions varied, depending upon political circumstances in the White House and the degree of involvement on the part of key individuals in the Pentagon. From the Washington guidance provided through JCS channels, CINCPAC prepared a target list, which was drawn on by MACV and CTF 77, who coordinated carefully to ensure that national and JCS priorities were followed, that all assigned targets were covered, and that Air Force and Navy units were given targets that best suited their special capabilities.[16]

General Momyer noted that he, as 7th Air Force commander, had little choice in which targets could be struck inside his own theater: "[I]ntelligence analysis led to the nomination of targets to the JCS that the president approved and then sent to CINCPAC for strike." He added that the leaders in North Vietnam knew exactly which targets were left off of the approved lists and therefore knew where they could "hide" these resources, often in plain sight. According to Momyer, "All residential areas of Hanoi and Haiphong were filled with supplies stacked on each side of the street. Photos showed vehicles lined up bumper to bumper." Finally, Momyer lamented that the North Vietnamese could easily discern which targets were going to be attacked. "We had little opportunity to surprise or deceive the North Vietnamese about strike force targets and times. They fully understood the creeping release of targets, and therefore could predict from day to day what was next on the list."[17]

While Momyer fumed at his inability to strike useful targets, McNamara seemed to believe that the interdiction effort [had] "caused North Vietnam increasing difficulty in supplying their units in Laos and South Vietnam." However, he could not quantify the degree of that difficulty. For a man known for his preference for numbers, he had none in this case. Furthermore, there was also no indication that bombing missions had any effect on the number or severity of ongoing attacks in South Vietnam by the Viet Cong. It seems clear that McNamara looked for ways to show the president that the bombings were having an impact, but had difficulty in doing so. McNamara attached a tab to the memorandum that showed the number of targets, the number of those targets already struck, as well as "percent of national capacity destroyed," but this still did not provide ample evidence that the bombing of North Vietnam was having any effect on the war.[18]

Strikes in North Vietnam as part of the Rolling Thunder campaign continued throughout the summer of 1965, although no one inside the administration could "point to any specific evidence that the bombing in the North had as yet had any impact on the war in the South." Despite this, the list of targets chosen in Washington, DC, proliferated from the initial 94 to 236. This accounted to roughly 750 strike sorties occurring in North Vietnam per week, which continued unabated through the summer and fall months of 1965, until a pause in the bombing took place between December 1965 and January 1966.[19]

Although the number of targets increased, the locations of targets that *could not* be struck did not change. Around the city of Hanoi, a circle extended from the city center twenty miles out. A ten-mile ring extended around the port city of Haiphong. CINCPAC Admiral Sharp noted that "foreign shipping would continue to resupply the system, and the U.S. air effort could harass but not effectively deter infiltration." One report noted that as much as 67 percent of North Vietnam's external supplies came through the ports of Haiphong, Hon Gay, and Cam Pha, each of them off limits for strikes. The rest of the supplies came over rail lines originating in China.[20]

Two rail lines moved the rest of the materiel south that did not come through the ports. Along the border with China, a prohibited zone existed, stretching twenty miles south. This provided another sanctuary for materiel and prohibited American airmen from interdicting North Vietnam's supply routes. Between Hanoi, the port cities, and the rail lines that were off limits to attack, North Vietnam imported their war-making capacity with near impunity. The CHECO reports note that "these constraints provided the enemy an open-ended funnel at the top, into which they could pour the supplies necessary in their attempt to obtain what they needed at the bottom—South Vietnam—regardless of U.S. interdiction efforts against the LOCs [lines of communication] in between." Short of an expanded war to interdict Chinese rail traffic or Soviet shipping, the United States was incapable of hindering North Vietnam's supply chain.[21]

As early as 1966, the USAF recognized the Rolling Thunder campaign was not working and that the NVN forces were applying countermeasures to increase their effectiveness against the American forces. This presented a further problem for the Americans—namely, that North Vietnam air defense forces knew where strikes would occur and could prepare for them.

> The buffer zones and sanctuaries were readily apparent to the enemy and the communists took full military advantage of [them]. The buffer zone alone, for instance, gave Hanoi thousands of square miles of territory they did not need to defend. This allowed them to concentrate AW [automatic weapons]/AAA [antiaircraft artillery] and SAM [surface-to-air missiles] in a far smaller area, increasing their ground fire base tremendously. At the same time, the buffer zone reduced U.S. strike pilots' flexibility by funneling ingress and egress routes into narrower, more predictable channels where the enemy could further concentrate his defense forces.[22]

When bombing resumed in January 1966, nothing had changed. Still no discernible results could be seen against North Vietnam nor against the efforts to interdict supplies flowing south. In 1966 John McNaughton, assistant secretary of defense for international security affairs, sent a memo to McNamara in which he wrote: "The present US objective in Vietnam is to avoid humiliation. The reasons we went into Vietnam to the present depth are varied; but they are now largely academic." McNaughton recognized the United States was in a dilemma with no clear way out. The only thing that did seem certain? The bombing was not working. The fliers of these missions soldiered on with grim resolve.[23]

During the Rolling Thunder missions, a typical preplanned strike package composed of tactical fighters and fighter-bombers in North Vietnam was nothing short of massive and consisted of dozens of jets. The strikers that took off from bases in Thailand had to attack targets in North Vietnam but were forbidden from hitting any targets or ground support in South Vietnam. One pilot remembered, "Aircraft from Thai bases were forbidden to deliver any kind of ordnance for any reason (into South Vietnam). How foolish of me to think the war was there. . . . It was isolated, fortressed, and revetted against a fighter pilot in Thailand doing anything to support the American ground forces engaged against the Viet Cong. The battlements were bureaucratic."[24]

Prior to the entrance of the fighter-bombers, two Wild Weasel F-105Fs preceded the strikers by one to five minutes. On both sides and above the strikers flew two flights of four MiG combat air patrols (MiGCAPs) whose sole mission was to find and keep any MiG aircraft away from the bombers. This did not always work. If MiGs could find their way near the striking aircraft and force them to jettison their bombs, the MiGs had accomplished their mission. The attack force itself was typically composed of eight to sixteen aircraft flying in flights of four. A variety of jamming and escort aircraft supported the strikers. Later missions, especially during the Linebacker Operations, would see the inclusion of escorts and fighters that performed the chaff mission, creating a corridor to confuse the SAM radars. These "gorilla packages" usually had more support aircraft than actual bombers. A Navy Alpha Strike followed similar procedures and consisted of a large number of the aircraft in the carrier air wing.

Captain Steve Ritchie remembered that a Rolling Thunder mission could include hundreds of aircraft: "[T]he total force generally included eight to sixteen strike airplanes, eight to sixteen escorts, eight to sixteen chaff airplanes, twelve to twenty MIG-CAP, four to eight Wild Weasel, Barrier CAP, Tanker CAP, weather recce and photo recce." However, with the advent and employment of laser-guided bomb (LGB)–equipped aircraft in later campaigns, the size of a mission and the need for so many aircraft greatly diminished. Fighter-bombers dropping LGBs had a greater accuracy against targets and thus did not need as many bomb-carrying aircraft. LGBs proved especially effective at dropping what was the bane of an attack pilot's existence: bridges. Prior to the use of LGBs, bridges proved to be an especially difficult nut to crack.[25]

Attacks on the bridges bring into focus the weight of effort air planners used against these fixed targets. Due to their fixed nature, bridges have always been particularly attractive targets. Throughout October of 1965, the air force and the navy sent dozens of aircraft against the Long Het, Kep, and Bac Can bridges. In each strike the bridges suffered damage to either the spans or the bridge itself. However, the North Vietnamese either repaired them or found ways to bypass them. Sometimes this meant repairing the bridge itself or using pontoons that could be pulled to shore to bypass the damaged bridge. Either way, despite their attractiveness as targets, destroying bridges remained easier said than done.[26]

Throughout the fall and into the winter of 1965, members of the Johnson administration debated the utility of a bombing pause against targets in the North. The pause, finally approved in December, went into effect on Christmas Eve. This halt in bombing lasted exactly thirty-seven days. Since becoming involved in Vietnam, the USAF had lost 311 aircraft to ground fire, surface-to-air-missile, or air combat, and most of those losses occurred in North Vietnam. In 1966 alone, those numbers were about to increase dramatically.[27]

1966–1968

The year 1966 began with a bombing pause in place in North Vietnam. In Washington the New Year saw administration officials continuing to debate the utility of resuming those paused missions. Robert McNamara and George

Ball continued to worry about drawing China into the conflict once the bombing campaign of Rolling Thunder resumed. On January 25, Ball wrote to the president in a memorandum titled, "The Resumption of Bombing Poses Grave Danger of Precipitating a War with China," saying, "sustained bombing of North Vietnam will more than likely lead us into a war with Red China—probably in six to nine months." Ball went on to give a particularly damning critique of the entire Rolling Thunder campaign to this point:

> Admittedly, we have never had a generally agreed upon rationale for bombing North Vietnam. But the inarticulate major premise has always been that bombing will somehow, some day, and in some manner, create pressure on Hanoi to stop the war. This is accepted as an article of faith, not only by the military who have planning and operational responsibilities but by most civilian advocates of bombing in the administration.[28]

The bombing of North Vietnam resumed six days later.[29]

More than a year into the Rolling Thunder campaign, the assessments of the bombing operations continued to pour in both from Vietnam itself and from other organizations, including the CIA and the DIA (Defense Intelligence Agency), which produced a report titled "An Appraisal of the First Year of Bombing in North Vietnam." The report gave the clearest indications of exactly what the bombing accomplished—very little—and indicated the targets hit as well as the ascertained results:

- Power plants: "Did not reduce the power supply for the Hanoi/Haiphong area."
- Manufacturing: "Loss of explosives plant of little consequence since China furnished virtually all the explosives required."
- Bridges: "NVN has generally not made a major reconstruction effort, usually putting fords, ferries, and pontoon bridges into service instead. Damage has neither stopped nor curtailed movement of military supplies."
- Railroad yards: "Has not significantly hampered the operations of the major portions of the rail network."
- Ports: "Impact on economy minor."
- Locks: "8 targets . . . only 1 hit."
- Transport equipment: "Destroyed or damaged 12 locomotives, 819 freight cars, 805 trucks, 109 ferries, 750 barges, and 354 other water craft. No evidence of serious problems due to shortages of equipment."

The report concluded that none of this mattered because even if strikes and resultant bomb damage assessment increased, North Vietnam remained "predominantly agricultural." As the authors of *The Pentagon Papers* summarized it, "North Vietnam was an extremely poor target for air attack."[30]

This then begs the question: If, instead of the escalatory strikes of Rolling Thunder, a bombing program of heavier strikes against North Vietnam's industrial base had been employed, would it have had a different impact in 1965 or 1966? The answer is an unequivocal no. North Vietnam had only a limited number of industrial targets, and even if these had been bombed into oblivion, the bulk of North Vietnam's war-fighting logistics came into the country from China and the Soviet Union, and these targets were never considered as possible opportunities to hit for the justifiable fear of the war spilling over into an East vs. West conflict. It was a war fought with imports, but the United States only attacked domestic targets.

Toward the end of 1967, it was becoming readily apparent that air power was accomplishing very little in the North. Although every indication up until this point seemed to show the same thing, and everyone involved in the selection of Rolling Thunder targets had often stated the same, a note in the Foreign Relations of the United States made it perfectly clear:

> As of October 1967, the U.S. bombing has had no measurable effect upon Hanoi's ability to mount and support military operations in the South. North Vietnam supports operations in the South mainly by functioning as a logistical funnel and providing a source of manpower, from an economy in which manpower has been widely under-utilized. Most of the essential military supplies that the VC/NVA forces in the South require from external sources are provided by the USSR, Eastern Europe, and Communist China. Furthermore, the volume of such supplies is so low that only a small fraction of the capacity of North Vietnam is required to maintain that flow.[31]

The air force blamed the failure on the administration's unwillingness to initiate attacks against the original ninety-four-target list in one fell swoop. Testifying in front of a Senate Armed Services Committee subcommittee for preparedness investigations, the USAF chief of staff, General John P. McConnell, stated:

> The original concept of the Joint Chiefs of Staff was to go in there with a very severe application of airpower. In fact our first target list was 94 targets which we intended to destroy in a total of 16 days. That process was disapproved. . . . It was the 2nd of March, 1965, and we recommended what we called a sharp sudden blow which would have in our opinion done much to paralyze the enemy's capability to move his equipment around to supply people in the South. That was disapproved as a concept.[32]

McConnell was wrong. As noted by the Foreign Relations of the United States, the official collection of US foreign policy documents, the fact was that the amount of supplies needed by forces in the South was so small that no amount of air power interdiction was going to stop them from arriving at their destination. The problem of interdiction on that supply route fell not to boots on the ground, but to specialized aircraft flying at hundreds of miles an hour, looking for telltale signs of a vehicle crossing a river or a sliver of movement beneath the jungle canopy. The men who flew these aircraft did so largely unbeknownst to the American people.

Commando Sabre and the Misty Fast-FACs

In the North it was called the Truong Son Strategic Supply Route. The Americans called it the Ho Chi Minh Trail. It began at the Mu Gia Pass and farther south at Ban Karai Pass. From these two points of entry it ran into Laos, flowed south and on into Cambodia, finally turning southeast with strategic offshoots into South Vietnam. It continued south to as far as the outskirts of Saigon. One report, "A Method for Finding Targets on the Ho Chi Minh Trail," described it as more than just a trail. It was an entire system composed of "geography, physiography, and enemy habits."[33]

The trail also proved notoriously difficult to interdict. The same report noted that closing the trail was nigh impossible, and equated it to attempting to pick up a "puddle of mercury" with your fingers. If a particular piece of the trail was cratered or if a bridge was destroyed, the trail simply morphed and used another tendril to reroute itself. It surmised that

> [t]here do not appear to be any choke points which, if kept closed, could reduce traffic through the complex appreciably; road and bridge destruction would ordinarily cause only diversions and delay. Although this LOC might be called austere by U.S. standards, it is nevertheless flexible because there are a great number of alternate routes, the use of which would cause inconvenience but not stoppage.

The best that American forces could hope for was for the enemy to be "seriously inconvenienced, and certainly delayed, but just as certainly not logistically embarrassed."[34]

None of this stopped the United States from trying to use air power against the trail, against its entrances in North Vietnam, or its routes through Laos and Cambodia and its exits in South Vietnam. Despite the fact that much of the trail was mostly invisible from the air, aerial observers proved to be the most effective way of interdicting the heavier items—trucks—moving down the trail. In the early years of the war (1964–1967), prior to the introduction of jets, propeller-driven O-1 and O-2 aircraft proved effective observers. They were small, low, slow, and cheap to operate, which was a fine method of observation until North Vietnam pushed their AAA further south. The air force needed something significantly faster and sturdier if they were going to find targets in North Vietnam and along the entrances to the trail in Laos.

The F-100 Super Sabre (more commonly referred to as "The Hun") replaced the slower propeller-driven aircraft in June of 1967. Since August of 1966, it proved impossible for the traditional FAC aircraft—O-1s and O-2s—to operate in either Route Pac I or in the northern areas of South Vietnam. To that end, the USAF moved toward an "experiment with the use of jet aircraft to perform visual reconnaissance" under the top-secret program called Commando Sabre. Initially conceived of as a program using F-4s, it was later given over to the F-100Fs, which were cheaper to operate.

The F-100F was a two-seat version of the Hun allowing for an extra pair of eyes during the reconnaissance missions. Major George "Bud" Day commanded this new unit, the 416th Tactical Fighter Squadron, based at Phu Cat, and also gave them their call sign: "Misty," after the Johnny Mathis song, a favorite of Day's. It was an all-volunteer unit. According to Misty-94, Merrill McPeak, the unit rapidly became a "haven for the hard-core." The Misty's F-100Fs were also reconfigured with two external fuel tanks and an LAU-59 rocket launcher on each wing capable of firing seven rockets each. Misty pilots used the white phosphorous rockets to mark targets for other strikers.[35]

In total, 157 men became designated as Misty Fast-FACs. Of these, 34 percent were shot down and five of them became prisoners of war. The purpose of the Misty Fast-FACs was to control tactical air strikes either in North Vietnam or in Laos, when operations shifted to that country. FACs found targets, marked them, and controlled the other air assets used to attack these targets. To find the targets, Misty pilots had to look for the "hand of man," as Bill Douglas, Misty-2 remembered, "a little different shade of color, a little dust on the foliage, a straight line, or a curve, or circle . . . anything that showed man's involvement." It was a dynamic environment with only the broadest of guidance given to them by the 7th Air Force. Charles B. Neel, Misty-22, stated, "In the early days we were unorganized, but learning fast." Upon arriving at the 416th, a new pilot flew his first five missions in the backseat of the F-100F. On one of these missions, the new pilot was given a threat identification check ride. Ron Fogleman, Misty-86, and later chief of staff of the USAF, said, "Believe it or not, we had training aids that we never killed. These were [North Vietnamese] gunners that were so bad that we kind of had a truce."[36]

The early primary focus for the Misty Fast-FACs was in route package 1. These early Mistys only flew into Laos during bad weather that precluded accomplishing anything in North Vietnam. The first fifty Mistys (Mistys 1–50) found that Laos was a secondary target. Besides, flying in RP 1 was preferable: Wide-open roads and rice paddies provided better opportunity for finding the "hand of man." This also allowed the aircraft to fly at a higher altitude and a slightly lower speed (4,000 to 5,000 feet, at 450 knots). They could also find, observe, and mark targets on the ground more easily. However, this changed as Soviet technology pushed south into RP-1 to the detriment of the Mistys.[37]

The Misty pilots inadvertently discovered that the surface-to-air-missile sites installed in and around the DMZ were fully operational. Major General Don Shepperd, Misty-34, said that "the clouds broke and we discovered they were setting up a SAM site." Shepperd and his back-seater Jim Fiorelli refueled and headed back to take a closer look at the site. "We're letting down 14,000 feet . . . 10,000 feet . . . 9,000 feet coming back to the SAM site when WHAM! a SAM comes up. It never occurred to us that it actually might shoot at us." Of course, an active SAM site was a valid target to attack. McPeak remembered, "When North pushed SAMs south Misty took care of them."[38]

During a typical day of work for the Misty pilots, fourteen of the seventeen assigned pilots flew with an average mission length of between four to five hours. The first aircraft to take off was Misty-11, followed by Misty-21, and so on until Misty-71 at the end of the day. The first and last flights of the day were typically the most effective and had the highest likelihood of discovering trucks recently pulled over in the morning or attempting to get a head start in the twilight period. The day began with a 0400 wake-up followed by a quick breakfast before the morning mission brief. Aircrew then "stepped" to the aircraft, started the engine, and taxied the aircraft—all before sunrise. If the timing was right, the aircraft and its two occupants descended into North Vietnam along RP-1 while it was still dark.

The Misty pilots were on the deck in North Vietnam or sometimes Laos at first light. Looking for the hand of man was one thing, but there was also the daily hope of coming across an easy find, particularly trucks that had broken down and could not get off the road. The sun broke with first light between 0500 and 0530, and from that point forward there was a Misty aircraft in RP-1 or Laos until the last Misty departed, once it became too dark to do any further reconnaissance. Seven sorties in a fifteen- to sixteen-hour period. There was always one and usually two Misty aircraft over the area during the day. To accomplish this, each F-100F needed two air-to-air refuelings.[39]

Flying Mistys and discovering enemy activity required good use of tradecraft and sometimes guesswork. Ron Fogleman recalled, "You'd look at stream crossings and look for water splashed up on the banks of the rivers. You'd follow those south and once you found a river with no water splashed up, you'd know there was a truck parked near there." Pilots also had to continually "jink" their aircraft to avoid any potential AAA, even when they could not see it. Ed Rasimus, an F-105 pilot, remembered, "Don't be lulled by the fact that you don't see any shooting. They're shooting at you all the time. Keep your speed up. Keep your aircraft moving. Don't be predictable. Don't be stupid. Keep your head on a swivel. They're shooting every mission."[40]

The first Misty commander, Major George "Bud" Day, was shot down on August 26, 1967. That morning, Day and Corwin "Kipp" Kippenhan, in the backseat of the aircraft, were in RP-1 looking at a newly emplaced SAM battery. Just after spotting the SAM, AAA struck their F-100F. Day, in control, noticed they were losing hydraulic pressure even as he tried to nurse the stricken aircraft to the coast. The plane pitched over into a dive and both Kipp and Day knew their only chance of survival was to get out, so they ejected. Under canopy they floated down toward North Vietnam. Even as they had struggled to save their aircraft and radioed a Mayday call, rescue forces were dispatched to pick them up.

Kippenhan was lucky; he was picked up almost immediately. Day was not. He had no sooner untangled himself from his parachute than he was captured. Just moments later, stripped of his boots and other personal belongings as he was being marched north, the rescue helicopter, already carrying Kippenhan and desperately looking for Day, passed directly overhead. Day escaped his initial capture and then evaded to the South for ten days before being recaptured. It was the beginning of an arduous stint as a POW.[41]

There is no doubt that Misty proved fairly conclusively that jet aircraft performed just as well, if not better, than traditional slow-moving FACs. Bomb damage assessment after completed missions spiked when a Fast-FAC was used, increasing by more than 50 percent. In other words, more targets were destroyed when a Misty FAC was present to guide in strikes. Because of the extensive amount of time that Misty pilots spent in RP-1 and on the Ho Chi Minh Trail, they also proved to be a valuable resource for evaluating the logistics patterns of the enemy. The area they flew in was relatively small, allowing for the Misty pilots over time to become intimately familiar with the area. In addition the Misty unit provided 7th Air Force with better intelligence. Charles Neel said, "We discovered we were giving 7th Air Force more intel than they could give us." The 7th Air Force eventually ordered the creation of a second jet FAC squadron at Da Nang in 1968, and "Fast-FACs" proliferated throughout the war.

Proliferation of another type caused 7th Air Force significant concern, and that was the emplacement of a continued increasing number of surface-to-air-missile sites. The USAF, USN, 7th Air Force, and pilots assigned to squadrons in-theater started looking for solutions to the SAM threat.[42]

In-Theater Solutions: SAMs, Iron Hand, and Wild Weasels (YGBSM)

The war in the North fundamentally changed in 1965 with the introduction of Soviet air defense weapons into North Vietnam. By this time the Americans were already contending with large amounts of antiaircraft artillery that ranged in size from small four-barreled .50 caliber guns up to 37-, 57-, and 85-millimeter artillery. The AAA effectively covered the surface of the Earth up to 15,000 feet. One fighter pilot recalled arriving in-theater and having a more-veteran pilot discuss the AAA threat this way: "It's the flak. It doesn't know who you are, whether you're good or weak. It doesn't care. It's the flak. The goddamn guns. There's so many goddamn guns. They just shoot everywhere, and you get hit by the golden B-B. You can't jink, you can't avoid it." AAA proved to be the most lethal weapon at the hands of the NVA throughout the war.[43]

As Soviet technology proliferated inside North Vietnam in the form of the SA-2 missile and the associated radar systems, the US Air Force looked for a way to defeat these air defense systems. At Takhli Air Base in 1965 an event occurred that underscored American perceptions of what type of war was being fought. A fighter pilot casually walked through his squadron operations area and announced that the North Vietnamese were "building a SAM site about 25 nautical miles south of Hanoi." Another pilot replied that the North Vietnamese had elephants, and it was the American forces who had "all the high-tech stuff."[44]

The technological advantage held by the Americans was suddenly reversed. This proved problematic because many of the pilots inside the fighters and fighter-bombers currently flying inside North Vietnam had "no RHAW [Radar Homing and Warning Receiver], no training, and no clue about the SA-2s." Also, simply destroying the SAM sites was not going to be an easy task. There existed no tactics for a prolonged suppression-of-enemy-defenses campaign, and the combination of AAA (below 15,000 feet) and the SAM threat (above 10,000 feet) presented fliers with a damned-if-you-do, damned-if-you-don't scenario. Besides, even if the SAM sites were attacked, there was the very real possibility a Soviet advisor might be killed in the process. The pilots were initially told to "not bother the Russians."[45]

SAM sites were basically a collection of missiles tied back into a missile van where air defense operators attempted to manipulate their radars to gain a lock on an enemy (American) aircraft. While Fan Song remains the most-understood radar—it was a ground-controlled radar used to acquire targets and fire a missile—it was only one of several radars employed by North Vietnamese forces to track American aircraft. The others included early warning (EW) radar under the NATO code names Tall King and Bar Lock, and altitude-finding radar, including Rock, Sponge, and Stone Cake. Other radars that helped tie this net together included Flat Face, Fire Can, etc. All of these radars worked together to pass information to the SAM operators who could then use the Fan Song to track an aircraft and fire a missile.[46]

On May 27, 1965, less than three months after the start of Rolling Thunder, the Joint Chiefs sent a memorandum to Secretary McNamara in which they recommended destroying the SAM sites and the MiG aircraft parked on the ramp at Phuc Yen, west of Hanoi, but McNamara worried about an "embarrassing international reaction to such attacks" (e.g., killing a Soviet advisor). McNamara then asked other departments about attacking the sites. The CIA believed there would be limited to no response, but the State Department thought otherwise and believed there could indeed be a response—not from the Soviets, but from the Chinese and their air bases just across the border. McNamara later called Dean Rusk at the State Department and told him that pilots in Vietnam had been instructed that no SAM or air bases were on the approved-for-attack list. The biggest threats to American pilots were off limits.[47]

Meanwhile, in South Vietnam, Momyer recognized the fallacy in not attacking the SAM sites, but due to American "restraint, the system was able to expand without any significant interference until the spring of 1966." Momyer advocated attacking the sites especially in their "embryonic state," but was rebuffed. John T. McNaughton, an assistant secretary of defense, scoffed at both Momyer and Westmoreland when they brought up attacking the sites: "You don't think the North Vietnamese are going to use them! Putting them in is just a political ploy by the Russians to appease Hanoi." This proved to be an egregious mistake.[48]

Calculations changed on July 24, when a Soviet-made SA-2 shot down an American F-4 (call sign Leopard 2) roughly thirty miles west of Hanoi. It should be noted that the Fan Song radar attached to the SA-2 site—and used to track American aircraft—radiated before, during, and after the shoot-down. At that point SAM operators had no fear of American reprisal attacks against the radars. Two days later the president met with a large group of advisors including CJCS General Wheeler, McNamara, Bundy, Lodge, and Rusk. For much of the next two hours, they discussed the surface-to-air missile threat and whether or not to strike the sites in reprisal for the shoot-down. Again, the fear was in inadvertently killing Soviet personnel who were almost certainly aiding and training the North Vietnamese at these sites. Wheeler reported that the Joint Chiefs all recommended hitting the sites as soon as possible, which concurred with Ambassador Taylor's assessment as well. President Johnson asked the group, "What will be [the] reaction of [the] enemy if he can knock down U.S. planes and we do nothing about it? The sites are put there to destroy us. Are we going to sit and let them knock down our planes?" For the time being, no one seemed to have an answer.[49]

The same group met again two days later and discussed striking at the SAM sites, numbered one through seven. General Wheeler advocated for attacking all seven SAM sites, but McNamara was against striking site four, the closest to Hanoi and Haiphong, out of a fear that it "would vex the Soviets." President Johnson ordered an attack only on sites six and seven, stating, "Take them out." The resulting attack on July 27, 1965, was a disaster, and resulted in the loss of six of the forty-six F-105s sent to strike the SAM sites. In addition to the forty-six F-105s, twelve F-4s, eight F-104s, three EB-66s, and six USMC EF-10Bs joined in the raid. After-action analysis also proved that the North Vietnamese expected a reprisal attack and were ready for it. Of the two sites attacked, number six held dummy missiles and site seven was empty. The North Vietnamese also surrounded both SAM locations with a mix of 37-, 57-, and 85mm AAA. It was a trap.[50]

The US Navy suffered a similar event on the night of August 11–12 when an A-4E was shot down and another heavily damaged. In the low-level reprisal strikes against the SAM site, the USN lost five aircraft to a similar withering AAA fire. Worse, by the time the reprisal attack occurred, the North Vietnamese military moved the SA-2 site. It was gone. One senior navy official back in Washington, DC, called it a "truly black Friday the 13th" for navy forces in the region. Clearly, a change in tactics was required to deal with the growing SAM threat.[51]

Initially, the only defense against the surface-to-air missiles was the "SAM break." Fighter pilot Richard Hamilton recalled, "[T]he pilot that was attacked would wait until the missile had committed itself to his aircraft and then break, turning sharply down and into the missile. If he timed it right—the key word being 'if'—this usually caused the missile to overshoot and explode harmlessly." If a pilot survived his SAM engagement and returned to base he could report the location of the SAM battery. USAF units based in Thailand began keeping F-105s on alert to go after these sites, but the response time took several hours. One USAF report noted that "three hours was sufficient time for a SAM battalion to pack up and thread its way over narrow roads to a new location."[52]

What is commonly called the "kill chain" (find the target, fix its position, track it, target it, engage and destroy it) in modern military parlance needed to be significantly shortened. Giving the NVA time to shoot at American aircraft and then move their missiles needed to end. Aircrews needed to be able to find the site and target it immediately. Back in the United States, the USAF was hard at work on this problem under a program named "Wild Weasel."

The air force took F-100Fs, a two-seat trainer version of the fighter and the same ones used by the Misty fast-FACs, and equipped the rear seat with a panoramic scan receiver and a vector homing and warning system. Both pieces of equipment interpreted enemy radar signals being received by antennas installed around the aircraft. In basic terms, if a Fan Song was "painting" the fighter, the attached antennas displayed "lines of light" on the radar operator's viewing scope and pointed back in the general direction of the enemy radar. This gave the aircraft a general location of the SAM site more than seventeen miles away, which also happened to be the maximum effective range of the SA-2. As the F-100Fs approached the target—inside the lethal SAM envelope—they relied on their vector homing radar, which provided a more-accurate location of the enemy radar and associated missile site.[53]

Since it was the job of the Wild Weasels to locate the SAM site, effectively being tracked by the enemy radar the entire time, this led to the creation of one of the more famous emblems and patches of the USAF, albeit an unofficial one. Crews of the Wild Weasel missions sported a patch featuring a frazzled-looking weasel. On the upper end of the patch were the words "Wild Weasel," and on the bottom, the letters "YGBSM," which stood for "You gotta be shitting me." F-100F Wild Weasels could then be paired with a flight of F-105 Iron Hand SAM killers. In November of 1965, the first of these specially equipped F-100Fs arrived at Korat RTAFB as part of the Wild Weasel Task Force.

In August of 1966 the commander of the Pacific Air Forces, General Hunter Harris Jr., sent a message to the USAF's chief of staff, General John P. McConnell, with the subject line "Wild Weasel." In the memo Harris noted that Wild Weasels provided "SAM warning/suppression and suppression of gun laying radars in support of strike forces; conduct around the clock SAM and radar search/destroy operations, and support special operations such as Arc Light missions in or near possible SAM areas." It was a long and, more importantly, time-consuming mission. Harris noted that at its aircraft and manpower levels, the aircraft equipped for the Wild Weasel missions could not produce the necessary sortie numbers in comparison to the increasing SAM systems. Harris noted that an additional eighteen F-105F aircraft would be ready and equipped by October of 1966, but this did not meet the emerging—and emergency—need in-theater at that moment. Harris asked the chief of staff to take "immediate action" and order the deployment of twelve additional Wild Weasel aircraft and crews to Southeast Asia.[54]

"Hunter-Killer" Tactics

The use of the F-100F as the Wild Weasel had a short life span. The problem with the Hun manifested itself in two distinct ways. The older F-100s proved problematic when flying with newer 105s. The lead F-100 cruised at a slower speed, which forced the accompanying F-105s to fly "S" patterns behind him in order to keep from overtaking and passing the flight lead. The second problem stemmed from the first. The 2nd Air Division (later, the 7th Air Force) became convinced that the F-100s "were too old and too slow to survive in the hostile skies above the Red River Delta." The F-100s were soon replaced with the newer and faster F-105s, but again, the two-seat trainer "F" model of the Thuds were used.[55]

A serious problem developed early in the tactics, techniques, and procedures used as part of Iron Hand/Wild Weasel. A December 1966 memo from the 388th Tactical Fighter Wing commander noted that "the primary purpose of IRON HAND is to provide protection to the strike force." More importantly it noted that an overall SAM suppression campaign would not take place. Instead, the Wild Weasel pilots were instructed to provide warning to the strike force of possible SAM activity and use their AGM-45s against the Fan Song radars. If a SAM site became an "immediate threat" by firing a missile, the strike force commander was instructed to divert members of the strike package to the Wild Weasel pilots to attack the SAM site itself. In other words, the suppression of SAM missiles could only occur once a missile had been fired, and then members of the strike package—already headed against a different target—were broken off from their primary mission to strike the SAM missile site. It was a less-than-ideal solution to the missile threat. To counter this, the USAF started pairing flights of F-105s into "hunter-killer" teams.[56]

The initial hunter-killer teams were led by the two-seat F-100Fs and later F-105Fs, mentioned earlier. The aircraft that began operations in November of 1965 had significant improvements. Each F-100F now had a radar homing and warning (RHAW) system as well as a missile guidance warning receiver. Each F-100F or F-105F back-seater was also now a certified electronic warfare officer. The hunter-killers used American technology against the Soviet missile sites.[57]

Pilots flying Wild Weasel SAM suppression missions homed in on enemy radar emissions (hunters) and marked the SAM site with rockets so the follow-on F-105s could attack the site (killers). The killer F-105s then had to dive toward the missile site and wait for the AGM-45 Shrike (an AIM-7 missile converted to seek out radar emissions on the ground) seeker head to lock on to the transmitting radar. Pilots then pulled up and "lofted" the Shrike toward the enemy radar. Since the AGM-45 had a small warhead, this meant that anything short of a direct hit was not going to destroy the radar. A message from CINCPAC to the USAF chief of staff on August 28, 1966, noted that the current stockpile of available AGM-45s was a "matter of grave concern in review of increasingly hostile air defense environment [in] NVN."

He also asked the CSAF to take "immediate action to expedite all deliveries of subject missiles."[58]

Of course, North Vietnam's SAM operators modified their own tactics to decrease American success rates in SAM suppression. NVA radar operators used a complex network of ground-based observers and long-range acquisitions radars to limit the time a Fan Song radar needed to be active to take a missile shot, sometimes as short as three minutes. The radar operators of North Vietnam also learned that American hunter-killer teams flew in a recognizable four-ship formation, which differed from larger strike packages, and instead simply chose not to turn their radars on when these teams were in the vicinity.[59]

This changed over time when two F-105F Wild Weasels were attached to two dedicated F-4E Phantoms. Rather than range out in front of the strike package, these hunter-killer teams attempted to place themselves in between the SAM sites and the strike package. None of this mattered if the SAM crews decided to launch a missile ballistically (i.e., without radar support or guidance). The 105s launched AGM-45/78 and the F-4s followed up at the impact site with conventional munitions in hopes of destroying the radar and the SAMs as well.[60]

The success of the hunter-killer tactics in 1966 also forced the North Vietnamese to constantly move their SAM sites. For North Vietnam, this hindered missile maintenance and increased general wear and tear to the missiles themselves, but the process of continually moving the missiles made it more difficult for American intelligence troops to know which SAM sites in North Vietnam were occupied and operational during any given mission. It was a back-and-forth game between the missile shooters on the ground and the missile shooters in the air in a battle for air superiority over North Vietnam.

Back in Washington, the Joint Chiefs of Staff continued to implore McNamara to make a concerted effort to destroy the surface-to-air missile sites which continued to shoot down American aircraft. On September 15, 1965, McNamara sent a memo to General Wheeler and stated again, "At this date I am not persuaded by the reasoning of JCSM 670-652 that the military advantages the Joint Chiefs of Staff state would flow from the proposed strike effort outweigh the military and political risks involved in implementing the proposal." McNamara was often concerned about the "political risks" that would occur if the United States took a heavier hand against the SAM sites or the MiG airfields.

A week after his rejection memo to the Joint Chiefs, the SECDEF sent a memo to the president where he outlined these fears, which included Chinese air intervention: "It is possible that Hanoi and Peking already have an agreed plan for the Chinese to intervene from their own bases in response to the kind of US attack assumed in this estimate."[61]

Although McNamara rated this type of response by the Chinese as very unlikely, it was a possibility, and further escalation could bring the Chinese into the war as an outright combatant. He also spoke of the possibility of the Soviet Union either intervening in Vietnam or making a move against the United States in Berlin. Again, he rated this possibility as unlikely, but given the Soviet Union's secrecy and America's insecurities in their grasp of the leadership situation in the Soviet Union, McNamara believed anything was possible. No matter what the response, McNamara clearly indicated that attacking SAM sites, MiG airfields, and targets closer to Hanoi and Haiphong would have serious adverse effects, saying "Hanoi, Peking, and Moscow would all view the strikes as initiating—and in large part, executing—the highest level of militarily significant escalation available in the DRV short of ground invasion."[62]

Later in the War

By the middle of 1967, the Air Defense System in North Vietnam reached its most robust state. A typical SAM site consisted of a Fan Song radar and guidance facility with as many as six missile sites surrounding the control area. From the air the entire site resembled a large flower made of earth and machinery carved into the ground. North Vietnamese SAM operators became quite adept at countering the tactics of the United States. Once the Iron Hand/Wild Weasel missions became commonplace, the North Vietnamese SAM operators began practicing strict discipline in their operations. Rather than have their radars actively emitting—sure to draw an anti-radiation missile down on them—they used other methods like optical and passive tracking methods until the strike was within range. SAM operators also turned on their radars, waited until the AGMs had been fired, then turned off their radars, which effectively eliminated the ability of the HARM (high-speed anti-radiation missile) to guide or home in on the radar. Once the NVA crews deemed all or most of the air-to-ground missiles had been expended, their radars came up emitting full-time to track and shoot at the strike package.[63]

It was a tit-for-tat, back-and-forth game between the Americans and the North Vietnamese SAM operators, and it all occurred in a matter of minutes. If an American strike package flew into a SAM threat ring, a "good" North Vietnamese operator only needed five to ten seconds of active radiating to fire a missile. One thing was for sure: The North Vietnamese soldiers, with the help of their Soviet allies, proved their ability to negate and counter any American technological advantage.[64]

As all of this occurred in the sky over North Vietnam—attacking targets and responding to SAM escalation—the USAF struggled to understand what exactly was occurring to the organization. As early as 1968, an idea had formed inside the USAF. It was not that the USAF was underperforming or that they were not having the desired effect; it was that an outside agent, namely the Johnson administration, was hamstringing their efforts. A top-secret report written at the Air War College, titled "Target Selection Process: Categories and Decision Levels" and detailing the target sets in 1965, noted that the reason the air force, and air power writ large, had not already succeeded was that "[o]ne of the most significant limitations, admittedly the most significant to the North Vietnamese, is the United States resolve not to inflict the threat of national destruction upon the government of North Vietnam." The report went on to note that "as long as this self-imposed political restraint continues, the United States will not, as one observer remarked, 'see a victory in Vietnam of the kind we gained in World War I or II.' " Here was the Lost Cause ideology in an embryonic form.[65]

Already by 1968, the US Air Force was creating its own Lost Cause mythology. Rolling Thunder was not a tactical or operational failure incapable of providing victory, but a missed opportunity at higher levels to allow the USAF to seriously attack the nation of North Vietnam. If only more bombing had been done earlier, the result would have been different; at least, this is what the USAF came to believe. The truth is that the USAF was wrong in this assertion.

Even as this report lamented the restraints placed upon air power by the administration, it also ironically noted that its desired path to victory was, in fact, not a path at all. The author noted that even though bombing in North Vietnam and against the trail network in Laos and Cambodia was limited, the supplies for the Viet Cong and regular army forces were still flowing south:

> In spite of this [bombing] effort men and supplies continued to infiltrate SVN over a complex network of enemy lines of communications (LOCs). The problem was twofold. First, the network of LOCs did not compare with the well-defined systems encountered on the continent during WWII. There was no prime interdiction target such as the road massed armor experienced in Germany.[66]

This displays a major problem of cognitive dissonance in air force thinking at the time. First, some in the USAF believed that more bombing earlier against the government of North Vietnam was the solution. Second, they also recognized that no amount of bombing already accomplished or even conceived of could have a direct impact on supplies flowing south. The USAF brought first-world aircraft and munitions meant for industrialized warfare into a country and against an enemy that moved its meager supplies by truck and bike, but was buttressed in the field by an equal amount of advanced equipment from the USSR and China.

Bombing Pause (1968–1972)

Throughout 1968, bombing operations became more and more restricted until in November of that year, President Johnson ordered a bombing halt throughout North Vietnam as a means to aid in the ongoing peace negotiations in Paris. The pause, announced live on television to the American people, effectively ended Operation Rolling Thunder. The simple fact was that Rolling Thunder was not working. "Two of the prime political aims for Rolling Thunder failed to materialize, i.e., reducing the will of the people to fight, and coercing the Hanoi government to agree to negotiations on terms acceptable to the United States."[67]

However, this in no way actually stopped flights or attacks in North Vietnam; it simply ended the official program of bombing targets in the North. Pilots flying over the North as part of armed reconnaissance missions could still retaliate if fired upon. In 1969, the US Navy and US Air Force flew more than five thousand reconnaissance missions over North Vietnam, many of which resulted in attacks against ground targets in the North. These "protective reaction strikes" occurred regularly, with more than one thousand taking place in 1970 alone. One of these retaliatory strikes, Proud Deep Alpha—conducted in 1971 and consisting of more than two hundred USAF and USN aircraft—attacked sites only seventy-five miles from Hanoi. This was the single largest attack to occur since the "bombing pause" went into effect in 1968.[68]

The Final Campaigns: Linebacker I and Linebacker II

Much had changed in the years between 1968 and 1972. Technologically, the war was different. American flier Dick Anderegg remembered that earlier in the war, "We were way behind the power curve when these [SAMs] were deployed. We had no radar warning [RW] receivers and only rudimentary electronic-countermeasure [ECM] pods." By 1972, numerous technical changes had gone into effect: Project Teaball used American ground control intercept (GCI) sites to track enemy aircraft from the moment they became airborne and eased the restriction on visual identification. Aircraft were equipped with radar homing and warning and gun pods. Tactics and training had also changed with the US Navy's Top Gun school and the USAF's Coronet Organ exercises better preparing pilots for combat. In 1972, the US military launched two massive aerial campaigns known to history as Linebacker I and II. Chapter 5 covers these campaigns from the perspective of the strategic importance and their results in full, but if the war in the North is treated as separate from the rest of the war in South Vietnam, some explanatory material is needed here.[69]

In March of 1972, North Vietnam launched a massive three-pronged invasion—the Nguyen Hue Offensive, more commonly called the Easter Offensive in Western literature—into South Vietnam with the aim of crippling the Army of South Vietnam and gaining bargaining position at the ongoing Paris peace talks. The attacking force moved on the South along three axes of advance: south through the demilitarized zone; from southern Laos, east toward the central highlands; and south through Cambodia in the direction of Saigon.

In response, the Nixon administration began a deployment of large numbers of USAF fighters, bombers, and support aircraft, and the US Navy repositioned four carriers. The NVA forces in the South suffered tremendous losses. A USAF report surmised that "the NVA underestimated the vulnerability of massed forces to air power, where tactical air is most efficient."[70]

Fighters and bombers not only hit targets in the South, but moved north of the DMZ for the first time since November of 1968. Much had changed since the bombing pause went into effect. US Navy tactics had changed, and technological developments aided in the attacking of targets in the North; this included the introduction of laser-guided bombs (LGBs) and electro-optical weapons.

Linebacker I was followed closely by Linebacker II. In this follow-on portion of the overall 1972 campaign, Nixon removed the restrictions against the targets found inside the areas around Hanoi and Haiphong. Over one million tons of ordnance was dropped in an eleven-day period. Both sides claimed victory. The United States lost only twelve tactical aircraft, but the loss of sixteen B-52s sent shock waves through the Strategic Air Command and forced a reevaluation of existing tactics, techniques, and procedures (TTPs). In the first nights of the operation B-52s approached in three-ship cells, hit their targets, and immediately conducted a standard turn away from the target. This turn changed the B-52's ECM pattern and allowed SAM operators a moment of opportunity to better target, track, and engage the bombers. Later in the campaign, the B-52 crews were allowed to adjust their ingress and egress routes, a stark departure from normal SAC procedures.

Precision-Guided Munitions (PGMs)

During World War II, under the code name "Aphrodite," the US Army Air Forces packed B-17s with explosives and equipped them with radio-controlled systems which allowed the "pilot" to fly the aircraft from a secondary mother ship. No less a personage than Hap Arnold placed his hopes on these B-17s—that they would see success as precision-guided munitions. The technology proved too advanced. None of the B-17s hit their targets. Some spun out of control; one exploded prematurely before the launch and arming crew could parachute to safety; and weather hindered other missions. Still, the USAF and USN continued to look for scientific and technological developments that might increase the accuracy of their munitions. Vietnam proved to be fertile ground for the employment of these developments. Air forces used two primary variants of what would come to be known as precision-guided munitions (PGMs): laser-guided and electro-optically guided.

LGBs took a dumb bomb and mated it with a laser seeker. While one aircraft "painted" the target, other aircraft in the strike package attacked the target. The laser reflected (refracted) off the target and created a cone or "basket" into which the attacking aircraft dropped their bombs, which then homed in on the target. Later updates placed gimbals on the laser designator which allowed the painter aircraft to attack the target as well.

Although both types of PGMs saw development and even early employment in the later part of the 1960s, the bombing halt prevented their use in significant numbers in North Vietnam. The Easter Offensive and the opening of the Linebacker Operations allowed for their wide use in 1972.

The introduction of PGMs had a significant effect on the dropping of bridges in the late stage of the war. The two most famous bridges put out of action in 1972 were the Paul Doumer Bridge (Long Biên) across the Red River in Hanoi and the Thanh Hoa Bridge across the Song Ma River, which was a strategic crossroads allowing for movement of men and supplies throughout North Vietnam. Besides both of these bridges being unserviceable after attack, American forces also used PGMs to strike five other bridges and heavily damaged each of them. Further bombing using both PGMs and conventional bombing damaged more than four hundred bridges connecting the routes from China into North Vietnam.

The use of PGMs proved to be a turning point not only in the Vietnam conflict, but in the development and use of other "smart bombs" after the conflict ended. The air arms began the slow transition from precision *delivery* of bombs to using precision-*guided* weapons. The first relied on a pilot placing a bomb precisely where he wanted it; the second melded pilot skill with technological advancement. Another advance in technology seen toward the end of the conflict was the use of the first of the post-Vietnam fighters. Commonly remembered for its strike against Libya during Operation El Dorado Canyon, the F-111 first saw employment during the air wars of Vietnam against targets in the North.[71]

The F-111

The F-111A offered the USAF a wide variety of benefits. As a "low-level, night, all-weather, single-ship penetrator," the USAF finally had an equal to the navy's A-6 and A-7; although it carried the fighter designation and is sometimes listed as a "fighter/bomber," the F-111 Aardvark was really an attack aircraft. It also offered an order-of-magnitude increase in weapons delivery. A single F-111 carried the same bomb tonnage as four F-4s, and a four-ship carried the equivalent of twenty F-4s. To that end, the USAF, perhaps unwisely, rushed the F-111 into Southeast Asia. The initial aircraft bound for Thailand departed Nellis Air Force Base on March 15, 1968, and arrived at Takhli on March 17.[72]

It became apparent to the USAF that the F-111 had been rushed into combat. As Marcelle Knaack stated, "[T]he F-111A's entry into combat was not a success." The USAF lost three of their newest aircraft in less than a month. Most troubling was that none of these losses were to enemy activity. There was something wrong with the aircraft itself. The F-111s unceremoniously returned stateside. Four years later, the F-111 returned to SEA during Linebacker Operations, again to Takhli RTAFB. As soon as the aircraft arrived, they were prepped for combat operations and launched on their first mission, just four hours after arriving in-theater. F-111s flew only at night and attacked in high-speed, low-altitude, single-ship formations. The actual mission profile called for F-111s to go high-low-high: high-level penetration; low-level TFR (terrain-following radar) bomb run; high-level withdrawal from the threat area. The 7th Air Force used the F-111s against SAM sites, radio communications facilities, railroads, troop concentrations, and during Linebacker II, attacks against MiG airfields prior to the B-52 bombing runs.[73]

Over the course of the next four months, six F-111s were lost during combat operations. The first of these occurred on September 28, 1972, when the aircraft of Major William Clare "Bill" Coltman and First Lieutenant Robert Arthur "Lefty" Brett Jr., call sign RANGER 23, was lost due to a problem with its terrain-following radar. This aircraft loss occurred on the first night of F-111 operations.[74]

Eighteen days later another F-111 was lost near the Phuc Yen airfield in North Vietnam. This aircraft, piloted by Captain James Hockridge and First

Lieutenant Allen Graham, was possibly hit by an SA-2 missile, although the cause of the aircraft loss was never conclusively proven. Different USAF reports note that it could have been a TFR problem or an ordnance issue, as well.[75]

According to one CHECO report, the NVN had a difficult time engaging F-111s with SAMs due to their low-level penetration during their bomb runs. When fired upon, F-111s turned "into the missile and rapidly climb[ed] 1,000 to 1,500 feet (a vertical 'jink' maneuver) followed by a TFR descent to the lowest practical clearance above the terrain." The ability of F-111 crews to operate safely at extremely low altitudes offered protection against the SAMs.[76]

Although used to great effect during Linebackers I and II, the USAF acknowledged that the F-111 was employed in a "learning situation" in the waning days of the conflict, and that anything accomplished by the F-111 would be applied in a manner to "influence further studies of F-111 employment concepts. Development of effective high-speed, low-altitude deliverable munitions for area targets will broaden its existing role as a night all-weather penetrator at low altitudes." Entering more fully into combat later in the war also protected the F-111 crews from those crews who had a more-protracted experience operating in North Vietnam, namely the possibility of becoming an American prisoner of war.[77]

The Experience of American POWs

It is difficult to know exactly how many Americans became prisoners of war during the Vietnam conflict. Nearly 600 were repatriated in 1973, but official tally still lists more than 1,350 US personnel as POW/MIA. Those 591 that returned home in 1973 were housed at thirteen different POW camps located inside and immediately adjacent to the city of Hanoi. These included Hoa Lo prison, still more commonly referred to as the Hanoi Hilton, as well as Skid Row, the Zoo, the Plantation, and nine others. Their day-to-day existence was brutish and nasty.

American fighter and rescue pilots did everything within their human ability to save their fellow fliers once they had ejected. One F-100F that was burning badly made it just over the beach before pilot and co-pilot ejected. An F-4 circling overhead dove on North Vietnamese boats sent to pick up the two downed aviators. One of the two men in the water, Guy Gruters, remembered it this way:

> An F-4 wingman spotted them, set his switches to "Arm-All, Fire-All," and dove to the attack. . . . More than one hundred rockets left the pods under his wing. . . .

The F-4 pilot fired so low that Charlie [the second American in the water] was sure he would not make the pullout. He just narrowly missed colliding with the water, overstressing the aircraft with a max-G pullout.[78]

This pilot risked his own life in an attempt to protect fellow aviators. In this instance, both pilots were rescued. Hundreds of others, including Gruters, who was shot down a second time, were not as lucky.

If rescue failed—never from lack of effort—a downed pilot's transportation from the site of his landing to his prison experience began. Most pilots were stripped to their underwear, bound, blindfolded, and made to walk, often through a village of angry citizens, before boarding a truck or boat and shipped north. The first of these prisoners was Lieutenant (junior grade) Everett Alvarez Jr. Flying from the USS *Constellation* he was shot down while attacking patrol boats at their harbor in the immediate aftermath of the Gulf of Tonkin incident. His airplane was hit at low altitude and began coming apart. He knew he had no choice but to eject. Fracturing his back in the process from his ejection at high speed and low altitude, North Vietnamese troops captured him almost immediately. He would spend the next eight and a half years in captivity. An additional 590 would join him and be released in 1973 during Operation Homecoming. Several more pilots were shot down, captured, and later died in captivity.[79]

Some POWs are remembered for their resistance to capture, their attempts to evade and escape, and their leadership in captivity, including Bud Day, James Stockdale, and Lance Sijan. The services back in the States did all they could for the POWs. In between his two tours in Vietnam, Fred Smith worked in the Pentagon for the deputy chief of staff for personnel (DCS/P), General Robert Dixon. Dixon was a notoriously difficult boss. Years later, as TAC commander, his subordinates named him the Tidewater Alligator. Smith remembered, "There was not a lot of love for Dixon anywhere. He was brutal to his staff. People were either disgusted or scared stiff of him." Smith also remembered Dixon once snapping at a brigadier general, "You were a lot fucking smarter when you were a colonel." That being said, Dixon was an experienced air power advocate and himself a prisoner of war during World War II. Later, he helped usher in significant changes to training after the war in Vietnam ended.[80]

Between 1969 and 1971 the POWs automatically promoted up through the rank of lieutenant colonel. This stopped at the O-6, or full colonel, level, and a rumor began to circulate inside the Pentagon that POWs were being passed over. Smith drafted the staff summary sheet and went with Dixon to see the chief of staff of the air force, General John D. Ryan. After the pitch Ryan asked Dixon, "Bob, how can we promote a guy without any record of performance to O-6?" Dixon looked at the chief of staff and said, "Chief, I was a POW, and I'm asking." That decided the issue. General Ryan sided with Dixon, and prisoners of war in their primary promotion zone with the rank of lieutenant colonel promoted to colonel.[81]

The experiences of the pilots, aviators, and marines who became POWs were not isolated instances that were simply expected circumstances of war. The American air arms looked closely at the prevention methods and search-and-rescue training and employment. The desire to prevent American airmen from becoming POWs became a hallmark of air power during Operation Desert Storm and afterward, in no small part because of the POW experience in Vietnam. The twenty-first chief of staff of the US Air Force, General David Goldfein, was himself rescued in a daring search-and-rescue mission in 1999.

The American aircrews who survived their ejections only to become prisoners of war missed the events of the world around them from the time they ejected until they returned home in the spring of 1973, sometimes obtaining snippets from newer prisoners. This included Super Bowls, World Series, political assassinations, Woodstock, the *Apollo* space program and moon landings, racial strife, and political protests that included protests to the war they were currently serving as prisoners of. During one mistake, the North Vietnamese prison guards allowed a letter in to one of the POWs; although the letter was heavily redacted, the guards had missed the "first man on the moon" stamp.[82]

Senator John McCain remembered Hanoi Hannah's "Voice of Vietnam" unintentionally letting the news of the moon landing out when she informed the prisoners that "President Nixon can put a man on the moon, but he can't end the war in Vietnam." McCain recalled: "In that one screwup, that brief mention of glorious news, our morale soared. We felt almost physically strengthened as we communicated with each other in whispers and tap code: 'Did you hear that? Did you? We put a man on the moon. My God, we did it.' "[83]

It should also be noted that there remains a possibility, if not probability, that all of the POWs were not released in 1973. Several sources indicate that it is possible an unknown number of American POWs were transferred to the USSR during the Vietnam conflict. In 1992, Alexander Zuyev, a Soviet fighter pilot who defected in 1989, wrote that he was told some Soviet nuclear weapons release procedures for the Soviet air force [VVS] were developed and "improved upon" due to contributions from captured American airmen. Also in 1992, Russian president Boris Yeltsin stated in an interview to NBC News: "Our archives have shown that it is true—some of [the POWs] were transferred to the territory of the former USSR and were kept in labor camps."[84]

Conclusion

By 1966, the war in the North more closely resembled—at least for the combined air arm of the USAF and US Navy—a peer-on-peer conflict against an enemy well prepared to check American advantages in technological might. While the war in the South remained an interdiction and close air support war, the war in the North freed the air force and navy to attack targets in what they believed to be a more-classical use of air power: a "strategic" air campaign that would, eventually, force North Vietnam to reexamine their support of the Viet Cong and their desire to reunify the country. However, throughout the war, the combined integrated air defense mechanisms of MiGs, AAA, and SAM systems hindered American control of the sky. Later in the war, this IADS system wreaked even more havoc on America's strategic bombers during the Linebacker I and II campaigns.

The combined aerial strength of the American military blanketed North Vietnam with more than one million tons of munitions. Everything from 750-pound general purpose bombs, larger 3,000-pound bombs, to napalm, white phosphorus, and, later in the war, the first precision-guided munitions. The effectiveness of the bombing campaigns continues to be debated in the twenty-first century. Don Shepperd, Misty-34, said in his book *Bury Us Upside Down*, that Vietnam is "a conflict that now seems primitive and barbaric" compared to the engagements of Desert Storm and afterward. Still, much of the success that occurred in Desert Storm and later in the Balkans was only possible because of the events, tactics, and trial and error that took place in North Vietnam.

The Foreign Relations of the United States was less sanguine, and commented:

> The bombing campaign against NVN has not discernibly weakened the determination of the North Vietnamese leaders to continue to direct and support the insurgency in the South. Shortages of food and clothing, travel restrictions, separations of families, lack of adequate medical and educational facilities, and heavy workloads have tended to affect adversely civilian morale. However, there are few if any reliable reports on a breakdown of the commitment of the people to support the war. Unlike the situation in the South, there are no reports of marked increases of absenteeism, draft dodging, black market operations or prostitution. There is no evidence that possible war weariness among the people has shaken the leadership's belief that they can continue to endure the bombing and outlast the U.S. and SVN in a protracted war of attrition.[85]

The American bombing of North Vietnam did not work.

However, the debate has raged for decades regarding whether "more bombing earlier" would have had a negative effect on North Vietnam's prosecution of the war, perhaps forcing North Vietnam into some type of negotiation in the late 1960s—if, rather than a Rolling Thunder, an "instant" thunder could have produced decisive results to force North Vietnam to negotiate for some type of peace sooner. While it can never be conclusively proven whether if the JCS target list had been used for an across-the-board attack on North Vietnam the country would have been forced to the negotiating table in 1965 or 1966, the preponderance of evidence indicates the answer would be "no."

The fact remains that the war's focus in the United States, in North Vietnam, and by North Vietnam's supporters in China and the Soviet Union had shifted significantly since the days of Rolling Thunder. For all parties involved, the context of the war had changed. By the early 1970s the participants had different motivations. For the United States, it was time for an exit. For North Vietnam, it was a waiting game until American withdrawal, but this was a hand played too early during the Easter Offensive. For the larger players in the Cold War it was a time of differing concepts of communism and a thaw in relations with the West. The war, and the global context, of the early 1970s was different from the war of the 1960s.

Some historians and participants in the struggle have come down on the side that a heavier bombing campaign in 1965 could have changed the outcome of the war. Admiral U. S. Grant Sharp Jr. stated, "Once the decision has been made to wage war that leadership must permit the war to be engaged in expeditiously and full-bore, not halfway." Many other pilots who flew during Vietnam have subscribed to this "more bombing earlier" mantra. Historian David Pike stated, "Had a similar campaign of all-out bombing been made in early 1965," then the Johnson administration might have been successful in ejecting communist forces from South Vietnam.

This author disagrees. In all likelihood the bombing of ports and airfields could have drawn either the Soviet Union or China into the fray. Assurances that this would not happen did not come until the Nixon administration, thus giving Nixon significantly more freedom of action than his predecessor had. Also, if a similar bombing campaign along the lines of 1972 had been conducted in 1965, it is doubtful this would have been enough to cripple the supplies necessary to stop the North's support to the South.[86]

Furthermore, historical cases also demonstrate that the "more bombing earlier" school of thought was erroneous as far back as World War II. Historian Antulio Echevarria II noted:

> Controversy still remains as to whether an American victory, or at least an earlier settlement, might have been achieved had the Johnson administration not insisted on employing a gradualist approach. It is not clear, however, that the North Vietnamese would have responded any differently to massive bombings than the Japanese or the Germans (or the British) had in the Second World War.

The bombing surveys for that war . . . provide no evidence that such an approach would have worked three decades later.[87]

The Misty pilots, the other Fast-FACs, the bomber crews, and air force fighter and navy attack pilots—defended by their air-to-air brethren—all conducted their duties to the best of their abilities. Still, it was asymmetric. Despite North Vietnam's introduction of SAMs and MiGs, the United States was still trying to use conventional weapons designed for conventional war against an unconventional enemy, whose supply needs were so minuscule that it is doubtful any bombing campaign—exhaustive, attritional, or otherwise—could have stemmed the flow of supplies and ideas to the insurgents in South Vietnam.

While this chapter has focused almost entirely on the experiences of US Air Force pilots flying in the North, an entirely different air war took place in route packages 2, 3, 4, and 6B. This was the US Navy's air war in Vietnam, and it proved to be an attack pilot's paradise.

5

The US Navy's Air War

An Attack Pilot's War

S OME SOLDIERS IN THE US ARMY shared the perception that the US Navy did not *really* participate in the war in Vietnam. US Navy officer Commander Joseph Kiel was quoted in Stephen Howarth's history of the US Navy, *To Shining Sea*, discussing his experiences serving aboard the aircraft carrier USS *Hancock*. He noted that North Vietnam did not have a major navy, and that most naval personnel aboard ship enjoyed a relatively agreeable experience compared to their army—or even air force—brethren serving in country. Kiel stated, "I never felt any uneasiness at all in the ship." Howarth went on to state that "[m]any thousands of other US servicemen then and now would envy that—might, indeed, feel it suggests the US Navy had no real war to fight in Vietnam." Howarth points out that this is an unfair statement to be laid against the navy. While the US Navy enjoyed control of the sea and life afloat might have been preferable to life on land, the same enjoyment was not felt by naval aviators.[1]

Naval aviation is an extremely risky endeavor, even the routine tasks of taking off and landing aboard an aircraft carrier. In one seventeen-month stretch, the USS *Hancock* lost twenty aircraft to deck crashes alone. The inherent danger faced by naval aviators in their every task was not lost on aircrews: taking off; navigating to their targets, often only to find the target covered by weather; proceeding with an attack mission where they faced AAA and SAM threats; and then returning to the ship for the perilous landing. Commander Kiel remembered thinking, "Why did I risk my life taking off in this 1,500-foot ceiling, go there, when I'm just going out here to do what I consider to be very little anyhow?"[2]

The reason was simple, and it was found in how the US Navy perceived their role in the employment of air power in the 1960s and 1970s. At the time, the carrier air wing had two primary missions: fleet defense and attack. While the USAF converted its Century Series, designed to be interceptors and nuclear delivery platforms, into fighter-bombers, the US Navy already had dedicated attack squadrons: A-4 Skyhawks, A-6 Intruders, and later in the war, A-7 Corsairs. A navy A-7 attack pilot said, "With all due respect to the [navy's] MiG killers, the air war in Vietnam was an attack pilot's war." Another A-6 unit boasted, "If you're not attack, you must be support." There were also the USMC attack pilots. Historian Peter Mersky noted that the USMC took the concept of attack aviation to a different level: "As far as the Marines were concerned, interdiction was fine, but the men on the ground came first; that was the way it had always been and that was why the Marines had airplanes."[3]

The US Navy's role in the air war, including its contributions to the Rolling Thunder and both Linebacker campaigns, traditionally viewed as air force operations, is easy to miss despite the rich literature on the subject, especially in recent years. Historian Carol Reardon lamented, "Unfortunately, even the most detailed studies of this air offensive—most of which adopt the Air Force perspective—accord little attention to naval aviation's contributions to the total effort." Sadly, the study of the US Navy during Vietnam has been traditionally overlooked in favor of the USAF; this is not to say the role of the US Navy has been in any way ignored, just obfuscated. Naval air operations conducted out of Yankee (Gulf of Tonkin) and Dixie (Mekong Delta) Stations are explored in the following pages. Interestingly enough, it was not a historical account that brought attention to the navy's war. One of the more famous novels to come out of the conflict was the story of navy attack pilot Jake Grafton, a story lucidly detailed in Stephen Coonts's *Flight of the Intruder*. What James Salter's *The Hunters* was to the fighter community after Korea, Coonts's *Intruder* was for attack pilots.[4]

Unlike the US Air Force, the US Navy conducted attack missions using aircraft specifically designed for those missions, the aforementioned A-4s, A-6s, and A-7s, as well as the versatile F-4s, the latter created as a US Navy plane to begin with and only somewhat begrudgingly accepted by the air force. Although the two air arms had the same primary air-to-air fighter, the two services rarely worked together during the war. Rather than work jointly—a term that did not come into widespread use until after the war—the air arms divided Vietnam into the famous "route packages" that the air force and navy used to separate Vietnam into areas of responsibility for each service. One USAF fighter pilot noted after reading the rules of engagement, "The ridiculous gave way to the absurd. I couldn't discern whether the enemy was the North Vietnamese or the US Navy."[5]

The US Navy conducted operations from two locations. The first was Yankee Station in the north, and near the exit to the Gulf of Tonkin. The second was Dixie Station located further south in the South China Sea, nearer to Saigon. The navy's aviators participated in all of the same missions as did the pilots of the US Air Force, and flew in North and South Vietnam, Laos, and Cambodia. While the missions and locations were the same, they were certainly not done in a concentrated effort.

Gulf of Tonkin Incident

On the afternoon of August 2, 1964, five North Vietnamese torpedo boats approached the USS *Maddox* at high speed. The first visual contact came at 1334 as the *Maddox* sailed near the island of Hon Me off the coast of North Vietnam. The boats were 18,000 yards away, but were on an intercept course with the ship. Two of the torpedo boats broke off, but at 1630 the *Maddox* sounded the general quarters alarm as the other three boats made no attempt to alter their course. At 1708, the *Maddox* opened fire with warning shots and the torpedo boats returned fire. At 1718 and 1721, two of the boats launched a pair of torpedoes at the *Maddox*, both of which missed, before attempting to return to the safety of port in North Vietnam.[6]

A flight of F-8 Crusaders attacked the escaping boats with a strafing gun and rocket run, likely sinking one and damaging another. Two nights later, under cover of darkness, five torpedo boats approached the *Maddox* with both sides exchanging indecisive gunfire. There remains great debate about the authenticity of both attacks against the US Navy vessels, particularly the incident on August 4. James Stockdale, who participated in both incidents, remembered of the engagement on August 4 that he saw "[n]o boats, no boat wakes, no ricochets off boats, no boat gunfire, no torpedo wakes—nothing but black sea and American firepower." Whether or not the attacks happened as described, happened in a different manner, or never happened at all is largely irrelevant to this story. What does matter is the direct effect of these attacks—the expansion of the war in Vietnam especially as the navy was concerned.[7]

On August 4, Secretary of Defense Robert S. McNamara held a news conference where he stated,

> US Naval aircraft from the Carriers *Ticonderoga* and *Constellation* in the Bay of Tonkin area where our destroyers have undergone two deliberate attacks by the North Vietnamese have already initiated air strikes against the bases from which these PT boats have operated. Our naval aircraft have conducted strikes against certain other targets directly supporting the operation of the PT boats.[8]

The US Navy's air war in Vietnam began in earnest. As an immediate response the navy carried out aerial attacks against five separate locations, including the ports of the patrol boats and areas that provided logistical support.[9]

Naval Aviation Operations

In response to these attacks, the navy moved more assets into the theater, including another carrier battle group, which transferred from the First Fleet to the Seventh Fleet in the Western Pacific. In the air, the navy held the responsibility for conducting operations in route packages 1 (jointly with the USAF), 2, 3, 4, and 6B from the aircraft carriers operating in Yankee Station in the north and Dixie Station in the south. The two stations, Yankee and Dixie, and the aircraft carriers operating in those areas, combined to make up the Combined Task Force 77.

To conduct their strike missions, the US Navy operated numerous "attack aircraft," airframes specifically designed for all-weather strike missions to be conducted day or night, something the USAF lacked, instead being forced to use the F-105 and F-4 in ground attack roles. The workhorse for the US Navy was the A-6 Intruder, fielded in the early 1960s and on all carrier air wings by the time the navy entered the war. In later operations, after 1967, the navy also operated the A-7 Corsair. But these were only two of the attack aircraft fielded and operated by the navy during the Vietnam War, albeit the two most famous. The USN also flew the A-3 Skywarrior (the USAF flew a variant of this that was the B-66 Destroyer), and the A-4 Skyhawk.

While the USAF initially used rated pilots for its backseat radar operators, the navy instead elected to train and use dedicated radar intercept officers (RIOs), another program the air force later adopted when it transitioned its GIBs from the rated pilots to dedicated Weapons Systems Operators (WSO) in 1968. "GIB"—meaning "Guy in Back"—was the preferred air force term for the rear seater, regardless of pilot qualifications. This also applied to navy pilots flying the F-4, but not so the navy's A-6, where the pilots sat side by side rather than in tandem. In the A-6, however, the man in the right-hand seat was a "bombardier/navigator," and both RIOs and B/Ns were classified as naval flight officers (NFO). Histories often slight the GIB in favor of the pilot flying the aircraft. One USMC GIB remembered in a memoir, "The 'GIB,' or 'Guy in Back,' has often been overlooked or ignored," despite the fact that "the radar intercept officer played an integral part in enemy aircraft intercept and ordnance delivery."[10]

Life as a Naval Aviator and the SAM Threat

In the summer of 1965 as the war rapidly expanded, higher headquarters, most notably the office of the secretary of defense, demanded data to quantify attacks against North Vietnam. As one report put it, the navy needed to provide "tubular and statistical data." It made sense for the Defense Department to want to keep tabs on what pilots faced in Vietnam, but the presented data remained relatively antiseptic. Life for US Navy fighter and attack pilots was decidedly more savage and terrifying. From Hanoi to Yankee Station was 435 miles. North of Hanoi sat the MiG air base at Phuc Yen. Astride the direct line from the navy to the capital sat an SA-2 SAM site.[11]

The spring of 1965 witnessed increased SAM activity leading to a top-secret April 1965 message from the JCS to CINCPAC which stated, "Request you initiate planning for air attack against SA-2 site . . . Advise as to force composition, tactics, ordnance to be employed." Flying into RP VI-B was sure to bring a response from the North Vietnamese missile operators.[12]

Later, surface-to-air missiles could be found throughout North Vietnam. These were especially concentrated around the cities of Hanoi and Haiphong and other high-value targets, but also as far south as the DMZ. The navy pilots used the same tactics their air force brethren did in the early stage of the war. A navy pilot had one of two options: fly low enough to avoid SAM detection, which also placed the attacking aircraft into AAA threat rings; or, if the mission compelled the aircraft to fly high enough that it could be tracked and fired upon, use defensive maneuvering to avoid being shot down. If a SAM was observed to be guiding on a flight of aircraft, standard tactics dictated that aircraft perform a "High G turn into the SAM," more commonly called the SAM-break.[13]

Navy aircraft were equipped with the ALQ-51 track-breaker electronic countermeasure, the same type used to counter the SA-2's Fan Song fire-control radar used by the USAF. When the ALQ-51 was used in conjunction with high-speed maneuvering, this dropped the probable kill rate (Pk) rate of the SAM by a considerable margin over a heavily defended target—"to no more than 4 percent," according to one report. Pilots were given the following instructions and employed the following tactics: "airplanes receiving warning from . . . onboard warning systems execute sustained High-G maneuver such as roll-ahead, split-s, or steep spiral terminating as close to the ground as possible considering terrain and gun defenses." However, if at the same time as being fired upon by an SA-2 pilots were also receiving heavy AAA, they were instructed to "remain above 10,000 feet where optical and barrage gun system AAA is less effective." These instructions indicated that a SAM-break should terminate as close to the ground as possible unless AAA was present—and AAA was always present. It was a pure catch-22.[14]

Reports of SAMs on attack missions were frequent. Pilots described these in the mission reports upon return to the carrier. These included where and when the SAM was sighted, how the missile performed (guided vs. unguided), and how it approached the formation. An example follows: "Three SAMs came from 9 o'clock posit [position] and one from 11 o'clock posit, all missiles appeared unguided and passed approx. 5,000 feet above acft." While these missiles missed literally by a mile, the same flight of aircraft were fired upon again, and this time the missiles passed only 200 feet away, which should have caused the SAM to detonate by proximity, but in this case the missiles failed to explode and the aviators returned to the safety of their ship.[15]

Navy aircraft were warned to not fly in a standard four-ship formation, but rather to break up into two mutually supporting elements. Each element was further recommended to fly in a "two-plane section . . . with separation 500–700 feet vertically 200 feet aft and 400 feet abeam; this formation readily permits High-G maneuvers recommended for SAM avoidance." A separate memo from the chief of naval operations, Admiral Thomas H. Moorer, to CINCPACFLT, Admiral Roy L. Johnson, stated, "SAM defense formations of greater than two planes are unwieldy, provide no advantage over two-plane sections, and are not recommended."[16]

In November of 1967, the US Navy began noticing a disturbing trend in SAM activity, namely that the North Vietnam missile operators were using their Fan Song radars to track American aircraft at lower altitudes. This resulted in loss of attacking aircraft either by SAM engagements at lower altitudes or aircraft maneuvering into the ground while performing SAM avoidance measures. Again, as American pilots changed their tactics, so too did the defenders of North Vietnam, and navy losses correspondingly increased.[17]

The navy used operations reports to inform higher headquarters of aircraft losses. A fairly typical OPREP reported the downing of a navy aircraft, stating the aircraft type and call sign, if a search-and-rescue (SAR) effort was initiated, and if said SAR effort was successful. For example, "Helo BIG MOTHER 70 ordered into area. RESCAP [Rescue Combat Air Patrol] suppressed ground fire prior to and during BIG MOTHER Pickup."[18]

Not all rescue attempts ended in success. As one report indicated, the co-pilot was picked up, but

[a]fter ejection pilot and co-pilot were on opposite sides of a ridge. RESCAP had only limited communications with pilot during initial search effort. Co-pilot heard shots and voices and words "surrender-surrender" over radio. No communications established with pilot by SAR forces during night recovery attempt or subsequent daylight effort. Consider probability of rescue extremely remote.[19]

The navy approached attacking SAM sites in much the same way the air force did. Initially, it used the existing tactics in response to missile activity, but after losses mounted, naval aviators found they needed to engage the SAM sites in a direct manner. One report noted, "We must attack the system rather than ignore it. We must destroy the radars, the missiles, and, above all, kill the trained crews."[20]

All services took the SAM threat seriously and looked for solutions to the problem that went beyond the tactic of a "turn" into the missile, and hope. CINCPAC Admiral Roy Johnson noted that the North Vietnamese forces were in no danger of running out of SAMs. The Soviet Union shipped their missiles, radars, and associated equipment south by rail through China. Even though China continued to allow their Marxist brothers to ship materiel into North Vietnam, the USSR, as Soviet-Sino relations worsened, began shipping a portion of their SA-2s by sea. Admiral Johnson also noted that between 1966 and 1967, but especially through the spring of 1967, the North Vietnamese forces showed a proclivity for firing more missiles. He stated, "An examination of firing trends suggests that expenditures have drastically increased since July 1, 1966." Johnson went on to note that North Vietnam required a resupply of roughly 200 to 300 missiles per month, which indicated they were on pace to fire as many as 2,400 missiles that year. Clearly more needed to be done to counter the SAM threat.[21]

Countering the SAM threat received a boost when on May 30, 1967, members of the III Marine Amphibious Force recovered a portion of an SA-2 missile. Components of the missile included "the electronics package, the battery, the control fin actuating mechanism, the turbopump assembly, and the sustainer engine." This partial missile was placed on a C-141 and shipped to the Redstone Arsenal in Alabama for exploitation, although the threat of SAMs remained a potent one throughout the remainder of the war. While tactics changed and American pilots' ability to know when they were being tracked by SAM radars improved, no exploitation ever provided a silver-bullet solution to the problem of the Mach 3 telephone poles, especially for the attacking pilots rolling in on their bombing runs in the heavily defended RP-6B.[22]

MiG Threat

The MiG threat was as potent for the US Navy as it was for the USAF. As previously noted, early 1967 still found the MiG airfields on prohibited strike lists, leading Robin Olds to "entice" the MiGs into combat as part of Operation Bolo. This prohibition changed as the war progressed. Throughout the summer of 1967, there were "signs of increased aggressiveness during recent engagements" by the NVAF and a new "willingness to stay and fight."[23]

In October of 1967, a combined USN/USMC/USAF strike went after the MiG airfields at Phuc Yen and Kep for the first time. One American newspaper from California reported after the attack that "American pilots were so anxious to attack Phuc Yen that when it was removed from the restricted list pilots of all three American air arms volunteered for the raid—Navy, Air Force and Marines." The attack on Phuc Yen saw more than one hundred aircraft participate, including strike aircraft, CAP, AAA and SAM suppression, and ECM. Both runways were completely cratered and six MiGs on the ground either damaged or destroyed. American forces attacked the MiG air bases two more times in the coming months, but after each attack, the North Vietnamese forces quickly repaired the runways. Although the runways and taxiways were cratered and the aircraft revetments were also destroyed, there was one item not significantly damaged in these later attacks: Most of the MiGs survived. The MiGs had sought sanctuary inside China prior to the attack, and after each strike and repair operation, the MiGs moved back into the base. The only way to be sure the MiG aircraft were destroyed was to engage them in the air. While the attack aircraft plied their trade against ground targets, support aircraft, including MiGCAPs, existed for the sole purpose of protecting the strikers.[24]

The US Navy earned its first official air-to-air victory on June 17, 1965, when Commander Louis C. Page and Lieutenant John Smith downed a MiG-17 with an AIM-7 Sparrow. This was not only the US Navy's first aerial victory, but the first official air-to-air credit of the Vietnam War. The first official air force victory did not occur until July 10.[25]

The navy ended 1965 "up" with a kill ratio of 3:0, although this number does include the several engagements with MiGs belonging to China's People's Army Air Force. From 1965 forward, the US Navy engaged in aerial engagements with the NVAF over their assigned route packages. These ran the gamut from non-dogfights, "blue bandits observed" but not engaged, to short, quick air-to-air kills. "Showtime 602 fired one Sparrow in head-on run . . . missile observed to guide well, impact observed." However, if the American fighter pilots ended up in a turning dogfight, the reports turned decidedly more narrative as the pilot's actions and words flowed through his typewriter.[26]

These engagements were always followed by the necessary debriefs and after-action reports, the less-glamorous side of the life of the fighter pilot. These AAR messages were written by the flier for posterity, but also to portray any MiG sighting or engagement in as few words as possible. The language of the AAR was unique to the flying community. After stating the date and aircraft involved, the narratives were more often than not conveyed in a nearly indecipherable language. For example, the complete text of one message reads: "Hostile ACFT ALT 14 Thousand Closure Rate 1100-KTS/Deepest Penetration Hostiles 18-23N4/Firing Point VIC 18-45n8-23E3H5."

In some cases a city might be mentioned: "Vic [vicinity] of Vinh." Location was usually given by a reference to a "Bullseye" point. Bullseye was "an established reference point from which the position of an object can be referenced." For example, if Bullseye was the city of Hanoi and a message read 180/50, then the location of an event or a MiG engagement occurred 180 degrees—due south—of the city and 50 miles away from the city's center.[27]

These reports also indicated that, as the air force also learned, air-to-air weapons could only be fired inside of certain parameters. For example, early in the war, the heat-seeking radar head on the front end of an AIM-9 had a limit of three Gs and could not track if a target was in a higher-G turn or if the aircraft to which it was attached was also performing a high-G maneuver. One message noted that a flight of F-4s from the USS *Hornet* ended up in a turning fight with a pair of MiGs. In the course of the fight, "Rootbeer 212 slid in for a tail aspect sidewinder shot. MiG broke hard and Rootbeer 212 fired Sidewinder while pulling 5.0G. Sidewinder dropped out of sight." This was another example of missiles failing when fired beyond prescribed envelopes. As this F-4 turned and attempted to kill his MiG, two other MiG-21s appeared and attempted to pull in behind Rootbeer 212 while he was distracted with the aircraft in front of him. His wingman, Rootbeer 202, rolled over behind this second pair of MiGs. Rootbeer 202 called 212 to break-turn. Rootbeer 202 was one mile behind this second flight of MiGs in a nearly textbook position to shoot. The after-action report noted that the "MiG was . . . range one mile, tail-on aspect." Rootbeer 202 loosed an AIM-9, and since he was well within weapons parameters, the "Sidewinder guided up tailpipe, exploded and pilot ejected almost immediately." This engagement demonstrated the importance of placing your aircraft inside a proper weapons employment envelope, an issue the US Navy began covering in a new schoolhouse at Miramar in 1969.

However, North Vietnam's MiGs were not the only ones naval aviators had to contend with.[28] While North Vietnam proved to be a dangerous airspace, pilots also had to be careful not to accidentally stray into China, which occurred on more than one occasion. There was of course a buffer line which extended south from the Chinese border, but while this was clear on a map, it was less obvious from the cockpit of an aircraft.

On one strike into North Vietnam, Murphy's Law reared its head. The night of August 21, 1967, a flight of four A-6 Intruders—call sign Milestone 410, 405, 400, and 402—attacked the Duc Noi rail yard; the four-ship was part of a larger strike package that attacked the Hanoi power plant. On his bomb run, the flight lead, Milestone 410, was shot down by a SAM. The crew, Commander Leo T. Profilet and Lieutenant William M. Hardman, were both captured and spent the next five years as POWs. The three remaining aircraft turned east, heading for their "coast out point." In the midst of their egress North Vietnam troops fired more than twenty SAMs at them. In the ensuing "jinking" to avoid the SAMs, Milestone 405 called out he was "blind," which indicated he had lost visual contact with the other two aircraft. To make matters worse, a large thunderstorm was directly in front of their route. Although the A-6s were "all-weather" attack aircraft, they prudently turned north to avoid the storm.

Milestone 405 regained sight of the other Intruders, who were by this time ten miles to the north, and called for them to steer further east. Although they acknowledged his radio call, the A-6s continued in a more northerly route apparently in an attempt to fly between the storm and the border of China. Milestone 405 reiterated his call for a turn a few moments later. A later memo to the secretary of defense stated, "The delay in commencing this turn plus the gradual turn radius apparently positioned Milestone 400 and 402 . . . inside CHICOM [communist China] territory 5–11 miles."[29]

Milestone 405 next heard a radio call of "MiGs, MiGs, Farmers, Farmers, Farmers." ("Farmers" was the North Atlantic Treaty Organization's designation for the MiG-19. MiG-17a and MiG-21s were the Fresco and the Fishbed, respectively.) Looking to his left he saw a number of People's Liberation Army Air Force (PLAAF) MiG-19s making an attack run on the rest of his flight. Milestone 405 took evasive maneuvers by making a hard bank to the right and diving down into cloud cover. He never saw the MiGs down his crew mates. Both A-6s were lost. Three of the four crew members were killed: Lieutenant (junior grade) Dain Scott, Lieutenant (junior grade) J. Forrest Trembley, and Lieutenant Commander Jimmy L. Buckley. The fourth member, Lieutenant Robert J. Flynn, spent the next five years held as a prisoner of war in China.[30]

Peking did not miss the opportunity to inform the world of the downing of the A-6s. In a press statement released the same day of the incident, the Peking International Service noted that a pair of A-6s "of the US Imperialists" and piloted by "two air pirates" were brought down by "an Air Force unit of the heroic Chinese People's Liberation Army" who were "armed with the invincible thought of Mao Tse-tung." This was not the only incident in which stray American aircraft were engaged by the PLAAF during the Vietnam conflict, but sometimes the threat was closer to home. Sometimes it was not AAA, MiGs, or SAMs that caused damage, but an unforeseen accident.[31]

Forrestal Fire

Although many in the army, or even the air force, might have envied the relative safety of their navy brethren, the US Navy had other enemies than those found in the skies and on the ground in Southeast Asia. In July 1967, while conducting aircraft launch operations, a Zuni rocket attached to an F-4 misfired and shot across the deck of the USS *Forrestal*. The rocket impacted two waiting A-4s parked across the deck as the deck crew maneuvered aircraft and prepared the carrier for that day's flight operations. The rocket did not detonate, but it did slice through fuel tanks attached to the wings of the parked A-4s, and the deck was immediately covered in JP-8 (jet fuel), which ignited. A conflagration ensued as jet fuel, rockets, missiles, and bombs all mixed together into a massive and uncontrollable firestorm.

That day's ship log reported the incident: "1046: Class Bravo fire in an aircraft on the flight deck aft . . . sounded fire alarm . . . Captain takes the conn . . . sounded general quarters. 1054: Experiencing detonations of bombs and other ordnance attached to aircraft in grouping on flight deck." The situation grew even more grave as personnel were reported trapped by smoke; orders went out to move the wounded forward of the forecastle and to push damaged aircraft over the side. The USS *Rupertus* pulled within feet of the *Forrestal* and used her own firefighting system to provide assistance. A request for medical assistance was sent to all ships in the area and other ships in the carrier's strike group came alongside to render aid. By the time night fell, the hospital ship USS *Repose* had pulled in front of the *Forrestal* and helicopters flew between the two ships, moving wounded and bringing in additional medical aid.[32]

In acts of heroism, sailors and marines fought to contain the fires, which were largely under control by early afternoon. By the morning of July 31, they were reported contained and put out.

This tragic event resulted in the deaths of 134 sailors and another 161 injured, and the US Navy lost twenty-one aircraft. It was the worst disaster on board a ship since World War II, the largest single loss of navy aircraft in the Vietnam War, and the worst casualty event for the US Navy during the Vietnam conflict.

Although it pales in comparison to the horrendous loss of life, the loss of twenty-one aircraft in the fire was significant. As one history noted, "The unlucky *Forrestal* (CVN-59) spent only five days on the line as she suffered serious damage and heavy casualties during the fire on July 29, 1967." Although the *Forrestal* fire is arguably the most well-remembered carrier fire, it was only one of three major fires to occur during the course of the navy's involvement in Vietnam. In October of 1966 a lit flare caused a massive fire on the USS *Oriskany*, resulting in the deaths of 44 sailors; and in 1969 another Zuni rocket ignited on the USS *Enterprise*, leading to the deaths of 28 sailors.[33]

The Navy Attack War and the Ault Report

Whether AAA, SAM, MiG, or the dangers encountered on board the ship, the entire point of the navy's role was to put bombs on target in South Vietnam, Laos, Cambodia, and North Vietnam. Fighter pilots flew MiGCAP, but again, their mission was to protect the strike aircraft. Some targets necessitated a massive combined effort. According to Stephen R. Gray, an A-4 Skyhawk pilot, "[T]he more important, and therefore more fortified, targets required a more concentrated effort, and the entire wing would work in concert against these targets, attacking in 'alpha strikes.' "[34]

As previously mentioned, the attack pilots of the Vietnam War believed they produced results while the fighter pilots received the glory. Carol Reardon's memoir of one A-6 squadron dropping bombs during the Linebacker missions noted that A-6 crews "did not chase MiGs through North Vietnamese skies or challenge enemy pilots to dogfights. They dropped bombs. Their story—to some—lacks the flash and dash of 1972's best known aviators. . . . [T]he attack community has languished too long in the shadow of the fighters." Again, the navy's dedicated attack aircraft, specifically designed for a particular type of mission, did what the USAF had to change their fighter-bombers in order to do. The navy pilots would argue they did it better as well, but inter-service rivalry aside, the A-4, A-6, and A-7 communities had a unique role in the conflict. A-6s could fly individual attack missions—in pairs, larger flights of four, or as part of the massive alpha strikes. Reardon also noted, "At night and in bad weather, the Navy's A-6s filled the skies for months before the Air Force's heralded F-111s returned to air operations in late September 1972."[35]

Both the USAF and US Navy recognized by the late 1960s that aircrew performance was clearly less than desired, and both services produced a plethora of studies and programs aimed at improving combat capability—Combat Sage, Sparrow Shoot, and the Walker report, to name a few—but two studies stand out not only for their comprehensiveness, but for the direct impact they had on changing their service's combat preparedness. For the US Navy this was the "Air-to-Air Missile System Capability Review," more commonly called the "Ault Report," for its namesake, Captain Frank W. Ault. This report is best remembered as the document that led directly to the creation of the navy's Top Gun program. Although it did indeed accomplish this, the report was much greater than simply a review of air-to-air combat.

The Ault Committee convened their first meeting at the Naval Missile Center, Point Mugu, California, on August 8, 1968, and ended three months later, in November. The published report hit the fleet in January of 1969. The fundamental problem was that "[p]erformance in combat indicates a probability of achieving about one kill for every ten firing attempts in any engagement where air-to-air missiles are employed in an environment similar to that in Southeast Asia." During the time the Ault Committee conducted their interviews and prepared its report, US Navy fighters shot twenty-four *more* missiles with a resultant two MiG kills.[36]

The committee, led by Ault, started out with five questions to guide their quest for answers:

1. Is industry delivering to the Navy a high-quality product, designed and built to specifications?
2. Are Fleet support organizations delivering a high-quality product to the CVAs (Carrier Vehicle Attack) and to the forward area sites ashore?
3. Do shipboard and squadron organizations (afloat and ashore) launch an optimally ready combat aircraft-missile system?
4. Does the combat aircrew fully understand and exploit the capabilities of the aircraft-missile system? (Corollary question: Is the aircraft-missile system properly designed and configured for the air-to-air mission?)
5. Is the air-to-air missile system (aircraft/fire control system/missile) repair and rework program returning a quality product to the Fleet?[37]

These questions clearly indicate that the Ault Report was not only about aircrew performance, but also about the life cycle of the missile itself, starting with its production by industry and ending with a button press where it left the rails and either killed a MiG or failed to do so. The committee stated: "The review indicates that numerous design, procedural, and organizational changes can and should be made."[38]

These changes came in the form of fourteen separate areas requiring improvement in order to increase missile kill ratios: policy, management, production, performance vs. design, maintenance and test, aircrew training, personnel training other than aircrew, logistic support, documentation, surveillance, inspection, safety, rework, and evaluation by Fleet Missile Systems Analysis and Evaluation Group (FMSAEG). Several areas noted as problems in the Ault Report were also recognized by the USAF in its own self-evaluations going on at the same time.

One area that was indicated as problematic was the use of the F-4 as a "jack-of-all trades" aircraft. The F-4 was created with the ability, and had the capability, to perform in both the air-to-air and air-to-ground roles. While the aircraft itself was obviously designed and had the capability to perform both mission sets, using squadrons to perform both missions came at the detriment of performing either one well. "A key issue" in the area of training and readiness was "the commitment of fighter squadrons to air-to-ground missions in Southeast Asia and the consequent dilution of air-to-air training and readiness." In other words, fighter pilots needed to be allowed to focus on the mission of killing MiGs and not on bomb runs, strafing, and other attack missions. Conversely, attack pilots should *only* conduct those missions.[39]

Another area which required attention was the complexity of the aircraft itself. Radar tracking, the arrangement of controls inside the cockpit (switchology), and missile control and employment all led to the conclusion that "US fighter pilots have been required to fight a 'heads up' engagement in Southeast Asia with a 'heads down' system." This does not include the coordination needed between the aircraft commander sitting up front and the radar intercept officer in the back.[40]

Navy pilots (and their USAF brethren) also routinely fired their missiles outside of their prescribed envelopes. Although changes made during Vietnam indicated the importance of placing the fighter in a position of advantage over the enemy (i.e., the mechanics of dogfighting), the Ault Report showed that "much of this effort has been wasted because it did not stress one of the key elements of the problem: missile envelope recognition/identification." Navy fighter pilots flew better than their NVAF counterparts, but they continued to struggle with missile employment, the result being that although navy pilots might find themselves in an advantageous position over their enemy, their inability to place their aircraft in the proper weapon's employment zone (WEZ) meant that they did not achieve the elusive MiG kill. Their missiles' own inherent design problems also hindered them in this regard.[41]

The solutions to the problems proved to be simple and yet elegant. Outside of recommendations to industry and the US Navy writ large, the biggest impact from the Ault Report came in changes made to the training of navy aircrew, which began almost immediately. The overarching problem proved to be a "gradual loss of expertise and continuity in the field of fighter weaponry." The solution was the creation of a new organization whose sole purpose was to be a schoolhouse for "consolidating, coordinating, and promulgating the doctrine, lore, tactics, and procedures for fighter employment." This came in the form of recommendation number 11 under section IV, subheading B, area 6: "CNO and ComNavAirPac establish, as early as possible, an Advanced

Fighter Weapons School in RCVW-12 at NAS Miramar for both the F-8 and F-4."[42]

Throughout the Vietnam War—and this could be extrapolated throughout much of the military aerial developments of the 1960s writ large—the US Navy served as a leader in technology, pilot development, and assessment of changes that needed to be made during the crucible of combat. Although loathe to admit it, the USAF ended up adopting or adapting many of the USN's programs.

It would not be a stretch to state that many of the good concepts the USN developed or created during the Vietnam War eventually found their way into the USAF. These included the adoption of the F-4 (although admittedly this was more due to Secretary of Defense Robert McNamara than the USAF), the AIM-7 Sparrow missile, and the radar intercept officer (RIO), which became the weapon systems officer (WSO) in the USAF, replacing the "Guy in Back" program that caused both pilots and GIBs so much consternation. Although the air force already fielded a Fighter Weapons School of their own that traced its origins back to the Aerial Gunnery School of the 1950s, it was not meeting the desired ends of improving the combat capability of USAF fighter squadrons. The first officer in charge of the navy's school at Miramar, Dan Pederson, noted, "Sure, it bothered us to hear the Air Force claim it had created the first Fighter Weapons School. (If that was true in name, it wasn't true in substance—or result.)"[43]

USAF ace Captain Steve Ritchie wrote to the commander of TAC, General William W. Momyer, stating as much. Ritchie informed General Momyer,

> I cited the lack of training that we had even in the Fighter Weapons School in those days—the Fighter Weapons School was the best training we had available, but we were not allowed to fight other types of airplanes. The only kind of aircraft we could fight was the type we flew—the only airplane I ever fought against prior to Vietnam was an F-4.[44]

Junior officers in the USAF observed the training at the Top Gun school, and the results there began to cross-pollinate into the USAF. Pederson remembers that the USAF fighter pilots "were alive to the dynamism of the Navy's Loose Deuce cruising formation, and the offensive potential of exploiting the egg. The USAF also began to understand the value of dissimilar combat training. . . . The blue suits learned fast, and the training environment became one of mutual respect with a healthy exchange of ideas." The ability to train against dissimilar aircraft was an important tool the US Navy used at Top Gun; flying A-4s and other aircraft that performed as the MiGs did, the Air Force eventually adopted this concept as well with the creation of its own Aggressor squadrons in 1972.[45]

Conclusion

The US Navy's dedicated attack pilots bore the brunt of the air-to-ground war, but at least they flew aircraft specifically designed for the purpose, as opposed to the USAF who were forced to modify fighters or fighter/bombers designed for nuclear delivery to the purpose of conventional bombers. While the air-to-air fighter pilots gained the glory, the attack pilots trudged through the unforgiving war year after year, conducting their operations and completing their tours of duty.

The navy's creation of its own Fighter Weapons "Top Gun" School was based off of reports coming out of Vietnam, and the USN's Ault Report led to this development. The USAF made changes of its own in the creation of the Red Flag exercise, using its own Red Baron Reports (discussed in chapter 8), but the air force's changes did not occur until well after Vietnam had ended. Although Red Flag and its precursor, Exercise Coronet Organ, addressed many of the same issues that the navy dealt with, it seems obvious that the USN was ahead of the USAF in this regard. Even though the USAF already had a weapons school that traced it origins back to before the Vietnam War, it did not enjoy the same impact on the Vietnam conflict that Top Gun did.

During the course of the Vietnam War, the US Navy lost 1,631 sailors and 13,095 marines in combat operations. Of those numbers, 377 were naval aviators lost during the downing of some 530 aircraft during combat, and an additional 329 more to operational causes. The first commander of the navy's Fighter Weapons School stated fifty years later, "In the 1960s, America fought in Vietnam with the wrong planes, unreliable weapons, bad tactics, and the wrong senior civilian leadership. A lot of important things were broken. But we loved what we did." Of navy air power in Vietnam, historian John Darrell Sherwood stated in his official US Navy history, *Nixon's Trident*: "Despite the Navy's massive investment in the various bombing campaigns of the war, air power never proved strategically decisive."[46]

The war to bolster and protect South Vietnam from the Viet Cong counterinsurgency began as an "advise and train" mission. The Geneva Accords expressly forbade the use of "jet weapons"; thus, aircraft like the T-28 seen here was used to train the air force of South Vietnam. Even once jets were introduced, the T-28 saw wide use throughout Southeast Asia. (NMUSAF)

Helicopters saw extensive use throughout the conflict in Vietnam, serving as medical evacuation transport, special operations support, and search-and-rescue craft. The Hueys are best remembered for delivering troops to the field in rapid fashion as part of the US Army's Air Mobile Division. (USAF)

To look for traffic coming down the Ho Chi Minh Trail in North Vietnam, Laos, and Cambodia, the USAF created the "Misty Fast-FACs" (Forward Air Controllers) to find, mark, and engage enemy forces. Here is an early Misty two-seat F-100F. (NMUSAF)

During the Vietnam War, the B-52 conducted heavy bombing throughout the theater, but it also provided close air support at Khe Sanh and other areas. During Linebacker II, B-52s struck targets in Hanoi and Haiphong, but suffered tremendous losses. (USAF)

General William Westmoreland commanded the Military Assistance Command–Vietnam from 1964 to 1968, but admitted his "interest in the air war was somewhat incidental." (National Archives/Johnson Library)

In South Vietnam, the air forces of the USAF, USN, and USMC served principally in the close-air-support role. Here, marines at Khe Sanh observe an F-4 as it attacks targets along the base's perimeter. (USAF)

In the Oval Office (l. to r.): Secretary Clark Clifford, Secretary Dean Rusk, Geri Rudolph, President Lyndon B. Johnson, Tom Johnson, Walt Rostow, General Earle Wheeler, and Richard Helms. Johnson often personally selected targets for the Rolling Thunder campaign. (Johnson Library/National Archives)

As the United States conducted more attacks in North Vietnam, surface-to-air missile sites proliferated in the country. Here a reconnaissance photo from August of 1965 clearly shows the SA-2 missile and its associated Fan Song radar. (NMUSAF)

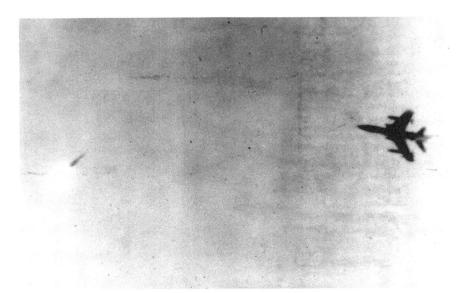

An F-105 attempts to dodge an SA-2 over North Vietnam. Early on in the war pilots were instructed to "execute sustained High-G maneuvers" or "SAM breaks" to avoid the missile. Later, the USAF and USN created special units to attack the missile sites. (NMUSAF)

The F-105 served as an air-to-ground bomber in North Vietnam. During the conflict 47 percent of the total F-105 fleet was lost, leading to the macabre joke, "Do you know what an optimist is? A Thud pilot who quits smoking." (NMUSAF)

General William Momyer was the first commander of the 7th Air Force and struggled to bring all air assets under his purview. After he left MACV in 1968, Momyer began making concrete changes to the way the USAF trained its pilots for combat as the commander of TAC. (USAF)

Unlike the USAF, the US Navy had aircraft specifically designed to perform "attack" missions. Here, an A-6 Intruder prepares to launch off of the USS Kitty Hawk in March of 1967. (National Archives)

Used by the USAF and USN, the F-4 Phantom served in both air-to-air and air-to-ground roles throughout the Vietnam War, but is probably best remembered as the principal fighter of the war and a supreme MiG-killer. (National Archives)

By the time Nixon came to office, the context of the war was beginning to change. In the early 1970s, with détente under way, Nixon had a wider choice of targets and did not fear the Soviet retaliation that Johnson had struggled with, allowing him to expand bombing operations in the North. Here, Nixon points to a map of Cambodia during a Vietnam War press conference on April 30, 1970. (Nixon Library/National Archives)

Bombs explode on and around the MiG base at Phuc Yen, northwest of Hanoi, in October 1967. Despite cratering the runway, the airfield was rapidly repaired. The only way to ensure that MiGs were destroyed was to shoot them down. Throughout the war, runways and bridges proved notoriously difficult targets to destroy. (NMUSAF)

The Air Force of North Vietnam proved equal to the task of engaging with American forces in the aerial arena. Here, MiG-19 pilots observe a lesson on air-to-air tactics. Rather than rotate out of the war as American pilots did, the NVAF either survived the war or flew until they were killed in combat. (NMUSAF)

One of the most famous images of the air war. Gun camera footage captures the moment an F-105 gains victory over a MiG-17 during a dogfight on June 5, 1967. (NMUSAF)

6

Strategic Air Power at Bay?

O PERATION ROLLING THUNDER, the bombing campaign against North
Vietnam, ended in November 1968. Although retaliatory strikes continued intermittently against targets in the North, no official bombing
campaign existed until the operations of Linebacker I and Linebacker II in
1972. Between 1968 and 1972 much had changed, not only in the Vietnam
War, but in a larger geopolitical sphere as well. The Linebacker Operations,
conducted during the Nixon administration, helped move the United States
into a better bargaining position against North Vietnam and aided in the
"Vietnamization" process. In short, the Nixon administration used these
bombing campaigns to move the United States into an improved position
to withdraw from the country entirely. Even though the air force had long
argued for heavier bombing earlier in the war, these two campaigns achieved
their limited success because of the *type* of war being waged and the nature of
the enemy at the time the operations were conducted. The nature of Nixon's
political objectives allowed for fewer bombing restrictions against more-
traditional targets. Assurances from the Soviet Union allowed more leeway
in what targets air power could strike. Furthermore, the North Vietnamese
leadership was also in a position to not only hasten the end of the war but also
to accelerate American withdrawal.

That being said, the second Linebacker proved to be almost prohibitively
costly to the American B-52 units and could not have continued many
more days. This chapter also explores Strategic Air Command's struggle in
the use of their "strategic" B-52s—those aircraft reserved for nuclear attack
against the Soviet Union—in a conventional war and the problem of a global

command-and-control structure conducting conventional attacks on the other side of the planet. SAC, more than any other organization, struggled with an identity crisis in the use of its aircraft. The B-52 proved to be capable of close air support to the beleaguered marine garrison at Khe Sanh and other locations throughout South Vietnam, but this was not a mission the strategic-bombardment community wanted to conduct.

The use of B-52s for close air support and interdiction, as part of the Arc Light missions, was covered in earlier chapters. As noted then, the Strategic Air Command in Omaha, Nebraska, was never in favor of using the B-52 in those unconventional roles. SAC was also not incredibly enthralled with the use of B-52s in the Vietnam period, noting that every B-52 at Guam or U-Tapao was one B-52 not standing alert or prepared to respond to Soviet attack. However, the use of B-52s as bombers conducting strategic bombing missions against industrialized targets in North Vietnam *did* fit preconceived notions of *how* bombers should be properly employed.

Linebacker I

As mentioned in chapter 3, the People's Army of North Vietnam, the conventional fighting force of North Vietnam, launched an immense three-pronged invasion of South Vietnam in the spring of 1972. The PAVN called it the Nguyen Hue Offensive, but in Western news outlets it simply became the Easter Offensive. It included regular PAVN soldiers as well as armor and artillery. Through the invasion of South Vietnam, the PAVN planned to degrade the Army of South Vietnam's ability to effectively resist future operations and gain a better bargaining position at the ongoing Paris peace talks.

The attacking force moved on South Vietnam along three lines of advance: south through the demilitarized zone; from southern Laos, east toward the central highlands; and south through Cambodia in the direction of Saigon. The United States used air power to help blunt this offensive and simultaneously launched an aerial campaign against targets inside North Vietnam. Historian Raymond Leonard noted that the first Linebacker Operation proved something different to each of the belligerents: to the United States, the efficacy of concentrated air power when properly applied; to South Vietnam, their vulnerability to attack in the absence of American air power; and to the North Vietnamese, the need to get the United States out of the conflict.[1]

With the beginning of the Easter Offensive, the United States needed a rapid response. By this point in the conflict, American troop strength had dropped from a high of 543,000 in 1969 to fewer than 25,000 in 1972. The drastic drop included a huge withdrawal of aerial assets, but by no means was America fangless.[2]

Much of the air power used during Rolling Thunder had already transitioned home as the Vietnamization process expanded. In order to bolster the air power still in-theater, the USAF executed a program under the name Constant Guard. The USAF rushed 36 F-4Es from Seymour Johnson AFB and another 36 from Homestead and Eglin AFBs. An additional 72 F-4s followed on the heels of the first deployment. The Strategic Air Command moved 120 B-52s to Guam and Thailand. To support the fighters and bombers, more than 100 KC-135s deployed. By May, the USAF had over 600 fighters and bombers ready to perform strike operations. By the end of July, that number was nearing 1,000. The US Navy ordered the deployment of an additional four carriers to support the two already on-station. This brought a substantial portion of the USAF and USN to bear on North Vietnam to stop the invading forces flowing into the South.[3]

Historian Earl Tilford noted that the plan called for Linebacker I to "halt the invasion and so devastate North Vietnam's military capabilities that Hanoi would be compelled to negotiate seriously for the first time since peace talks began in 1968." On April 2, 1972, for the first time since the bombing pause went into effect, American aircraft began flying preplanned and coordinated strikes against targets in North Vietnam as opposed to the retaliatory strikes after the end of Rolling Thunder.[4]

Operation Linebacker began in May of 1972 and signaled a renewal of the war in the air during the conflict. During the following five and a half months American aircraft lost during combat operations drastically increased: 134 American aircraft fell to North Vietnam's integrated air defense system (IADS). Conversely, only 63 aircraft belonging to North Vietnam were lost during the same period. The American loss rate was dispersed evenly throughout the services, primarily fighter and attack aircraft, but considering the bombing pause that had been in effect since 1968 and the sheer increase in sorties flown, the loss rate was to be expected. The USAF finished its first assessment of Linebacker I even before it concluded. A CHECO report published on September 27, 1972, stated that the "NVA underestimated the vulnerability of massed forces" to concentrated air power.[5]

The commander of the Pacific Air Forces, General Lucius D. Clay Jr., later told *Air Force* magazine,

> Initially they overwhelmed the allied defenses. The great unsung story of this invasion is the speed with which tac air [tactical air] was able to respond. I don't think that anybody can deny that the reason why the invasion was checked and the counter-offensive became possible is airpower, in the form of B-52s, tac air, the gunships, and the guided bombs.[6]

It is important to note that Clay mentions the use of guided bombs as evidence of success. The USAF already recognized the importance of these weapons on the conduct of future operations. The ability to guide a weapon to its target dated back to World War II and the ill-fated Aphrodite operations, but the maturation of the technology found useful employment in Vietnam and became a hallmark of how the USAF would conduct warfare in the future.

Both laser-guided and electro-optically guided bombs were used to great extent during Linebacker I. Beyond the destruction or damage of 400 bridges and 800 "road separations," these guided munitions also attacked tunnel systems and other means of transport between China and North Vietnam. Although these bombs cannot be underestimated, it is important to note that the context of the war had changed by 1972; thus, it was not just the use of these weapons but the targets they were used against that had also changed. Gone were the days of fearing Soviet or Chinese intervention or reprisal. Nixon's dual actions—diplomacy with China and détente with the Soviet Union—removed the fear of widening the conflict into a global confrontation. This freed American flyers to attack more targets leading from Hanoi north to the border with China.[7]

For the first time in the Vietnam conflict, air power was used not only with fewer restrictions, but the fliers from the USAF and USN were able to combine the changes and technological developments that were coming to the forefront in the late 1960s and were finally reaching maturity. Combined strike packages now included the strike aircraft, sometimes using laser-guided or electro-optical bombs, covered not only by fighters flying CAP missions, but also chaff (large concentrations of strips of zinc or aluminum capable of confusing enemy radar by providing erroneous radar signals which can mask the attacking aircraft) and electronic countermeasure (ECM) aircraft, and protected by Iron Hand and Wild Weasel SAM suppression. USN graduates of the new Top Gun school demonstrated the school's utility by drastically increasing the navy's air-to-air kill ratios. B-52s struck targets outside of Haiphong, including fuel storage facilities whose burning remnants could be viewed for miles in all directions.

Another change to tactics that greatly hindered the invading forces, or at least placed their ability to continue operations on a more-tenuous footing, was the mining of the harbors. That North Vietnam "did not believe the U.S. would resume bombing over North Vietnam, much less mine the harbors" brought realization to the government of North Vietnam that US willingness to apply pressure had changed.[8]

Historian Rebecca Grant went so far as to say of the first Linebacker Operation, "Linebacker's airpower halted the invasion" and "planted the seeds of success in future campaigns." This was undoubtedly true, but while

Linebacker I clearly stopped the North's invasion of the South, it did not bring the final resolution of the war at the peace table. One final operation cemented the end of the Vietnam War, but its utility and efficacy continues to be debated decades later.[9]

After Linebacker I ended, but before the official start of Linebacker II, a B-52 on a bombing mission over Vinh was struck by an SA-2 Guideline. The missile tore off part of the wing and knocked out all of the engines on one side of the aircraft. Miraculously, the pilot was able to turn toward the relative safety of Laos and cross into Thailand before calling on the crew to eject. All crew members bailed out safely and were rescued shortly thereafter. This was the first combat loss of a B-52. The official history of the People's Army of Vietnam noted that this attack "confirmed that our missile troops were capable of shooting down this American 'Super Flying Fortress.' " The missile battalions were soon to get a chance to prove they could do it again.[10]

Linebacker II

Linebacker II began on December 18, 1972, and set in motion an air operation designed to inflict the "maximum destruction of selected military targets in the vicinity of Hanoi/Haiphong." The execution order from the JCS to CINCPAC called for "a three-day maximum effort, repeat maximum effort, of B-52/TACAIR strikes." It lasted a scant eleven days, ending when President Nixon called a halt to operations on December 29. Linebacker II almost immediately developed into the poster child for the US Air Force on what air power was capable of accomplishing if given the leeway to conduct operations against the "right" kinds of targets. The truth of the efficacy of Linebacker II is somewhat more muddied.[11]

Linebacker II is best remembered for the use of the B-52s against targets in Hanoi and Haiphong. Interestingly enough, the lessons and practices from World War II were clearly visible in the first nights of the operation as B-52s, flying in cells of three aircraft each, conducted high-altitude precision (radar) bombing. This was in keeping with SAC doctrines and practices. As one historian noted, "Until Linebacker, SAC crews were not worried about being killed; they were worried about criticism from commanders and their staffs." The B-52 missions over Hanoi fundamentally altered this perception.[12]

Air force and navy planners now intended to use Linebacker II so as not to give the forces of North Vietnam a break. It was designed to provide relentless, around-the-clock, aerial bombardment. Fighters and attack aircraft from the air force and navy struck targets during the day and the strategic bombers attacked their targets at night. The first night of bombardment found sixteen separate cells of B-52s—forty-eight aircraft—from Guam and U-Tapao attacking the targets of Hoa Lac, Kep, and Phuc Yen airfields, the Kinh No complex, and the Yen Vien rail yard. In front of the B-52s, thirty-nine other aircraft supported their mission, including EB-66 electronic jammers, F-105s performing Iron Hand, and F-4s dropping chaff. However, while many American pilots in fighters and attack aircraft had flown in North Vietnam before and were familiar with the extensive IADS, B-52 pilots were flying into uncharted territory. Although the same pilots had flown Arc Light missions for years, the defenses over North Vietnam posed significantly more risk to the lumbering bombers.

The very manner in which SAC planned to use the strategic bombers invited catastrophe: Bombers flew along a predetermined route, at the exact same airspeed and altitude, each wave precisely timed and separated by four hours—giving the North Vietnamese forces more than ample time to prepare—and each cell making the exact combat break right-hand turn after bomb release with strict guidance to take no evasive action. No amount of MiGs or SAMs could cause the bombers to break formation, nor would an aircraft functioning at less than optimal conditions be allowed to abort or turn back; they functioned under SAC's "press on rules."

Robert Harder, a B-52 navigator-bomber, remembered the initial briefing for the first night's mission "was increasingly looking like a slow-motion train wreck." At 8th Air Force headquarters on Guam, the staff members "quickly saw the SAC plan contained the seeds of disaster." At bases in Thailand where the fighters and support crews were stationed, "all the fighter crews were sobered when they saw the B-52s' routes. It was immediately obvious to these veterans of many missions to Hanoi that having every B-52 coming in on the same heading, and then all turning to leave in the same direction, was a bad idea."[13]

According to Harder, leaders at SAC believed that "only they were capable of planning the Linebacker Two mission, never mind that Eighth Air Force on Guam had been successfully selecting and bombing tactical objectives virtually unhindered for seven and one-half years." Furthermore, the senior leaders and planners in SAC "managed to bungle the job so thoroughly it leaves one breathless to this day." Because those back at SAC in Omaha, Nebraska, were "insulated from the realities of the hot conventional war their primary weapons platform was fighting a half world away, SACHDQS not only dropped the ball, they kicked it out of bounds."[14]

The bombers from Guam and U-Tapao attacked that first night in a predictable pattern. Rendezvousing over Laos, the B-52s flew east, south of the buffer zone along China, and then turned south on their bomb runs coming at Hanoi from the north. The bombers, flying in cells of three, provided mutually beneficial support to each other and created their own electronic interference against SAMs. "Success depends on the B-52s staying in formation. Three aircraft the size of a [B-52] BUFF can put out a lot of jamming power. However, if one aircraft gets out of formation, one-third of the cell's mutual protection is lost, making it easier for the enemy to find both that aircraft and the others on his radar." When traveling together in a tight, mutually supported formation, the B-52's ECM proved effective against both the Bar Lock radar and the SA-2's Fan Song radars.[15]

In the early-morning hours of December 18, as the B-52s approached their targets, the North Vietnamese started firing their SAM missiles. In the Gulf of Tonkin, navy radar ships provided continual updates to the approaching bomber cells and support aircraft: "SAM Launch . . . SAM Launch vicinity of Hanoi." As the pilots approached their bomb release points, the pilots, co-pilots, and gunner—sitting more than 150 feet behind the crew in the front of the aircraft and facing to the rear—called out each time they sighted a SAM. "Two SAMs, nine o'clock visual low."[16]

One pilot in the first wave indicated there were as many as two hundred missiles fired against the first wave, although this was a widely exaggerated number. B-52 aircraft commander Lieutenant Colonel Hendsley Conner stated that as he started his attack run there were so many missiles in the air, "it reminded me of a Fourth of July fireworks display." Three B-52s were downed on the first night of the operation, and two other heavily damaged by SAMs; that same night the USAF lost an F-111A. Planners and SAC leaders were shocked, but lulled into a false sense of security the following night. The second night proved "uneventful" inasmuch as no B-52s were shot down, but this proved to be an anomaly. The SAMs returned with a vengeance on December 20, what historian Marshall Michel called the "Slaughter of the Gs."[17]

On the night of December 20, according to one USAF history, "all hell broke loose," and "the optimism that had accompanied Day Two's results was shattered." The first cells on that night did not suffer high losses; rather, the NVN missile battalions waited and used the first cell to "mark" the bomb release points and turning points. Subsequent cells faced much heavier missile fire. The USAF lost six B-52s, all to surface-to-air missiles. Of those six aircraft, five were B-52G models. The fact that more G models were shot down was not accidental. Those B-52s operated with less-sophisticated and older ECM packages and were significantly easier for the missile battalions to pick up and track. A later history co-authored by the wing commander at Guam during the operation said, "[I]t was now apparent that the unmodified Gs were neither protecting themselves nor their formation adequately, and were bearing the brunt of the losses inflicted by Hanoi's SAM sites." SAC commander General J. C. Meyer ordered six B-52s in the second wave to be recalled, but SAC staff members convinced him to allow the unmodified Gs on the third wave to "press on." Two of these were lost.[18]

On the fourth night, two more B-52s were lost over Hanoi from a smaller striking force. Targets changed the night of December 22 when a single wave of B-52s from U-Tapao bombed Haiphong. North Vietnamese forces viewed the change in target as a victory—and as the Americans being unwilling to suffer further losses. The final losses to B-52s occurred on the nights of December 26 and 27, even though by this point the attacks on Hanoi had undergone significant tactical changes. Four other B-52s suffered extreme damage during the operation. Today, remnants of the downed aircraft can be viewed at the B-52 Victory Museum in Hanoi.

The "official" count of B-52s lost during Linebacker II stands at fifteen. In addition, there was the first B-52 loss on November 22, bringing the total to sixteen B-52s shot down. This number is probably low. A number of the B-52s that landed at U-Tapao RTAFB were so damaged they never flew again. Captain Dana Drenkowski, author of the above study, counted nine B-52s parked on what was known as "wreck row" at U-Tapao in January of 1973. The USAF does not count these aircraft as a combat loss. One study notes that the USAF lost anywhere between twenty-two and twenty-seven B-52s as part of the Linebacker II Operation. Marshall Michel also put the number of damaged B-52s at nine, but only three as completely un-flyable. The official count by the USAF of B-52s lost during Linebacker II is undoubtedly not correct.[19]

Several reasons exist for the success in the use of SA-2s against the B-52s. The first was the sheer number of missiles fired, sometimes ballistically (i.e., fired without any radar guidance). A second reason was the predictable pattern in which the B-52s entered their target areas, particularly on the first three nights of the operation. SAC procedures had the B-52s approach their targets along the same azimuth and in sequential trails, each formation following the same bombing run as the flight before it. The ECM package carried on the unmodified G models also led to higher losses. Missions flown later in December eschewed all the cells flying in from the north and instead approached their targets from around the compass. However, the initial missions faced the problem of the B-52s approaching from the same direction and continuing along the egress route after the bombers had dropped their munitions. Again, following SAC procedure, each B-52 in the cell executed a 45-degree combat break-turn away from the target to begin its exit from the target area. This turn created two problems.

First, as each B-52 turned and encountered headwinds, it inevitably slowed directly over the target area and Hanoi's significant defenses. One flier called this "throwing out an anchor when instead we should be getting the hell out of Dodge." This tactic was used for nuclear delivery in order to get the bombers away from the inevitable detonation. Physics dictated that a B-52 releasing a gravity nuclear weapon would be closer to the bomb when it exploded if it continued traveling in the same direction as the free-falling bomb than if it conducted a break-turn after weapons release.[20]

Second, as each B-52 turned, its ECM systems turned as well. Historian Marshall Michel, himself a fighter pilot who flew missions during Vietnam, noted that

> the B-52's electronic countermeasure (ECM) systems were designed to face earthward to jam the guidance radars of the North Vietnamese SA-2 SAM (surface-to-air) missiles. As the B-52s commenced their 45-degree turns, their onboard ECM systems tilted skyward and away from any threatening SAMs at the exact time the radar cross section of the aircraft was to be maximized, all this over the heart of the North Vietnamese defenses.[21]

The B-52s in their post-bombing turn presented excellent radar returns to their North Vietnam adversaries. Those flying in the B-52s knew this. After the first night's mission briefing, one flight crew member quipped, "Do these people know a steep, slow turn over a million SAM launchers will cause all my electronic countermeasures to get pointed out into space?" Dana Drenkowski, himself a B-52 pilot from Vietnam, noted,

> [T]he post-release target turns over Hanoi during Linebacker II raids were simply left-over procedures that no one dared to change, regardless of the fact that the maneuver turned the belly-based, downward-pointing electronic countermeasures antennae away from the immediate target area, where the enemy defenses were thickest.[22]

There is no doubt or argument that Linebacker II proved costly not only for the USAF and Strategic Air Command, but also for the tactical fighter force as well. During Linebacker II the air force found that "146 aircraft were designated combat losses. Aircraft with the most losses were: 64 F-4s, 17 B-52s, and 24 FACs (O-2, OV-10). Recorded instances of battle damage not causing aircraft losses totaled 446 instances." Despite the heavy losses, the air forces of America could look to some positives from the operation. Operation Linebacker II proved successful where Rolling Thunder failed, but not for the reasons so often cited. Although Nixon used air power in a more-decisive manner, it was not air power per se that forced the end of the conflict.[23]

Two questions remain and continue to be debated by military and air power historians in the second decade of the twenty-first century. The first: Did it work? Did Linebacker II hasten the end of the war? The second: If the precepts of a Linebacker II–style operation had been applied earlier in the war, as noted by General LeMay, would the North Vietnamese have been forced to negotiate a peace at an earlier date?

The answer to the first question is, it depends largely on how you look at it. Retired air force general Curtis LeMay later argued that the USAF "could have ended it [the war in Vietnam] in any ten-day period you wanted to, but they would never bomb the target list we had." This is a problematic statement. Even if the United States had implemented a Linebacker II–style operation sometime between 1965 and 1969, it is doubtful the country of North Vietnam would have rushed to the negotiating table. The context of where the two belligerents stood in 1967 compared to 1972 could not have been further apart. In the 1960s, with strong backing from the People's Republic of China and the Union of Soviet Socialist Republics, North Vietnam had no real fear of strong US attacks along the order of Linebacker; furthermore, the United States was certainly in no position, and had no desire, to expand the war outside of Southeast Asia. By 1972, the calculus on both sides had changed. The United States was eager to finalize their exit from the region, and with diplomatic relations thawing among the USSR, China, and the United States, North Vietnam did not enjoy the same bargaining position they had had earlier in the war. So yes, Linebacker II hastened the end of the war, but only because numerous other contextual issues aligned to allow it to do so.[24]

The answer to the second question seems a bit easier to tackle at this juncture: No. There is no truth to the counterfactual notion that had air power been applied in the same manner earlier, the North Vietnamese would have been forced to seek an end to hostilities. First, as Mark Clodfelter noted, Linebacker II was a limited operation with limited objectives—simply to force North Vietnam into a position where the United States could exit the war with honor intact.

Second, at any point earlier in the conflict, it was not in North Vietnam's interest to end the war. However, by the time of Linebacker II, the North Vietnamese were prepared to meet the demands outlined in Paris to get the United States out of the war.

Third, the very concepts and doctrines of strategic bombardment were meant to apply against a highly industrialized society, which North Vietnam was not. Perhaps strategic bombardment applied against China or the Soviet Union would have wrecked North Vietnam's receipt of materiel and aircraft, but this was never within the realm of the possible. As such, North Vietnam was always receiving the necessary supplies from its industrialized partners.[25]

One recent article noted that despite the fact that Linebacker II nearly ended in disaster for the USAF, after the war ended, SAC "launched a massive media and public relations blitz (and internal witch hunt) to prove that

Linebacker II was an unqualified success that unfolded as planned." One way SAC did this was to use total sorties—over 700—as the basis for their 2 percent loss rate. However, the total number of B-52s available at Guam and U-Tapao was between 150 and 200. Even the most conservative estimate of 200 aircraft divided by 15 lost means that SAC lost 13 percent of the aircraft available. If the number of B-52s that landed but never flew again are included, the percentage of aircraft loss is even higher.[26]

The institutional memory of Linebacker II was that it "forced the North Vietnamese to negotiate." This view is so pervasive that it shows up in many sources, from Wikipedia to several popular histories. It has been written so often that it has become one of the fundamental "truths" of Vietnam: "[I]t would take one more massive air operation, Operation Linebacker II in December 1972, to finally convince the Vietnamese to come to an agreement acceptable to the United States."

An air force publication on strategic bombing noted, "The last B-52 strikes came in the night on December 29. . . . The North Vietnamese then agreed to resume negotiations." One historian noted that among USAF members, "it arises as a declarative statement, 'If the U.S. had used B-52s on Hanoi sooner, the U.S. could have won the war.' " This is the USAF's Lost Cause narrative. Many of the first-person accounts of those who flew during Vietnam seem to fall in line with this thought process. It provides a bookend to the war. If the Gulf of Tonkin incident started the war, then Linebacker II ended it— although as mentioned above, the realities of the operation are significantly more complicated.[27]

The fact remains that if Linebacker II did not occur in December of 1972, the Paris Peace Accords would have been signed in early 1973 anyway. It is also important to note that the country of Vietnam remembers Linebacker II as a victory for the North, where the name of the battle remains *Dien Bien Phu Tren Khong*, "Dien Bien Phu of the skies." According to Marshall Michel, in North Vietnam, the bombing "served to unify a population that was beginning to chafe under years of unending war."

An article written in Vietnam's *National Defense Journal* (*Tạp chí Quốc phòng toàn dân*) on the forty-fifth anniversary of the attacks emphatically stated, "The successful December 1972 air defense campaign shattered the US Air Force's B-52s, forcing the US empire to sign the Paris Agreement and to withdraw its troops." The official history of the People's Army summed up the battle this way: "The enemy's massive strategic offensive using B-52s against Hanoi and Haiphong had been crushed. Nixon's dream of negotiating from a position of strength had ended in total failure." This grandiose version of North Vietnam's success is surely slanted, but demonstrated that the USAF view of total victory is slanted as well. To paraphrase the space opera *Star Wars*, which side "won" the battle depends greatly upon your point of view.[28]

Henry Kissinger, negotiating on behalf of the United States, stopped short of saying Linebacker II hastened the signing of the Paris Peace Accords. Instead, Kissinger hinted, "There was a deadlock . . . in the middle of December. . . . There was a rapid movement where negotiations resumed . . . on January 8. These facts have to be analyzed by each person for himself."[29]

None of this should diminish in any way the heroic memory of the B-52 pilots who flew over Hanoi and Haiphong in December of 1972. A US Marine Corps history notes: "The courage and skills of the B-52 crews over Hanoi in those night raids of December 1972, against flak, SAMs, and MiGs, deserve telling in any account of Vietnam combat."

As a final thought on the Linebacker II operation, the USAF notes that one of the sticking points only settled after the bombing was the release of the POWs. One official history notes, "If Linebacker II was in any way responsible for validating national intent and for bringing our POWs back home, then we believe it was worth it."[30]

Conclusion

One of the most pressing problems facing SAC and one it steadfastly refused to address in the aftermath of the war—even as TAC was going through its own revolution—was its own rigidity when it came to changes in tactics. As historian Mark Clodfelter stated, "SAC did not alter its nuclear approach to conventional war." The same was true after the conflict in Korea two decades earlier and remained true after Vietnam. SAC simply refused to let go of its preferred method of war.[31]

Strategic bombing operations did little more than allow concepts of strategic bombardment to dig themselves deeper into institutional identity, especially back at SAC headquarters in Omaha. Despite the loss of sixteen B-52 bombers in eleven days, many in the air force pointed to these final operations as the reason the North Vietnamese agreed to terms at the Paris Peace Accords. In this view, strategic bombardment worked, but this, again, removes the more nuanced and contextual elements from when the operation occurred.

From Rolling Thunder and Arc Light (CAS and interdiction) to Linebacker I and II, the USAF drew a clear line from strategic bombing practices of World War II through Korea to Vietnam. From this view of history, strategic bombardment continued to work, and thus there was no need for SAC to reevaluate its doctrine or practices. Strategic air power in Vietnam, at least to those in SAC, proved conclusive. In other areas of the USAF matters were not so certain, and other lessons were being learned. Inside of the other senior USAF organizations, most notably Tactical Air Command—where the generation of pilots who left Vietnam came to the realization that tactical fighters were just as capable as strategic bombers of delivering higher-order effects—there was a massive focus on change. Change in tactics, change in training, and change aimed at ensuring the hard lessons of Vietnam did not repeat themselves.

Linebacker II is often the final signpost. On the highway of the conflict a road sign read: Exit here to leave Vietnam. The operation allowed Americans to leave with dignity, predated the ceasefire, and in the end helped to aid in the return of American POWs throughout the first months of 1973. However, North Vietnam violated every portion of the agreement and overran South Vietnam in 1975. It was America's swan song in Vietnam, but even though the American public believed this was the end of American involvement in Southeast Asia, air power had more roles to play. After Linebacker II and the Paris Peace Accords most Americans saw the end of the war, but the final defeat and fall of South Vietnam would not occur until 1975, and even after the signing of the Accords in January of 1973, the air war did not end. In the neighboring countries of Laos and Cambodia, operations continued unabated.

7

Laos, Cambodia, and the War against the Ho Chi Minh Trail

THE ONLY WAY TO WIN THE WAR in South Vietnam was to win the secret war that occurred inside Laos and Cambodia, the home to the Ho Chi Minh Trail. No treatment of this conflict could be complete without looking at the air wars that occurred inside the countries of Laos and Cambodia— what one pilot called "home of the shadow war—the war that doesn't exist but that kills you just as dead."[1]

From a certain point of view, these two separate but interconnected air wars came to represent Americans' conception of the way the American military conducted aerial attacks against other countries. American notions of "carpet bombing" so rarely used occurred here as strategic B-52s dropped full payloads against amorphous targets. In these two nation-states, victims of geographical closeness, the combined air forces of the United States conducted the Barrel Roll, Menu, Steel Tiger, and Commando Hunt operations (among many others). These operations consisted of search-and-rescue missions, close air support to ground troops, and reconnaissance, but were mainly an interdiction attack against the Ho Chi Minh Trail (Truong Son Strategic Supply Route) that ran north to south. Originating in North Vietnam, it flowed in a southerly direction through Laos and on into Cambodia. Most importantly, all of these aerial missions were covert and conducted without the knowledge of the American public. In Laos, the United States not only interdicted the Ho Chi Minh Trail, but also engaged in active operations against the communist organization Pathet Lao in the region known as the Plaine des Jarres, or PDJ to the pilots flying overhead.

Both of these Southeast Asian nations suffered a tremendous amount of depredation at the hands of the American "air pirates," but none more so than Laos. Between 1964 and through 1973, a year after the war "ended" with the Paris Peace Accords, US forces continued an unpublished air war against Laos. Exact tonnage and total bombs dropped is difficult to compute, and totals vary widely, but based on averages, the United States Army Air Forces (USAAF) dropped over 1.5 million tons on the continent of Europe during World War II, 600,000 tons on North Korea during that conflict, another 1 million tons in North Vietnam, and 4 million tons in the South. Laos, the entrance point to the Ho Chi Minh Trail, was on the receiving end of anywhere between 2 and 3 million tons of ordnance. An article in the *New York Times* quoted this figure as "nearly a ton for every person in Laos."[2] Throughout the war, a higher percentage of missions flew over Laos than North Vietnam; when the United States stopped bombing in North Vietnam in 1968, the focus shifted to bombing Laos.

Sitting farther south, but with strategic exit points north of Saigon and the Mekong Delta region, sat Cambodia. Air force historian Earl H. Tilford Jr. noted in his history *Setup: What the Air Force Did in Vietnam and Why* that the bombing of Cambodia was connected to the Vietnam War in three important ways:

> First, the areas bombed were an integral part of the Vietcong and PAVN logistical network supporting operations in the region around Saigon. Second, North Vietnam had not shown restraint in moving men and supplies southward through its panhandle and then into Laos and down the Ho Chi Minh Trail. Third, the bombing was tied to the overall US strategy of disengagement.[3]

Tilford also noted that for much of the early and middle portions of the war, from 1964 through 1970, Cambodian prince Norodom Sihanouk had successfully kept the country from becoming a full partner in the conflict. Sihanouk was caught between a rock and a hard place. He was incapable of keeping North Vietnam from using the borderlands as a supply route, but also had to, in some small measure, allow the United States to bomb these same regions. Furthermore, at least a portion of North Vietnam's supplies did not come down the Ho Chi Minh Trail, but rather came in through the Cambodian port of Sihanoukville and traveled up the American-built "Friendship Highway."[4]

In 1968, as the bombing pause was going into effect, the Johnson administration still wanted to continue to interdict supplies coming down the Trail. This meant the bombing attacks inside Laos and Cambodia's ill-defined border with South Vietnam drastically increased. Even though the American people were led to believe the pause was in effect, missions over the Ho Chi Minh Trail never stopped. Furthermore, March of 1970 saw the overthrow of Cambodia's Prince Norodom Sihanouk. The country descended into civil war. In April, American forces entered Cambodia as part of what Nixon called an "incursion," to attack communist forces that had been using the country as a stronghold and logistics hub. Prior to the incursion, American B-52s attacked the countryside. Nixon needed to destroy communist forces to allow time for American forces to continue to draw down, but he was constrained from opening up heavier attacks against North Vietnam while also negotiating with them. Thus, his attention turned toward the bombing missions in Laos and Cambodia.

The Truong Son Strategic Supply Route

After the war many inside the US Air Force indicated that their hands had been tied by politicians, most notably Johnson and McNamara. It was often said that political leaders had placed unreasonable constraints on air power, hindering it from attacking the needed target sets. Interestingly, no such restrictions existed in South Vietnam, Laos, or Cambodia along the Ho Chi Minh Trail, where air power was allowed to conduct bombing missions with near impunity. Attacking the Trail still did not stem the flow of supplies southward. While targets remained off limits in North Vietnam, any supplies headed south on the Trail were completely within the given rules of engagement.

Surely, the free hand given to attacking targets coming south on North Vietnam's resupply route in both Laos and Cambodia should have been enough to tie a tourniquet around the North's supply chain, halting the flow, but this never happened. If Hanoi and Haiphong were the beating heart of North Vietnam's supply effort, then the Ho Chi Minh Trail was the aorta; close off the Trail, and you've closed off North Vietnam's supply of blood. The heart might still pump, but the blood supply would never reach the vital organs. This never happened. The Ho Chi Minh Trail proved to be an aorta that could not be severed; too many other veins and capillaries continued to pump supplies south. No amount of bombing along the Trail could significantly hinder the supplies flowing south. If the amassed might of the American air arms could not—in any meaningful way—interdict or cut the logistics lines running into South Vietnam, how could any argument be made that more bombing by American forces would have been capable of securing victory or independence for the South?

The air wars in the countries of Laos and Cambodia represent the best examples of high versus low technological conflict. In Laos, there were no SAMs and there were no MiGs. AAA remained a potent threat on the Trail, especially around the strategic crossroads city of Tchepone. The US Air Force used Century Series fighters—designed to either intercept Soviet bombers or deliver nuclear weapons—as a means of reconnaissance and interdiction against a jungle-trail system. It was the US fighter and bomber aircraft going against the environment of the Ho Chi Minh Trail.

Chapter 2 discussed early Misty operations along route package 1 and the entrances of the Ho Chi Minh Trail in North Vietnam at Mu Gia and Ban Kari Passes, but to truly attack the trail, the Mistys had to get into Laos, the heavily forested, jungle, and mountainous regions where supplies traveled north to south. The terrain proved as much of an obstacle to operations as the enemy did—perhaps more so. No technology was able to penetrate the jungle cover, although the USAF attempted to do so, and while bombing opened up roads, the travelers simply bypassed the destruction. In Laos the only way to find targets was to get low.

Merrill McPeak, Misty-94 and a future chief of staff of the USAF, remembered flying along the Trail in the following terms: "It was hard to get a SAM down the HCM Trail, and the AAA threat was also very different." McPeak noted that in North Vietnam, American aircrews typically faced a broad mix of 37- and 57mm AAA and the occasional 85mm. Laos was different. "I never saw 57. I saw 37, which people called 57, but the smaller 23mm was the best gun they had."[5]

A myth also existed that RP-1 in North Vietnam was more dangerous for the Misty pilots, but Laos proved to be just as deadly, even without the surface-to-air missiles. This was due to the fact that Mistys were required to fly at a very low altitude over the Trail, which brought them into the deadly grasp of the AAA. Of the thirty-five Misty aircraft shot down, almost half of these (seventeen) occurred in Laos; of the seven Misty pilots killed in action, four were killed in Laos.[6]

Flying in Laos was tough work for both the pilot and the guy in back. Since the small arms threat was so significant, Misty F-100s kept their airspeed above 500 knots and continuously jinked the aircraft. It was exhausting work. The pilots had to fly low to observe the Trail, so speed was life. Merrill McPeak recalled, "I *never* got below 500 knots. If I hit 500 knots, I went into Afterburner."

Although the Misty pilots proved effective at finding targets and calling in strikes as part of the interdiction campaign, the USAF also sought to leverage emerging technologies against the enemy that flowed down the Trail.[7]

Igloo White

From January 1968 until February 1973, the USAF attempted to use a covert electronic warfare operation codenamed Igloo White in order to locate men and equipment along the Ho Chi Minh Trail. One report later named it "[e]xceedingly costly and complex." For a service which prided itself on the technologically advanced, this was something of an admission that perhaps technological advances could only provide so much. The concept was simple enough: "develop a system to interdict North Vietnamese infiltration into South Vietnam." This operation sought a technological solution to detect the trucks, men, and bicycles that flowed down the supply route. It utilized a highly sophisticated network of air-dropped electronic sensors, computers, and communications-relay aircraft in an attempt to automate intelligence collection.

There were three interconnected pieces to Igloo White: "the Infiltration Surveillance Center (ISC) at Nakhon Phanom RTAFB, Thailand, the remote sensor field, and the airborne relay stations." Theoretically the data gathered by the electronic system during the operation could be converted into operational intelligence and passed over to the strike units to disrupt the flow of supplies. It was a high-tech solution to a low-tech problem, and this represented another example of the US Air Force attempting to use technology to defeat an adaptable enemy capable of circumventing the air force's systems.[8]

Under Igloo White, the USAF dropped an electronic picket line across the Ho Chi Minh Trail. The line used a series of air-dropped seismic and acoustic sensors to detect NVA forces moving along the Trail. Data was picked up by nearby aircraft (EC-121), transmitted to Nakhon Phanom, and turned into actionable intelligence to provide targets along the Trail. The air force believed the program could provide a "real-time intelligence source which would result in rapid target acquisition and attack by airstrike forces." Since the USAF obviously did not want NVA or VC personnel to disable the sensors, a number of them were booby-trapped. One air force historian noted, "To discourage the North Vietnamese from removing electronic sensors or disassembling them for study and the possible development of countermeasures, ordnance technicians loaded some with explosive charges."[9]

Igloo White was beset with problems from the beginning. Besides being an enormously complicated system—even if everything worked as advertised— the technology itself often failed. The air-dropped sensors provided problems. Any "inaccurately emplaced, malfunctioning, or completely dead sensor within a string, often seriously inhibited the effectiveness of the entire string as a detection and prediction device." Devices timed out, batteries failed, and some died on impact. Between December 1967 and March 1968, the USAF dropped 855 sensors, both seismic and acoustic varieties. At the end of March, only 639 were actively transmitting data. The CHECO report covering this operation called the failing sensors a "continual reseeding program." This meant that the sensor buoys needed to be continually replaced, and although the air force had planned for this, it meant there were always gaps and seams along the detection system, sitting along a trail that was itself already amorphous.[10]

Other problems included target assessment officers back at Nakhon Phanom who "had great difficulty in distinguishing targets by identifying characteristic movement patterns, as they developed within the maze of apparently random activations." This stemmed from the fact that the Ho Chi Minh Trail was not a superhighway or even a singular road, but an ever-evolving system of trails which prevented easy analysis.[11]

Besides the Igloo White operation, there were easier ways to locate targets on the Trail, including the FACs, which forced the USAF to admit that the "air was often saturated with targets to strike, which had been acquired by already existent visual and mechanical means, *other* than the sensor fields." Strike aircraft operating in the Steel Tiger area of Laos "were fully occupied much of the time in conducting strikes on lucrative targets, whose nature and location were *already known*" (emphasis in the original). Even when Igloo White provided a target, a fighter aircraft in the region might not strike it in lieu of a different or more lucrative target. The 7th Air Force was unenthusiastic about assigning strike sorties to the sensor-generated targets; FACs pulled strike aircraft away even when they were assigned to strike an Igloo White target, or a pilot might visually locate a convoy on the Trail and strike that. A visually located target was better than a target that *might* be there.[12]

Later Igloo White operations aided in the prosecution of a bombing campaign in Laos under the name Commando Hunt. Once the bombing pause in North Vietnam had gone into effect, the air arms had no other choice but to increase the interdiction campaigns in Laos and Cambodia. The American military might not be striking targets in North Vietnam, but the bombing pause said nothing of Laos and Cambodia. Commando Hunt also sought to ensure that North Vietnam did not simply use Laos and Cambodia as areas to mass or hide their forces, although as evidenced by the Easter Offensive, American forces were not always successful in this regard.

The Igloo White operation certainly never produced the desired results—although it did help detect NVA forces moving toward Khe Sanh in 1968—and the fact that North Vietnam was able to use the Ho Chi Minh Trail with only prohibitive interference from the American air forces indicated that while there was certainly a technological goal of locating North Vietnam forces coming down the Trail, Igloo White failed to be an effective check against this. It should also be noted that not only did the Ho Chi Minh Trail increase its throughput over the course of the war, but North Vietnam was also able to prepare for two massive invasions of the South—the Tet Offensive in 1968 and the Easter Offensive in 1972—without the United States fully understanding that these buildups were occurring.[13]

In the end, Igloo White simply proved less attractive than other alternatives. A 7th Air Force report noted that

> the competitive priority of a contingency sensor system should be low compared to the priority of strike forces in a reduced budget environment. However, a minimal system could be maintained with little impact on strike force capability, considering the relative costs of a minimal sensor system versus the costs of strike aircraft, associated equipment and facilities.[14]

In other words, an *extensive* sensor system could not come at the expanse of further fighter aircraft, but a *minimal* system with a relatively lower budgetary impact would be supported.

In the end, even if the USAF had placed the Igloo White sensors with perfection, even if American forces had had a perfect understanding or diagram of the Ho Chi Minh Trail system, and even if the entire system had worked at a faultless level, the NVA still had a say in Igloo White's execution. According to a general officer in the North Vietnamese Army, the NVA could always "search out the individual sensors and destroy them, avoid them, or deceive them, perhaps by simply playing a recording of truck noises."[15]

Other than the secret air war which occurred in Laos, the United States had "boots on the ground" at numerous Lima sites, which provided forward basing and air traffic command and control, as well as serving as tactical air navigation system sites. In total, the USAF, along with the Central Intelligence Agency, operated numerous radar sites in Laos. It would be a considerable understatement to call it dangerous and life-threatening work. Here the enemy included North Vietnamese troops, but also the indigenous Pathet Lao.

The Lima Sites

To prosecute the secret air war in Laos, the USAF worked with the CIA and the Royal Lao Army by providing tactical air navigation system (TACAN) sites capable of providing range, bearing, and location to American aircraft operating the area. In total, more than twenty-five of these "Lima sites" existed in rural Laos. The Lima sites sat at strategically important locations, often on mountaintops. Each site contained a living trailer, a latrine, an operations building, and a communications center. Typically, a short walk down the summit or to an adjoining mountaintop led to a helicopter landing zone. Most sites provided TACAN, and that device was located nearby as well.

These sites often suffered back-and-forth engagements with the soldiers of North Vietnam and the Pathet Lao. One example was the continued handoff of Lima Site 36. The USAF used Lima Site 36 as a staging area that provided combat search-and-rescue for Jolly Green helicopters. In February 1966, North Vietnamese and Pathet Lao troops overran the site. It was retaken in May of 1966, but attacked again in January 1967. This back-and-forth continued until the site was abandoned in the spring of 1969. This is merely to demonstrate that holding these sites in a country the United States was not technically at war with was problematic and difficult.[16]

In January 1968, members of the tactical air navigation system (TACAN) radar team on top of the mountain at Phou Pha Thi, Laos, more commonly known as Lima Site 85, came under attack by a pair of North Vietnamese AN-2 Colts, marking one of the few times in the post–Korean War era that American troops on the ground came under aerial attack. The two AN-2 biplanes themselves came under attack from a CIA Air American Huey. In fact, this may be the last time American troops on the ground came under aerial attack, although the USAF uses Korea as the reference point for the last time this occurred; since neither North Vietnam nor the Americans were supposed to be operating out of Laos, this is technically correct. Although no Americans were injured in the attack and no damage was done to the TACAN site, it was a clear indication that North Vietnam personnel were actively observing the activities at the Lima sites.[17]

Lima Site 85 sat atop a mountain summit. The site also sat astride a steep cliff face that fell hundreds of feet to the jungle below. The cliff, and the isolation of the site, played an important role in the next attack. The main protection of the site came from the one thousand Hmong troops—ethnic Chinese people of the region recruited and trained by the CIA—but these troops were stationed farther down the hill, near the seven-hundred-foot landing strip/LZ. Since the cliff was considered protection enough from infiltration, the American troops at the site believed that the airstrip and the presence of the Hmong soldiers was defense enough against any type of concerted attack. A mixture of USAF and CIA personnel manned the site.

The next attack came not from the air, but from a concerted ground assault of the PAVN. Led by Lieutenant Colonel Troung Muc, a retired PAVN officer, a sapper battalion attacked and overran the site in the early-morning hours of March 11, 1968. The sapper unit scaled the cliff, disarmed a number of trip-wire mines, and then moved around the perimeter of the site, surrounding the camp and effectively pinning the Americans with their backs to the cliff. At 0230, Troung Muc's unit opened fire and took the camp by surprise. By 0500 the attack was over. The TACAN site was destroyed and twelve of the American personnel killed.[18]

The remaining six, including USAF chief master sergeant Richard Etchberger, now huddled just below the cliff face as the PAVN consolidated their gains and secured their own perimeter, now controlling the camp. Around dawn on March 11, Air America helicopters flew in to remove the remaining survivors. Etchberger aided in this operation by providing suppressive fire and ensuring that all other members of the Lima site were secured. As the final man to be rescued, Etchberger "had fought so tenaciously and had so heroically aided the rescue of his team, had survived untouched by enemy weapons' fire." Immediately after being pulled aboard the Huey, as the helicopter pulled away from the site, enemy fire strafed the bottom of the helicopter and Etchberger was critically wounded. Before he could be transferred to the medical facilities at Udorn, he died from his wounds. For his actions, he was awarded the Air Force Cross. In 2010, this was upgraded to the Medal of Honor.

As to Lima Site 85, USAF fighters attacked and destroyed the site over the course of the following week. This proved slightly ironic, since destruction of the site was Troung Muc's established goal in the first place. Both Igloo White and the use of the Lima sites demonstrate the heavy American presence operating inside Laos and the necessity of using advanced technologies in the attempt to stem the flow of supplies down the trail systems.

Nixon's War: Operations Menu, Patio, Good Luck, and Freedom Deal

On January 20, 1969, Richard M. Nixon was sworn in as president of the United States. He quickly set about implementing his own course for the Vietnam War. In December of 1968, Johnson announced the bombing halt against targets in North Vietnam. Johnson's attempt to bring the war to a close before he left office with the Paris Peace Accords were inexpiably torpedoed when South Vietnam walked away. Recent discoveries indicate it was Nixon's plan to throw a "monkey wrench" into the deal and thus ensure his victory over the Democratic nominee, Hubert Humphrey. Notes made by future Nixon chief of staff H. R. Haldeman show Nixon's direct involvement. Whether Nixon wanted to ensure his presidential victory or wanted to garner the exit of American forces for himself is irrelevant here. What mattered was that the air war against North Vietnam now belonged to Richard Nixon.[19]

From the beginning, the Joint Chiefs of Staff attempted to convince Nixon of the utility of bombing in Cambodia. Nixon hesitated, fearing an expansion of an already long war, a war he himself seems to have explicitly extended.

Nixon wanted to "quarantine" Cambodia, but the JCS and General Creighton Abrams convinced him of the utility of using aerial bombardment to attack the supply lines in Cambodia and also strike against the Central Office for South Vietnam (COSVN). On March 16, 1969, National Security Advisor Henry Kissinger sent Nixon a top-secret memorandum on a plan to bomb heavily inside the borders of Cambodia. Eventually known as the Menu Operations, this initial idea went by the name "Breakfast Plan."

In the memo, Kissinger stated, "Breakfast Plan will be treated as a routine military operation within the current framework of our military actions in Cambodian territory." It was anything but routine. Nixon and Kissinger envisioned Menu as a way to destroy the stockpiles of equipment North Vietnam kept inside the sanctuary of Cambodia. Few people knew about Nixon's intentions. One air force historian noted, "Strict secrecy concealed every aspect of the Menu bombing." Stanley Karnow, author of the acclaimed *Vietnam: A History*, noted that the secrecy extended to both the secretary of the air force and the air force chief of staff.[20]

There were also other purposes for the bombing inside Cambodia: to interdict North Vietnamese units interfering with the Vietnamization phase of the war, and, hopefully, to force North Vietnam to continue peace talks. Nixon approved the plan on March 17, and the bombings began the next evening in Cambodia. Nixon and Kissinger went to great lengths to conceal the bombings and limited the number of personnel who knew about the attacks, even going so far as to ensure that senior military officers were not aware of what was occurring. On the B-52s only the pilots and navigators knew that their bombers were conducting operations inside Cambodian territory.

The Menu Operations began in March of 1969 and continued for more than two years. The first strike, comprised of fifty-nine B-52s, used the Combat Skyspot radar installations to guide to the bomb release point. The Menu Operations eventually expanded to include six different locations, each named for a menu item—Breakfast, Lunch, Dinner, Supper, Snack, and Dessert—and each one a North Vietnamese marshaling or logistics storage area in Cambodia.

However, the American advantage in technology was checked by the Soviet Union, whose intelligence-gathering "fishing trawlers" provided advance warning to the North Vietnamese when B-52s departed Guam, or whose ground observers noted when B-52s departed U-Tapao in Thailand. Once North Vietnamese radars picked up the incoming aircraft, the Central Office for South Vietnam could move its forces or at least seek shelter in advance of the bombs raining down. Still, the attacks caused some measure of awe from the North Vietnamese troops. Troung Nha T'ang, a member of the COSVN, stated after a B-52 attack, "There was nothing left. It was as if an enormous scythe had swept through the jungle, felling the giant . . . trees like grass in its way, shredding them into scattered splinters."[21]

The Nixon administration, DOD, and USAF used subterfuge to keep the bombings secret. As previously mentioned, only the pilots and navigators knew their B-52s would be dropping bombs on Cambodia; the remainder of the crews had no indication. One DOD report from 1973 noted that the Menu strikes were carried out as follows:

> A B-52 strike on a target in South Vietnam would be requested through normal communication and command channels. Through the special security communication and command channel, a strike on the MENU [Cambodian] target nearest a requested target in South Vietnam would be requested. Upon approval, the mission would be flown in such a way that the MENU aircraft on its final run would pass over or near the target in South Vietnam and release its bombs on the enemy in the MENU sanctuary target area. On return of the aircraft to its base, routine reports on the mission would be filed in normal communication channels which did not reveal the MENU aspect of the mission. Separate reports were provided by "back" channel on the MENU aspect.[22]

Bernard Nalty noted that "strategic bombers designed for intercontinental nuclear retaliation served as aerial artillery." Another historian noted that the B-52s flying five miles above the ground "released a deluge of high explosives against the North Vietnamese hidden in the jungle below." B-52s flew 3,875 sorties and dropped 108,823 tons of bombs against targets in Cambodia as part of Menu; despite this, according to Troung Nha T'ang, the Menu bombings "had not killed even one member of the [C]entral [O]ffice."[23]

In addition to the bombing campaigns, Nixon also agreed to send American troops into Cambodia on May 1, 1970; Nixon announced the incursion the evening before in the United States. After the Cambodian National Assembly removed Prince Norodom Sihanouk in a coup and replaced him with Prime Minister Lon Nol, events spiraled out of control. Ironically, the coup took place on the same day that Nixon began the Breakfast portion of Operation Menu. In late March, North Vietnamese army units entered into Cambodia, and a month later South Vietnam and American units opened a limited campaign in Cambodia. Between April 29 and July 22, 1970, the war in Vietnam also had a ground component inside Cambodia. This American force could not only destroy any North Vietnamese units it came into contact with, but also serve as a blocking force for the North Vietnamese forces flowing south, attempting to hinder the Vietnamization process. Moving into Cambodia gave Nixon space and time to continue the American withdrawal.

The Americans called this Operation Shoemaker, for the assistant division commander of the 1st Cavalry Division. The ARVN forces called it Operation

Toan Thang (Total Victory). President Nixon announced on the night of April 30, 1970, that American troops were headed into Cambodia to find and destroy the COSVN, the North Vietnamese headquarters directing operations in South Vietnam. As happened so many other times in the history of the Vietnam conflict, this headquarters simply melted deeper into Cambodia to avoid contact with ARVN and American troops.

Air operations to support the American incursion increased during this time as well, and the Operation Menu strikes were augmented by Operation Patio. Patio, requested by MACV commander General Creighton Abrams, requested additional tactical assets in addition to the B-52s already dropping weapons in Cambodia. Thus, Patio was a subset of Menu and used tactical fighter-bombers. Whereas the B-52 strikes of Menu were preplanned against known NVA locations, the Patio strikes went against pop-up targets "of a more transitory nature." These targets had to be within a zone that extended from the border of South Vietnam to no more than eighteen miles inside of Cambodia. During the duration of Patio only 156 sorties were flown against targets including "a 125-man enemy column" and a "lucrative enemy truck park and storage area."[24]

While Operation Patio might seem an insignificant footnote, it really represented a period of transition. Initially, the Patio mission fell under the same strict control and secrecy measures that the Menu Operations used, but only eight days in, the DOD and Nixon administration decided to make the strikes into Cambodia part of "normal sustained operations." As to the results of these operations, one JCS report noted that "North Vietnamese forces operating with impunity in eastern Cambodia were forced to abandon their wholly open infiltration, resupply, and regrouping activities." This seems an odd statement given that at no time did North Vietnam enjoy a "wholly open" supply route, as well as the fact that the US air arms had been attacking the Ho Chi Minh Trail as far back as the mid-1960s. Once Patio became part of normal operations, the name changed and it became part of a "new" operation called "Freedom Deal."[25]

Freedom Deal, the continuation of bombing NVA targets in Cambodia, began on May 19, 1970, and lasted until the final bomb fell from an American plane in August of 1973. Initially, Freedom Deal was begun "to maintain surveillance of enemy activities in Cambodia, east of the Mekong River, and to attack these activities as necessary to protect US forces in the Republic of Vietnam." Freedom Deal served two purposes: to provide direct support to American troops on the ground supporting the Cambodian campaign; and as a larger interdiction effort against any NVA or VC forces in the area. As with the ground campaign itself, the results of the operation were mixed, with the USAF going so far as to say, "The overall results of USAF efforts in Cambodia during the period July through October can perhaps be best described as inconclusive."[26]

Further north in Laos, Nixon also allowed B-52 strikes in support of the Royal Laotian government as part of Operation Good Luck. This operation began after Laotian prime minister Souvanna Phouma requested air strikes to aid his ground troops engaged in combat against the regular forces of the NVA. In the region known as the Plaine des Jarres (PDJ), and beginning on February 17, 1970, B-52s bombed marshaling areas and North Vietnamese troop concentrations. Again, there were significant "restrictions on disclosure," and the Good Luck message traffic was all classified at the top-secret level. It proved to be a short-lived operation lasting only two months and ending on April 20, 1972, but it proved that SAC and 7th Air Force had become accustomed to using the B-52 as a tactical bomber. It still did not seem to matter. No amount of bombing inside Laos hindered what North Vietnam needed to get down the trail system. Even the JCS was forced to admit that "at no time was North Vietnamese control of eastern Laos seriously threatened."[27]

The story repeated itself in early 1971 when American and ARVN forces entered Laos again behind American air power as part of Lam Son 719. American forces played primarily a supporting role during this limited operation, with the American air arm providing B-52 and tactical air sorties as well as a significant number of rotary-wing assets to aid the ARVN forces in their attempt to interdict and destroy PAVN forces building along the Ho Chi Minh Trail. The campaign, despite American support, revealed the ARVN's shortcomings in the face of the PAVN, but Nixon did not allow the ARVN's failures to hinder American withdrawal from Vietnam.

American support during Lam Son 719 was used to slow the inevitable. As air force historian Bernard Nalty noted, "President Nixon looked on it as an opportunity to gain time for further Vietnamization and the withdrawal of additional US troops." As Vietnamization continued and American forces on the ground drew down, Nixon was left with air power as the military tool to finalize his position at the peace tables. Nixon also announced to the American people: "Tonight I can report that Vietnamization has succeeded," even though the ARVN forces in Laos had been forced into a retreat. Furthermore, it was blatantly obvious to all those involved that "the ARVN could not sustain itself on the battlefield without large amounts of American air power."[28]

Conclusion

The air war against Laos and Cambodia—or, more aptly, the air war against North Vietnam that occurred in neighboring Laos and Cambodia—never achieved the desired results. The interdiction campaign did not stem supplies flowing from north to south. The Ho Chi Minh Trail was never decisively severed, primarily because much of it was in fact a series of trails rather than an artery that could be cut. In 2016, an article appeared in the *Asia-Pacific Journal* titled "Making More Enemies than We Kill? Calculating US Bomb Tonnages Dropped on Laos and Cambodia, and Weighing Their Implications." According to this article, today Laos and Cambodia remain two of the most bombed countries on the planet. Their involvement in America's Vietnam War was a matter of geography.[29]

American air power over Laos and Cambodia experienced a catch-22. Bombing alone could not defeat either the PAVN or the Khmer Rouge forces, but the ability to place American combat troops on the ground was also off the table. The United States could have invaded Laos and Cambodia in a large ground offensive to cut the Trail once and for all, but a corresponding increase in large-scale combat operations would have meant a corresponding increase in American casualties, something that by 1969, the society of the United States of America was already vehemently against. This meant that despite over a decade of bombing the Ho Chi Minh Trail, supplies continued to flow south in ever greater numbers, and guerrilla forces in Cambodia increased as well. "During the four years of United States B-52 bombardment of Cambodia, from 1969 to 1973, the Khmer Rouge forces grew from possibly one thousand guerrillas to over 200,000 troops and militia." Air power continued to exacerbate the problems, creating more enemies in Laos and Cambodia rather than less.[30]

Even if the combined air might of the United States had been able to interdict 100 percent of supplies flowing into South Vietnam, this never would have been enough to stop the ongoing insurgency in South Vietnam. Thomas Thayer indicated that communist forces received as much as 70 percent of their necessary supplies from *within* South Vietnam. This never mattered anyway, because air power was incapable of stemming the flow of supplies down the Ho Chi Minh Trail. The manner in which America applied air power was essentially useless against the country of North Vietnam and in the fight inside Laos and Cambodia. It was an unwinnable interdiction campaign, or, as air force historian Bernard C. Nalty noted, "The price paid by the United States in attempting to interdict traffic on the Ho Chi Minh Trail took the form of diminishing support for the nation's objectives in Vietnam, as well as the continuing expenditure of aircraft, money, and lives." While the dropping of bombs in an interdiction campaign was part of the overall American strategy, it is often overshadowed by the "white scarves waving in the wind" history of the fighter pilot.[31]

8

The Air-to-Air War

IN SOUTH VIETNAM, AMERICAN PILOTS provided close air support. In Laos and Cambodia, interdiction. In North Vietnam, air-to-ground attacks struck everything from strategic targets to airfields, barracks, supply depots, and rail yards in an ever-shifting, on-again, off-again, on-again rolling campaign to change North Vietnam's perceptions of America's willingness to continue the war. B-52s provided CAS and interdiction. O-1s, O-2s, and OV-10s marked targets. American air power conducted operations for more than seven years, from the Gulf of Tonkin incident to the cessation of hostilities, but more ink has been spilled over the air-to-air engagements than any other aspect of air power used during the Vietnam War.

Many of these are memoirs, but a nearly equal number are academic studies—the author being a guilty party—on the effectiveness of air-to-air combat during the conflict. The air-to-air war was where technological and doctrinal problems were addressed most strenuously in the aftermath of the war, because those who participated clearly understood that North Vietnam's air force was, in certain instances and engagements, equal to their American counterparts. Many in the military establishment entered the Vietnam conflict believing the days of the dogfight were over. Technological advancements in beyond-visual-range (BVR) missiles indicated that classic "dogfights" were supposedly a thing of the past. Vietnam proved this to be false.

The air force, specifically its mid-grade officers, knew there was much to be learned from the dogfight engagements in Vietnam, and to this end produced an exhaustive study on each and every MiG sighting and engagement of the conflict. The USAF's Red Baron Reports took a holistic approach and cataloged every air-to-air engagement of the war (not just the air force's engagements), leading the USAF to create the Red Flag training exercise after the war to better train its junior aircrews for combat operations.

There is a generality that occurred in the skies over North Vietnam that bears mentioning here. While there were exceptions, it was generally accepted that USAF fighter pilots were more likely to engage MiG-21s, and the US Navy, more likely to engage MiG-17s. This was in no way preplanned or intentional by any of the participating parties, but according to USAF ace Steve Ritchie, it was purely "because the 17s work[ed] in the area where the Navy operate[d] most of the time." Again, this was a generality and not a hard-and-fast rule.[1]

What did an aerial engagement—a dogfight—look like in Vietnam? The USAF's Red Baron Reports, an exhaustive study of every one of these engagements, stated it this way:

> The complexity of real-world air-to-air combat is the result of the sequential decision processes of two or more pilots and the resulting series of maneuvers of the high-performance aircraft involved. Additional complexities result from the employment or attempted employment of the sophisticated avionics and weapon systems in the often rapidly changing offensive and defensive roles of the combatants.[2]

Put simply, air-to-air combat is difficult. So states an official USAF report that attempted to make sense of why American pilots did not enjoy the same margins of victory seen during World War II and the Korean conflict in the domain of the air.

Over the sky of Vietnam flew two mythical creatures: The first was the American fighter pilot, and he played a prominent role in both the air-to-air and air-to-ground war in Vietnam. Within this group of American airmen flew that rarest of aerial champions, the "ace." Vietnam saw the last of these crowned. The legendary status of these men continues to be taught and read about widely, although arguments over who could be considered an ace rose to the forefront of conversations with the advent of the radar operator/weapons officer in the rear of the F-4s. Working together, aircraft commander and GIB killed the enemy with radar-operated AIM-7 and heat-seeking AIM-9 missiles, with 20mm guns, and on several occasions, by maneuvering with the enemy until the latter ran into the ground. These aerial engagements developed in the summer of 1965 and lasted until January 1973, when an F-4D of the 4th Tactical Fighter Squadron shot down a final MiG-21. The USAF had 137 confirmed aerial victories in Vietnam. The US Navy had 63.

The second mythical creature was North Vietnam's MiG fighter pilots, flying for the Fatherland, Ho Chi Minh, and the VNAF. They are all but ignored in many Western histories, where their aircraft are viewed as targets rather than a melding of man and machine, the way American fliers and their aircraft are portrayed. The MiG pilots flew one of three types of aircraft: MiG-17, -19, or -21; flew with one of four air regiments; and flew from one of five air bases: Phuc Yen, Kep, Hanoi/Gia Lam, Haiphong/Kien-An, and Hoa Lac. On the ground at these airfields for much of the war, the MiGs "enjoyed a certain degree of immunity" due to political restrictions, and thus were able to choose the time and place of when to engage American aircraft—a valuable advantage. Using exit interviews and oral history reports collected by the services, this chapter explores air-to-air combat from both the American and, as much as possible, the Vietnamese perspectives.[3]

During the air-to-air war in Vietnam, jet dogfighting, as well as the employment of missile systems, was just coming into its own as a form of combat. While it is true that jet combat first took place during the Korean conflict, Vietnam became the proving ground for jet dogfights and missile employment. Technology, in the form of high-performance jets, missiles, radars, and fire-control systems, as well as the human element inside the cockpit—and in most cases this meant *two* individuals working together—had to perform seamlessly together in a manner never before seen in aerial combat. However, as they were the last of the American aerial knights to engage in protracted air-to-air war, profound questions about their performance still need to be answered. What was their impact on future tactics? Why did their weapons systems not work as advertised? Why did North Vietnam fighter pilots enjoy the success they did? Why did American-made missiles not kill the enemy with the precision and accuracy promised by the industry? Above all, why were American fighter pilots losing their deadly aerial jousts with the enemy in ways that many before the war, in all branches of the US Armed Forces, believed to be impossible?[4]

Prior to Vietnam, many in the USAF, including General Momyer, believed the age of the gun and the turning dogfight was over. Aerial kills would come from missile shots that occurred when the two aircraft were not even within sight of each other. This quickly proved to be erroneous. Since the advent of beyond-visual-range (BVR) missiles, only a small amount of aerial kills have actually occurred BVR. During Vietnam, a BVR kill, especially early in the war, was a rarity, since most MiG encounters began with the American pilots unaware the MiGs were even there.

Rules of engagement also dictated that American aircraft had to visually identify MiGs prior to employing weapons—weapons not designed to be employed in that arena—against the enemy. American fighter pilots flew into combat with missiles *capable* of killing beyond visual range, but hamstrung by a requirement to first *visually* identify the enemy. More than twenty-five years after Vietnam ended, a RAND report stated that of the 588 air-to-air kills with BVR-equipped forces, only 24 of those actually employed BVR. The US Air Force mainly employed the medium-range AIM-7 Sparrow missile. The AIM-7's probable kill rate (Pk)—the likelihood that a missile would hit its target—was billed as .70 (70 percent chance of hitting the intended target), but analysis conducted in the Red Baron and other reports showed the Pk rating to be no higher than .08, or about 8 percent. Enemy MiGs were one hundred times more likely to get close to dogfighting proximity (or "merge") with American aircraft than initially anticipated. The USAF, USN, and USMC also used the Aim-9 Sidewinder as a close-in missile, designed primarily for engaging a target from its six o'clock position. The North Vietnamese demonstrated proficiency at countering this threat, causing the probability of a kill with the Aim-9 to fall to slightly greater than one in ten by the end of the conflict.[5]

Dogfights in Vietnam had little to do with the perception of "knights of the air" engaging in duels. They were, in reality, complicated affairs combining geometry, physics, communication, and reflexes. The type of aerial combat over the skies of Vietnam was significantly different from predecessor conflicts, including World War II and Korea. It was faster, covered greater distances, and required not only luck and skill but teamwork to even get an aircraft into a firing position, much less gain a kill. Dogfights often occurred above Mach speeds. Unlike Korea, American fighter pilots used missiles.

Beyond these differences, the context, environment, and manner in which American pilots conducted their daily sorties also had an impact on the war. During Korea, American pilots sought out the enemy, flying north into a box known as MiG alley, and flying primarily offensive counter-air missions, whereas in Vietnam many pilots flew on the defensive, protecting a strike package. During Korea, both the Americans and the North Koreans used GCI for vectors; the American F-86s did not carry an air intercept radar. Dogfights, when they occurred, typically took place at high altitudes, between 30,000 and 40,000 feet. Furthermore, there was a limited surface-to-air fire and no SAM sites to contend with. All of these differences impacted the manner in which enemy aircraft were detected. The geography in Korea meant that, more often than not, American fighters flew toward their enemy with the MiGs being detected well in front of the pilot's 3-6 line (an invisible line extending from the wingtips of the aircraft covering the range in front of the aircraft). This was not the case in Vietnam, where visual detection occurred "around the clock," which ceded a certain advantage to the air force of North Vietnam.[6]

As noted in previous chapters, since the F-4 became the principal MiGCAP aircraft, most pilots in Vietnam had a second set of eyes to help them out, not only in visually detecting an enemy MiG, but in locating an enemy aircraft well beyond visual range, using the F-4's radar. The GIB's job was to run the aircraft's complex radar system. As historian Steve Fino noted, this was more difficult than simply looking at "blips" on a screen; there was also the operation of "PbS IR detectors, gigahertz radar frequencies, antenna train angles, [and] intercept geometrics." In the F-4 this was the APQ-100 or APA-128 radar and fire-control system.

The radar operator in the backseat of the aircraft had options when it came to how he chose to set the radar to search in the air-to-air role. "Gyro-Norm" was a straight radar sweep; "Gyro-Out" forced the radar to look forward along the wing-line of the aircraft, thus "pointing" the radar ahead in order to gain a better radar signature. In either Gyro-Out or Gyro-Norm, once a fighter had a target and was pointed at him, the GIB could—on his own volition or at the command of the aircraft commander—"go boresight" in order to snap the radar straight ahead like the beam of a flashlight pointed at an individual. This was all done in hopes of attaining a solid radar lock against an enemy MiG and to determine where he was in time and space. His range from the fighter, his speed, direction of travel (toward or away from the fighter), the azimuth, and his altitude (above or below the fighter), all contributed to placing the American fighter aircraft along a proper intercept trajectory, and ultimately, a favorable "weapons employment zone" (WEZ), the area where the missile was most likely to successfully hit the enemy. This all needed to be conveyed to the pilot, indicating that proper employment of the radar, the aircraft, and the weapons system required cohesive communication between the pilot and his GIB.[7]

The realms of speed, altitude, and physics all played into the pilot's job of placing his aircraft into the correct WEZ to take a missile shot. This was to say nothing of the necessary "switchology" that needed to be accomplished to ensure that a missile would actually fire when the trigger pull occurred. While the GIB was manipulating the radar, the aircraft commander needed to choose not only the correct weapon to fire, but also the particular weapon on the aircraft to fire. In an F-4, this meant the pilot had to remove his left hand from the throttle, reach forward just above his knee, and manually flip a switch either up, right, or down to switch between his missiles. This also meant the pilot's eyes needed to glance down in order to find the correct switch.

Many pilots took to taping the plastic length of an ink pen to the switch so they could flick the missile selector switch more easily. This particular switch, "Radar-Heat-Reject," toggled through his available suite of missiles: AIM-7 radar-guided or AIM-9 heat-seeking. Technology was both a help in destroying the enemy and also a hindrance when weapons did not work as advertised. It was not uncommon to fire two, three, or even four missiles at the enemy. Some fighter pilots even "volleyed" their missiles in sets of two to increase their probability of a kill. All during an intercept, as the GIB or RIO (radar intercept officer) sought radar lock, the overall element or flight commander needed to inform the other two or three aircraft in his formation what they were looking at. A call along the lines of "Olds 1, Bandit 2-ship, Bullseye 090-45, eighteen thousand" indicated that the aircraft commander (Olds 1) had a confirmed pair of MiGs (Bandit 2-ship), currently located at 90 degrees and 45 miles from a preestablished point, and flying at eighteen thousand feet. A flight lead could then assign follow-on actions to the rest of the aircraft in his element or flight.[8]

Into this technological morass entered one more problem: Most American fighter aircraft did not contain a gun, should missile shots fail and the fight devolve into a close-quarters melee. The missile vs. gun argument came down to disagreements over the role of technology in weaponry in modern jet aircraft, and two camps developed: those who accepted missiles as the way of the future, believing a gun was no longer necessary; and those who also accepted missiles as the way of the future, but still believed in the effectiveness of a gun for close-in combat and wanted one as a backup. Frederick "Boots" Blesse, a Korean War ace, noted that General William Momyer, himself an ace, was a member of the former group. "General Momyer, bless his heart, was one of the fuzzy thinkers in that area. . . . He was determined that the missile was the name of the game; guns just did not have any part in anything from then on."[9]

Although guns kills accounted for fewer overall victories than the AIM-7 and AIM-9, it would be unfair to call the number insignificant or without value. The Air Force Historical Research Agency, keepers of the USAF's official aerial victory lists, count over forty aerial victories as "guns kills." However, in the 1960s, Momyer was no fan of continuing to place a gun on a high-performance jet fighter, something that seemed to him an outdated and unnecessary practice. Momyer went so far as to state: "There will be a gun in the F-4 over my dead body." Though it did not kill Momyer, a gun was eventually added to some F-4 models during the Vietnam War, thus giving the pilots one more option with which to kill MiGs.[10]

Historian Steve Fino noted, "Air Force and Navy officials expected American pilots would have ample time to acquire the Soviet bombers, actuate the necessary switches, and maneuver the interceptor aircraft into an ideal position to employ their radar-guided and heat-seeking missiles." This proved to be simply not true in the aerial arena of Vietnam. Fighter-on-fighter combat inside North Vietnam happened faster than setting up an intercept on a Soviet bomber. The air force eventually recognized this when the July 1966 *PACAF Tactics and Techniques Bulletin* noted that "close-in fighting may become necessary."[11]

If everything occurred in the correct manner, air-to-air engagements began with either an airborne command-and-control aircraft, usually the USAF's EC-121 Warning Star, or the US Navy's sea-based positive identification radar advisory zone (PIRAZ) asset, picking up the enemy fighters. The PIRAZ ships were known by the call sign of "Red Crown." EC-121s used numerous call signs, including "Ethan" and "Disco." Early detection of enemy MiGs significantly changed the nature of the engagement and was cited by ace Steven Ritchie as "one of the primary reasons that we were able to engage MiGs and effect kills." Once detected, Red Crown/Disco called the MiG or bandit aircraft in a color-coordinated hierarchy: "Red Bandits" were MiG-17s, "White Bandits" were MiG-19s, and "Blue Bandits" were MiG-21s. There was also a "Green Bandit" indicating a VNAF pilot who appeared to be practiced and knowledgeable at his trade, and a "Black Bandit" indicating a MiG low on fuel, and thus one that could be ignored. Then began the time-consuming job of plotting an intercept, locking on with radar, and working with each aircraft's unique fire-control system to prepare for missile employment.[12]

Aerial combat in the Vietnam War, but in particular over North Vietnam, is typically divided into three phases. Phase one lasted from 1965 through the summer of 1967; phase two, from late 1967 until the bombing pause in December of 1968, and finally, the third phase, beginning in April of 1972 and lasting until December of that year. Phases one and two compose the Operation Rolling Thunder campaign, and phase three, the Linebacker Operations. The air-to-air war began fitfully in April of 1965. Over the next eight months, only eight enemy MiGs were shot down. A gap existed between the aerial victory in July of 1965 and the resumption of air-to-air combat in April of 1966, but from April of 1966 until the announced bombing halt in November of 1968, engagements occurred frequently. Historian Michael Hankins notes that once the bombing pause went into effect, "air-to-air combat was nearly absent in Southeast Asia from the end of 1968 until 1972." Air-to-air combat was not completely removed from the conflict at this time, it was just rare; but rare does not mean the same thing as absence.[13]

On March 28, 1970, a flight of F-4s from the USS *Constellation* shot down a MiG-21. Aircraft commander Lieutenant Jerry Beaulier was a graduate of the navy's first Top Gun class, where he had learned the tactics and techniques he had lacked earlier in the war to place his F-4 into an advantageous shooting position, from which he fired an AIM-9D after the MiG-21 reversed in front of him. Beaulier's RIO, Lieutenant (junior grade) Steve Barkley, remembered thinking "Bad move" as the MiG moved into a perfect weapons employment zone. This shoot-down occurred during the bombing pause in the North and was the first MiG kill by any service since the bombing pause became effective in 1968. The navy did not have another aerial victory until 1972.[14]

Air-to-air combat progressively increased from the introduction of jets through the bombing pause in 1968. Air engagements in 1967 were "marked by an intensity of battle unmatched in the entire two previous years of airstrikes to the north." As Rolling Thunder intensified, so did MiG encounters, particularly in RP-5 and RP-6. MiG activity increased to the degree that it began to hinder F-105 operations attacking targets in the North. MiGs waited on the ground at their airfields or in predetermined holding patterns aloft and waited to be vectored to F-105 strikes. Since the F-105 carried a unique QRC-120 jamming pod, North Vietnamese radar operators were capable of distinguishing between F-105 flights and F-4 flights. The MiGs preferred to attack the F-105s, which forced the American pilots to jettison their bomb loads and thus end the mission. An attempt to counter this led to one of the more famous aerial engagements in the history of fighter combat.[15]

Bolo

Many air-to-air engagements of the Vietnam War earned a place in the great air battles of all time, but perhaps the best remembered of the Vietnam War was Operation Bolo, led by legendary fighter pilot and ace Robin Olds. During his time flying in Vietnam, Olds scored four confirmed kills; this brought his total to sixteen, which included twelve kills from World War II, making him a rare triple ace. Olds masterminded the Bolo Operation and even received permission to spring his trap from 7th Air Force commander General Momyer. It was a blend of chicanery, subterfuge, and technology that decimated a sizable portion of North Vietnam's available MiG-21 aircraft.

Olds gathered a group of his most seasoned junior officers in his office, including Captain John B. Stone and First Lieutenant Ralph Wetterhahn. Envisioning two groups of F-4s, Olds broke each group down into seven flights. Each flight had four aircraft, for a total of twenty-eight aircraft in each group, and fifty-six aircraft total. One group was to act as an aerial blocking force to ensure that none of the MiGs escaped to China. The other group planned to simulate a strike package of F-105s. To make sure the ruse worked, the F-4s were outfitted with the same QRC-120 jamming pods carried by the F-105s. With any luck, the MiG-21s at Phuc Yen airfield would take the bait and attempt to take off and attack the "F-105s."

Each flight of F-4s used a particular car for their call sign. Robert Olds, leading the attack, would naturally be the Olds flight. The other flights were: Ford, Rambler, Lincoln, Tempest, Plymouth, and Vespa. The flights of F-4s set up at five-minute intervals, which allowed for maximum coverage of the airfields and also ensured that once engaged, the MiGs would have a difficult time breaking off contact.[16]

On January 2, 1967, Olds led the attack, and the MiGs fell for the ruse. As the MiG-21s broke through the cloud cover, between the first (Olds) and second (Ford) flights, they discovered not the bomb-laden F-105s on another run, but heavily armed F-4s and a group of American fighter pilots with their "fangs through the floor," each one spoiling for a kill. The Battle of Phuc Yen lasted for only a few minutes. The surviving MiGs eventually used the cloud cover to dive beneath and away from the attacking F-4s, but not before Olds's pilots destroyed seven MiG-21s during the dogfight, each with either an AIM-7 or AIM-9 missile kill. Olds later remembered, "We returned home triumphant." Although the NVAF husbanded their MiG-21s after Bolo, this did not mean they were unwilling to engage in combat; rather, "[a]fter January 1, 1967, the NVNAF displayed an aggressive commitment of a large fighting force."[17]

In March 1967, the JCS finally approved strikes against some of the MiG airfields, and MiG attacks in the air increased accordingly. In the first half of 1967, the air-to-air engagements fell in favor of the Americans, leading General Momyer to state, "We have driven the MiGs out of the sky for all practical purposes. . . . If he comes up, he will probably suffer the same fate." The MiG pilots recognized their deficiencies and began to change tactics during the summer of 1967. The MiGs, taking advantage of increased Rolling Thunder strikes, and thus, higher numbers of American aircraft to target, took off at low level, approached under American radar coverage, and popped up to attack. While Momyer was correct in asserting that the MiGs had been driven out of the skies, the NVAF was a learning organism capable of overcoming American advantages. As one CHECO report noted, after losses in the early part of 1967, the NVAF adapted: "By midyear, however, MIG pilots had come up with a better idea and had acquired the air discipline to stick to their plan. Henceforth, they would fight only on their own conditions."[18]

As the war progressed, there was a dawning recognition that the American missiles—despite engagements like Bolo—did not work as advertised, and that their Pk rates (probability of kill) were significantly lower than originally expected. In August of 1966 a message from the chief of naval operations (CNO) to the CINCPACFLT noted that an ongoing program by Raytheon aimed to fix the following issues in both the AIM-7 and AIM-9B: "provides increased missile tuning reliability . . . improves missile durability and launch reliability," and "minimizes radar break lock during air combat maneuvering by relaxing 3G rate limit." This eighty-five-day quick-fix program was only a first step toward improving missile reliability. The CNO also stated, "It is recommended that longer-range efforts to enhance overall fighter-to-fighter capability of current and follow-on Sparrow missiles be initiated earliest since such efforts will necessarily entail some re-design and modifications." Even as the USAF and USN struggled to improve missile effectiveness, another improvement in air-to-air capability finally arrived. At this point in the war, and against Momyer's earlier pronouncements about the F-4 having a gun "over my dead body," the SUU-16 gun pod was finally equipped on the air-to-air F-4s.[19]

American fighter pilots badly needed better missiles and the addition of the gun. The air-to-air war reached a peak of intensity in the later part of 1967. Neither side was able to gain distinct air superiority, nor were the MiGs swept from the sky. Instead, improved tactics allowed the North Vietnamese Air Force to battle American forces into near parity. Although aerial kill rates continued to favor the USAF and USN, by the bombing pause in December of 1968, when significant air-to-air combat went on hiatus, the USAF was forced to admit, "The air war against the MiGs had drawn to an inconclusive end."[20]

War in the Air (1969–1972) and the Last American Aces

No American pilot achieved ace status until the spring of 1972. In the later part of the Vietnam conflict, but especially in 1972, tactics, context, and technology had altered the air-to-air war. The US Navy had established its Fighter Weapons School, and new adaptations greatly increased American aerial success. One of the adaptations was the advent of the Combat Tree system which allowed American aircraft to "interrogate" enemy MiGs and determine if the aircraft was friend or foe. Thus, visual identification was no longer needed and American aircraft—finally—had the ability and clearance to fire AIM-7s in their prescribed and preferred BVR envelope. However, this came with a drawback; even when the system worked, the technology could work against American airmen. As air force historian Richard Hallion noted when investigating a case of fratricide, "[F]iring BVR is also risky, and the system of rules in place today is the direct result of experiences from air battles" during the Vietnam War. That being said, five individuals worked through the myriad problems to reach the status of an ace.[21]

Training was important, but so were technological and practical adaptations. By 1972, the navy and air force had adopted numerous technological improvements. Combat Tree allowed F-4 weapons systems officers (WSOs) and radar intercept officers (RIOs) to positively identify MiG aircraft. Newer F-4Es arriving in-theater were also equipped with the Target Identification

System Electro-Optical (TISEO) system for long-range identification—thus fixing the problem of visual identification—and finally, the USAF's Project Teaball provided pilots with near-real-time MiG locations and intentions and greatly increased the USAF's air-to-air kill ratios in the later part of 1972.[22]

Five Americans became aces during the Vietnam conflict, all of them in 1972. They were Captain Charles B. "Chuck" DeBellevue, USAF (six confirmed victories), Lieutenant Randall "Duke" Cunningham, USN (five), Lieutenant J. G. William P. "Irish" Driscoll, USN (five), Captain Steve Ritchie, USAF (five), and Captain Jeff Feinstein, USAF (five). Cunningham and Ritchie were both pilots, DeBellevue and Feinstein were USAF WSOs, and Driscoll, a USN RIO. Although he did not achieve ace status during the war in Vietnam, Olds earned confirmed victories fourteen through seventeen during the conflict, thus becoming a "triple ace" during the war, having achieved twelve victories during World War II.

Perhaps equal to that of Bolo, the events of the aerial engagement which occurred on May 10, 1972, are infamous and, in a way, proved the US Navy was learning from its experiences in the Vietnam War. On this date, Lieutenant Randall "Duke" Cunningham (five confirmed victories) along with his RIO, Lieutenant (junior grade) William P. "Irish" Driscoll (five), engaged in one of the most daring aerial engagements in the history of air warfare. Flying off the USS *Constellation*, Cunningham and Driscoll, under the call sign "Showtime 100," supported a larger strike package composed of thirty-five aircraft attacking the Hai Duong rail yard by providing flak suppression to the striker aircraft. At this point in the war, Cunningham already had two confirmed MiG kills. That day, he would add three more to his total.[23]

The May 10 engagement resulted in six destroyed MiGs and two F-4s shot down—including Cunningham's and Driscoll's, whose aircraft was struck by a SAM while egressing the engagement, *after* they had downed three MiGs. Cunningham stated in his after-action report, typed shortly after the engagement, "The only reason 6 F-4s battled 20 MiGs without a scratch and bagged 6 of them is that everyone had been through an adversary program . . . and knew the tactics from ACM [air combat maneuvering] training. We may lose one aircraft in training, but look how many lives it saved on May 10, [1972], and other times."[24]

The American aces of the Vietnam War imparted their skills to the next generation. Although these men racked up an impressive amount of "kills," they each knew the pain of losing fellow airmen in the arena of combat. For the US Navy, the creation of the Fighter Weapons (or Top Gun) School aided fighter pilots in melding training and technology into a lethal combination. After the war, the US Air Force used its newly created Aggressor squadrons, a revamped Fighter Weapons School, a secret program where Americans flew

Soviet-made MiGS, and a newly developed training exercise known as Red Flag to train its pilots for combat.

The North Vietnam Aces

On the other side of the battlefield and in the same sky where the Americans became aces, numerous fighter pilots of the North Vietnam Air Force also plied their trade against the best the American military pilots had to offer, and even more than on the American side, several became aces. Each and every MiG pilot flew with one of the four fighter aviation regiments—equivalent to an American squadron—the 921st, 923rd, 925th, and 927th Fighter Regiments. These four regiments represented the entirety of the NVAF that engaged against dozens of American squadrons. One Soviet source put the complete number of MiG-15, -19, and -21 aircraft available to North Vietnam at 187, with only a portion of these ever in a combat-ready status.[25]

Without a doubt, though, the most famous of all NVAF fighter pilots was the mythical "Colonel Tomb." Tomb was a legend invented by sightings of a MiG-17 with number 3020 painted on the forward portion of the aircraft and signals intelligence collected by various sources during the war. Cunningham and Driscoll were credited with shooting down 3020; Cunningham noted in his after-action review that the third aircraft he shot down that day was indeed Colonel Tomb. The fact that Tomb did not actually exist hardly matters. For all the attention Western historians have given to Vietnam sources—as far as the air war is concerned—he might very well have been their leading ace.[26]

The ability of Americans to study the air war from the perspective of the North Vietnam Air Force has been, at best, limited, and at worst, nearly non-existent. From the perspective of the historian, the ability to access official sources has been quite challenging, for several reasons. The first, of course, is the language barrier. Whereas many graduate students are required to learn a foreign language, the ability for Americans to study the Vietnam language as part of an officially sanctioned program is limited. Second, it's difficult for American scholars researching in Vietnam to get through a painful triple-tiered approval process to look at documents in their National Archives. One archivist called the collections of materials in Vietnam a "largely unexplored corpus of Vietnamese textual resources in research institutions and libraries." Third, even the secondary source material is limited; very few works look at the war from the perspective of the Vietnamese pilots, and the few books that do so do not juxtapose their own findings with the American sources. The United States and Vietnam normalized relations in 1995, but this has not led to a wellspring of American scholars publishing works using Vietnamese records. Very few authors have even attempted to look at the air war from the perspective of North Vietnam.[27]

Still, recent work by Istvan Toperczer has pulled back the curtain on the NVAF aces. His research demonstrates the difficulty in achieving historical consensus where two combatants are involved. In total, the Air Force of North Vietnam had sixteen pilots who achieved the status of ace, a term and milestone recognized by pilots on both sides of the conflict. The leading ace of the Vietnam conflict was from North Vietnam: Nguyen Van Coc, whose air-to-air kills totaled nine.[28]

The other aces of the North Vietnam Air Force included Nguyen Hong Nhi (eight confirmed victories), Pham Thanh Ngan (eight), Mai Van Cuong (eight), Dang Ngoc Ngu (seven), Nguyen Van Bay (seven), Nguyen Doc Soat (seven), Nguyen Ngoc Do (six), Nguyen Nhat Chieu (six), Le Thanh Dao (six), Nguyen Danh Kinh (six), Nguyen Tien Sam (six), Le Hai (six), Luu Huy Chao (six), Vu Ngoc Dinh (five), and Nguyen Van Nghia (five), bringing the total number of NVAF aces to sixteen.[29]

The pilots of North Vietnam did not rotate in and out the way American aircrews did. They simply flew until they died or they survived until war's end. The NVAF never had more than two hundred MiG aircraft at any given time throughout the American involvement in Vietnam. Since many of their bases were never on target lists, it was often impossible to destroy them on the ground. The fear of possibly killing a Soviet advisor far outweighed the military necessity of destroying their air force on the ground.

MiG Tactics

MiG formations were different than the common American four-ship group. MiGs flew in "hi-low pairs," with one pair one mile in front of a second lower pair in trail; in "stacked three," with the aircraft again separated by roughly a mile in a "high, low, high" group; and in a more-common "pair patrol." For the most part, MiG tactics did not change throughout the war. MiG flights were closely coordinated by ground control intercept (GCI) sites, which vectored MiGs toward their targets.

While this was standard procedure throughout the war, different approaches toward targets did change. Using the GCI sites to vector them toward American aircraft, MiGs typically employed the following intercept methods: a pursuit curve from a 30-degree offset to the rear in an attempt to close directly behind the American aircraft unseen; a parallel course attack from the front, but offset by distance in order to then turn for a tail attack;

and a lead cutoff attack. These were usually accomplished from medium to low altitude, which proved problematic for Americans when it came to gaining radar acquisition or employing their missiles. Early infrared missiles, the AIM-9B, routinely could not differentiate between a MiG and the ground clutter of planet Earth below. This was further exacerbated by MiGs continually closing inside American missiles' effective envelopes. "Inside these minimum ranges—about 3,000 feet—the missile's proximity fuse warhead would not arm; a missile fired inside that range was simply a large, dumb, and expensive bullet."[30]

It can be argued that MiG tactics proved successful because American tactics became repetitive. As a *Tactics Review* report noted, "The predictability of the chaff and strike force route may be responsible for the success they have experienced." Since North Vietnamese GCI sites knew roughly from which direction the strike package was going to come, it made it that much easier to intercept the American fighters using the tactics detailed above.[31]

"Hit and run" is the most appropriate term for MiG tactics during the Vietnam conflict. As reports coming out of the conflict noted, "MiGs do not engage unless they have the advantage." It was rare for MiGs to attack without the element of surprise. If an American flight turned to engage a MiG flight head-on, the MiGs more often than not chose to disengage. However, in their element, MiG pilots could be aggressive and determined. The MiG-21's speed advantage allowed them to attack and disengage almost at will especially in the horizontal plane. Captain Steve Ritchie, the USAF's only pilot ace of the war, remembered that MiGs always "turned in the horizontal. Therefore, we planned to work in the vertical, which gave us [an] advantage."[32]

MiG aircraft initially engaged with a high-altitude (30,000 feet) attack from the six o'clock position, hoping to catch the strike package unaware of the danger approaching behind them. When the Americans countered with dedicated MiG combat air patrols, the North Vietnamese pilots began using low-altitude intercepts, still from the rear, but would instead "snap up" to the American fighter aircraft. As American strike packages grew larger with separate flights of strikers, electronic support, escort, MiGCAP, and chaff dispensers, MiGs loitered either over the bases or inside predetermined holding areas, often over Hanoi, and then made an afterburner approach, hoping to hit one of the more-vulnerable aircraft on the edge of the strike package, such as a member of the chaff flight. Again Ritchie recalled, "The MiGs prefer to attack supersonic, disengage, and just keep right on going. So their general tactic was take off, stay in full [after]burner, [. . .] attack supersonic and then disengage, go back and land."[33]

Occasionally, MiGs attacked the MiGCAP aircraft directly, but only when enough aircraft could be generated for a coordinated multidirectional approach. This was the preferred method of attack of the MiG-17 pilots, who could strike in greater numbers. The MiG-21 was in such short supply that heavy losses to this aircraft seriously degraded their operations. This was the case after Operation Bolo shot down at least five—but probably closer to seven—of the fifteen aircraft in North Vietnam. Attacking as part of a large force and in a coordinated manner was a rare occurrence, however; MiG pilots typically did not want to become engaged in a turning dogfight with American fighter pilots, especially those with the express mission of killing them. MiGCAP pilots also tended to be the most capable aircrews with regard to engaging MiG aircraft. MiG-17s also used the "wagon wheel" tactic to hinder American tactics, where two to four MiGs turned in a wheel pattern, offset from each other, to ensure that no American fighter could get a tail shot on one without exposing his own aircraft to the next MiG in line.[34]

During Linebacker II, MiG pilots claimed to have shot down two of the B-52s lost during that campaign. Although bolstered in accounts given by Roger Boniface in *MiGs Over North Vietnam* and Istvan Toperczer in *Air War Over North Vietnam*, this claim is problematic and highly unlikely, although not impossible. For starters, the VNAF claims of B-52s shot down by either SAMs or MiGs seems wildly exaggerated. North Vietnam claims to have downed thirty-four B-52s—an impossible number, even when one takes into account the B-52s struck by SAMs that returned to base, but never flew again. Each B-52 lost can be accounted for by its tail number; the USAF could not have lost an additional eighteen B-52s without having to account for the missing tail numbers. The USAF's *Southeast Asia Management Summary: Final Semiannual Review* from 1974 puts the total number at eighteen.

Historian Wayne Thompson noted in his book, *To Hanoi and Back*, that during Linebacker II "the MiGs seemed able to do little more at night than gauge B–52 altitude for surface-to-air missiles." Although Thompson admits that North Vietnam sources "claim" to have shot down two B-52s, his source remains the work of Istvan Toperczer. Other historians including Marshall Michel agree with Thompson's assessment. Michel notes, "North Vietnamese histories indicate that the MiG pilots had a great deal of difficulty locating the B-52 flights." One former North Vietnamese officer interviewed by Michel, when asked about the possibility of MiGs approaching the B-52s, noted, "If our MiG had been that close, why wouldn't he have shot the B-52 down?" It seems if a B-52 had been shot down by a MiG, this would be generally recognized by those who participated in the events.[35]

In the end, and throughout the air-to-air contest in North Vietnam, NVAF pilots continued to routinely challenge American notions of superiority. Historian Marshall Michel, himself an F-4 pilot in Vietnam, stated, "The North Vietnamese MiG pilots again demonstrated they were equal to the Air Force

F-4 crews, and when the air war over North Vietnam ended at the end of December [1972], only the most ardent chauvinists could say the U.S. fighter force had achieved air superiority." Both the USAF and USN set out during the war to figure out exactly why and how North Vietnam's fighter pilots were able to accomplish this.[36]

Red Baron Reports

In October of 1966, the USAF instituted a study group to report on all encounters between American and NVN MiG aircraft. "Encounters" were defined as any "sighting of enemy aircraft (either visually or by radar), either US or enemy aircraft initiating hostile or evasive maneuvers, either US or enemy aircraft expending ordnance, and loss or damage in combat of either US or enemy aircraft." The long title of the report was the "Weapons System Evaluation Group Report #116: Air-to-Air Encounters in Southeast Asia (Volumes I–IV)," but the project is better remembered as the "Red Baron Reports."[37] Over the course of the conflict in Vietnam, a total of four volumes were published. These were eventually declassified in the early 2000s:

- Volume I: Account of F-4 and F-8 Events prior to March 1, 1967 (78 events)
- Volume II: F-105 Events Prior to March 1, 1967 (151 events)
- Volume III: Events from March 1, 1967, to August 1, 1967, and Miscellaneous Events (346 events)
- Volume IV: Analyses

Initially comprised of only four members, the group rapidly expanded to dozens of active-duty officers from the USAF, USN, and USMC, as well as psychologists and graphic artists. Eleven of these group members were trained to be interviewers and aided by the psychologists in the "reconstruction" of the events in question. The resultant interviews of each encounter were exhaustive, and when produced in the reports included mission and tactical situations, mission routes to targets, aircraft configurations (ordnance carried by each aircraft, also known as a standard conventional load [SCL]), flight conditions including altitude and weather, actions of friendly aircraft, actions of enemy aircraft, time marks, visual representation of the engagements, which included tactics and flight paths, and also narrative descriptions of each engagement. In each engagement, rather than using an aircraft's actual call sign, they were simply referred to as "Blue" for the American force and "MiG" for the enemy, so a flight of four F-4 Phantoms became Blue 1–4 and enemy aircraft, MiG 1–4.[38]

Some of the encounters proved to be relatively benign. Volume I, encounter seven, was a single paragraph:

> At 1520 local time Blue flight located approximately 21 degrees 55' N/00 53' E noticed two contrails heading SE. . . . Flight headed toward tracks, and jettisoned tanks and applied maximum power. The two aircraft in question made 180-degree turn and took an apparent NW heading to Meng-Tzu. When Blue flight determined that the two aircraft had crossed the Chinese border, Blue Flight returned to Phuc Yen area until BINGO fuel[ed] and returned to home station.[39]

Other encounters ran more than twenty pages with multiple charts, diagrams, and other breakouts to depict the engagement. The day before the "sighting only" report described above, four F-4s engaged two MiG-17s. In this engagement, the F-4s detected the enemy aircraft thirty-three miles to their front and separated into a "loose deuce" formation, with Blue 1 and 2 in front and Blue 3 and 4 in trail. The F-4s made a head-on identification pass and the fight began as the MiGs and Phantoms turned into each other. As the MiGs turned with the lead element, they noted that they had an easier firing position on the two rear Phantoms. Each "rolled out" of their turn and engaged Blue 3 and 4 with cannon at a "high angle off." Blue 3 and 4 both made a break-turn into the attacking MiGs, but the smaller, nimbler, more-agile MiGs continued to turn behind the F-4s into a more-advantageous firing position. Here, the Phantoms' engines aided their American occupants. Both F-4s lit their afterburners and gained separation from the MiGs, but this helped highlight to American aviators that it remained a bad idea to attempt a horizontal turning engagement with the MiGs.[40]

At this point, the pilot of Blue 4 chose to make a rapid "break-turn" to the right, away from Blue 3 in an attempt to "sandwich or split the MiGs." As Blue 4 made his hard turn to the right, one of the MiGs broke to follow him. Blue 4 went into a dive, falling from 22,000 feet to 12,000 feet, but at the same time increased speed to Mach 1.4, gaining a significant separation from his trailing MiG. The American then climbed and used his gained speed and energy to climb to 33,000. Rolling over and pointing his nose down, he was in a perfect firing position. Blue 4 loosed three sidewinder missiles, killing the MiG.[41]

In the meantime, the other MiG continued to turn behind Blue 3, who was forced to make a series of reversing turns to keep the MiG from being able to fire at him. This "scissors maneuver" eventually ended when the MiG made an overshoot out in front of the F-4. In this moment, the Blue 3 GIB made a communications call of "Go Heat," in essence telling the pilot to shoot an AIM-9. The aircraft commander responded back, "Go Boresight." Boresight snapped the radar to the F-4's centerline, looking directly out in front of the aircraft, which is where the unfortunate MiG pilot, in an advantageous position only seconds before, now found himself. In the next ten seconds, the Phantom fired three sidewinder missiles, also killing his MiG. The Red Baron Report entry noted that from the moment of the merge until the end of the engagement was probably no more than one to one and a half minutes.[42]

These two brief descriptions provide a good representation of the 575 encounters studied as part of Project Red Baron. However, it was the analyses volume that dictated what all of the data indicated. The simple fact, as concluded in the introduction to the analyses volume, was that the aerial environment in Vietnam had evolved "into a sophisticated, integrated air defense system consisting of MiGs, surface-to-air missiles, and intensive AAA, employed simultaneously with effective enemy early warning and GCI." A subtext to the problem was that if the IADS of North Vietnam could inhibit the American air arm, what would Soviet Union forces be capable of accomplishing in a Western Europe scenario? The answer was too clear. A Soviet IADS manned by highly trained Soviet troops and in far greater numbers posed an even larger problem than North Vietnam did. If war with the Soviet Union in Western Europe remained even a possibility, the war in North Vietnam demonstrated that significant changes to tactics, training, and equipment needed to occur for the American air forces.[43]

Whereas the US Navy's Ault Report made numerous recommendations, the Red Baron Reports eschewed this approach, and "carefully avoided suggesting specific solutions, so as not to prejudice the definition of the problem area." However, at least one generally accepted truth came out of the reports: If an American flier could survive his first ten combat missions, his chances of surviving his tour increased exponentially.[44]

The air-to-air war over North Vietnam was not a beyond-visual-range fight. American fighters did not lock up their enemy on radar and then lob AIM-7 medium-range semi-active radar homing missiles at the MiGs and destroy them, nor did they clean up the remaining fighters with direct-head AIM-9 heat-seeking missiles against non-maneuvering targets long before the merge. The assumptions the American air arms took into Vietnam were wrong. The air-to-air war in the skies of North Vietnam was "characterized by close-in combat, high-g maneuvering and visual cues."[45]

Although they made no specific recommendations, the Red Baron Reports indicated several areas that required immediate attention, and these became clear to those reading through the engagements: acquisition and identification of enemy aircraft in a timely manner, weapons reliability, weapons versatility, target discrimination, pilot training, pilot visibility, and man–machine compatibility.[46]

With regard to target identification, Red Baron Reports noted that the median range of all incidents was only two miles. Even worse, these engagements began in all quadrants. This meant air-to-air combat was initiated with little to no warning to the pilots and came from all sides, indicating that many of the aerial fights began with the Americans at a position of disadvantage or on the defensive. The reports noted this had happened in at least 25 percent of the engagements. The reports also noted that if an American aircraft visually acquired an enemy before the MiG was successful in moving into the rear quadrant, the American was successful 95 percent of the time in defeating his attacker by maneuvering. Again, although no specific recommendation was made, the reports noted that "the requirement for real-time information on the position of the enemy aircraft is apparent." Post-Vietnam changes, including the E-3 AWACS (airborne warning and control), were aimed at fixing this specific acquisition problem.[47]

The problem of weapons reliability was summed up this way: "The missile systems employed in SEA were not designed for use in close-in, dog-fight encounters." Without fear of being glib, one might imagine soldiers on the ground going into combat armed with weapons not designed for closing with and engaging the enemy. It would be similar to rifles designed to shoot a standing enemy combatant walking slowly in the other direction. The USN, USMC, and USAF were armed with air-to-air missiles designed to shoot down non-maneuvering Soviet bombers, and this led directly to the problem of weapons versatility.

The USAF and USN both recognized that current missiles, as well as any follow-on missile systems, needed greater parameters and envelopes. As mentioned previously, a pilot could call for the GIB to "Go Boresight" and snap the radar along the plane's centerline in order to shoot at a target in front of him. When done with the AIM-7, the results were terrible: "The boresight mode of firing the AIM-7, a degraded technique for 'snapshot' capability, has been unsuccessful in combat. In 65 attempts to fire in boresight mode, only one hit resulted." Both the AIM-7 and AIM-9 needed to be improved for use in any possible future combat operation.[48]

Trigger 4

The shoot-down of Trigger 4 in 1972 provides an engaging look at the complete chaos that erupted in the air-to-air arena, but also demonstrates how actions that occurred in the skies over North Vietnam stayed with the men who flew the missions for decades, even after they had returned home.

On July 29, 1972, during the Linebacker Operations, several flights (Trigger, Date, Plum, and Pistol) of air force F-4s became embroiled in a dogfight with a group of North Vietnamese MiG-21s. Into this fight, another flight of F-4s (Cadillac) turned to engage the two separate MiG flights. In total, there were twenty American F-4s and an unknown number of MiGs engaged in an aerial melee typically seen only in films. During the course of the engagement, two MiGs were shot down, and the Americans lost one F-4 (call sign Trigger 4) to a MiG's missile.[49]

Many pilots at the time believed there was a possibility that Trigger 4 was actually the victim of fratricide from an F-4 flying with the Cadillac flight. Years later, a USAF reservist came to the conclusion this was indeed the case, and the pilot of Trigger 4—who had survived his ejection, capture, and imprisonment—asked the chief of staff of the air force to open a case and determine exactly which aircraft (friendly or foe) had shot him down that July day over North Vietnam.

Every aspect of the air-to-air war over Vietnam was found in the recorded material of the Trigger 4 study. The engagement began over the port city of Haiphong when Red Crown confirmed MiG launches out of Phuc Yen and Kep airfields. "Cadillac, Crown, you have a bandit 231 at 28." Red Crown later informed Cadillac that these were "Green Bandits," indicating top-notch MiG pilots. For the next ten minutes, the radio erupted with chatter as each flight turned with and engaged the unknown number of MiGs and complete confusion reigned:

"Take it down, take it down. Triple launch 12 o'clock."

"Okay, I got some SAMs blowing up way out there at 9."

"Cadillac 4, you took a hit? Okay, let's go. Let's get outta here."

"Okay, bandits 300 at 9, Cadillac."

"Okay. Cleared to fire. Fire two."

At the height of the air battle, four flights of F-4s and two flights of MiGs turned and tangled east of Kep airfield. When the dust settled, two MiGs were down as well as the F-4 Trigger 4. An official study of all available records concluded, "Seventh Air Force credited Cadillac 1 and Pistol 1 each with a MiG kill. Project Red Baron and other official sources, including the North Vietnam Air Force, credited a MiG-21 pilot with shooting down Trigger 4."[50]

The study concluded that the MiG shot down by Cadillac was flying right to left across his nose, that Cadillac's missile exploded well before Trigger 4 was hit, and that the MiG kill awarded Cadillac was "in accordance with established kill confirmation policy." The importance to this study cannot be overstated. It demonstrates the lengths to which the American military will go to not only account for its airmen, but also to assuage the fears of fliers for an incident occurring decades in the past. The concluding statement of the report clearly shows that "[t]he body of evidence overwhelmingly supports the historical record. Trigger 4 was lost to a MiG-21 on July 29, 1972."[51]

Conclusion

The aerial arena remained a potent killer of American airmen during the conflict. One of the reasons for the success of the North Vietnamese pilots was that they conducted their operations in a target-rich environment with a plethora of American aircraft operating in the skies of Vietnam from 1965 to 1972. For the pilots who flew for the North Vietnamese Air Force, there were always targets to be found. The North Vietnamese pilots also had the added bonus of conducting operations close to their bases, in some cases—as at Phuc Yen—directly above them. This cannot be discounted.

The air-to-air arena in North Vietnam was one area where technology—although employed in different manners—tended to be relatively equal. The aircraft were of the same generation, although again, what was prioritized on American and Soviet aircraft was very different. For every advantage held by the Americans in aerial radar or command and control, the North Vietnamese Air Force had an equal measure of the same on the ground with their superb GCI system. Although the kill rates show American success in the air-to-air war, there were more aces on the VNAF side. Both sides can claim some level of victory. One thing remained clear: The VNAF met American airmen on equal terms and more than proved their worth. American fighters never had complete and total air superiority over North Vietnam.

Denouement and Conclusion

ONE OF THE EARLIEST CHECO REPORTS, "Punitive Air Strikes," published in 1965, noted, "For the past 10–15 years we have repeatedly asked for a chance to show what airpower could do. Now we are having our 'day in court.' When the verdict is in, we shall have little chance for appeal. Whatever the outcome . . . airpower has been given ample opportunity to prove its thesis."

The thesis was fundamentally not proven. Air power was not a decisive force in Vietnam, nor could it have been, but that is not how elements inside the services or those who participated in the conflict have chosen to remember it. Although air power certainly had moments that were critical at both the operational and the tactical levels, air power itself was not a determining factor.[1]

The overall experience of American airmen in Vietnam demonstrates that even though America had committed a significant amount of resources to the conflict, it was never a war America was prepared to win or capable of winning. Neither was it a war ideally suited to the contributions of American air power. America's air forces—the combined flying strength of the four branches of the armed forces—were best configured to face a conventional threat. The technologically advanced aircraft, the munitions, and the men who flew the machines were developed to face a peer threat, the most likely candidate at the time being the Soviet Union in a war for control of Western Europe. Even in the aerial arena over North Vietnam, the North Vietnamese proved to be more than a match for the United States. In the end, although the preferred American way of war might have been conventional, or peer on peer, the US air forces learned that the *preferred way* of war was not the *most likely*.

What can conclusively be said of air power during the Vietnam conflict? The facts are these. The US military flew 3.4 million combat sorties in South Vietnam, North Vietnam, Laos, and Cambodia, and in 1975, North Vietnam invaded the South for the final time.[2]

Navy historian John Darrell Sherwood said that during the Vietnam War, "air power . . . while occasionally influential, was never decisive." The interpretation from those who participated is no less opaque. Ed Rasimus, veteran of two tours in Vietnam in both the F-105 and F-4, noted,

> The view of the war today is only slightly clearer than it was then. We don't know yet why we were there or what the objective was. We can't define a national self-interest for involvement in Southeast-Asia, nor has anyone told us why we squandered such a valuable treasure of manpower and machines. We should know, but we don't.[3]

If neither the historian nor the participant can come to a final determination, then it is clear that our—American—interpretation and understanding of the war continues to be incomplete.

The close-air-support war in South Vietnam, the air-to-ground war against targets in North Vietnam—which also bred a separate air-to-air war—and the secret wars of interdiction in Laos and Cambodia were each separate air wars, but linked into the overall conflict that was American involvement in Vietnam. By and large, the war ended in 1973 with the signing of the Paris Peace Accords and the return of American POWs. Although bombing continued for a time in Laos and Cambodia, the American involvement in Vietnam had "ended," and the American military began a period of transition. This required each service to look at what had worked, but more importantly, what had failed during the conflict.

The US Air Force and the US Navy both experienced a watershed year in 1972. Both services introduced assets and technologies into the conflict. As American personnel in Southeast Asia decreased, there was a corresponding rise in the use of new technological developments. In the skies over Vietnam, these improvements became mainstays of aerial warfare that have continued to this day. The early 1970s witnessed a massive advance in aircraft avionics and munitions that found its way into Vietnam. In the waning days of American involvement, US troops employed the first precision-guided munitions, flew advanced aircraft including the F-111, and benefited from additions and updates to avionics systems, including the Teaball system. Advanced training methods were also employed, primarily in the navy, which more accurately simulated combat operations and tactics. All of this led to a more effective force on the battlefield, as is evidenced by the campaigns of 1972.

Aircraft coming into production after the conflict ended included technological and materiel changes around the pilot in the cockpit. Perhaps the best example of this was found inside the F-15 and F-16's "hands-on throttle and stick" (HOTAS) system, which allowed pilots to perform "switchology," including weapons selection, communications, and other pertinent functions without removing either hand from the aforementioned control instruments. These were all still in the development stages in 1972. There was also the introduction of the E-3 AWACS (Airborne Warning and Control System), which provided the battlefield control element so fundamentally important in locating and fixing targets and enemy aircraft.

But, in 1972, all that mattered to the Nixon administration and the Department of Defense was peace with honor, an exit from the quagmire. What is commonly missed in America's exit, stage right, was the fate of the very organization American air forces had entered into the conflict to begin training in the 1960s: the VNAF.

Vietnamization of the South Vietnam Air Force

It is all too easy to forget, especially after the introduction of jets in late 1964, that there existed another air force conducting operations in-country: the Republic of Vietnam Air Force. Prior to the fall of South Vietnam, the VNAF was the world's fourth-largest air force. America entered into the war with the primary goal of training the ARVN and VNAF to the point where they would be capable of defending themselves from an attack by the North. The USAF did not train their VNAF counterparts to that level, however, nor did it provide them with the capabilities and equipment needed to engage with and defeat the NVAF. Even though facing the NVAF was never part of the training mission—it was only ever envisioned that the VNAF needed to be able to handle things below the 17th parallel—once America removed its forces from South Vietnam, North Vietnam had no need to fear facing their brothers in the South in the air. The Soviet Union and China equipped North Vietnam's Air Force and Air Defense Air Force with their very best fighters and air defense systems, and trained them to use these tools effectively. The United States attempted to do the same in South Vietnam.

As one of the later CHECO reports noted, "The goal of the United States Policy in South Vietnam during 1970 and 1971 was to train and equip the Republic of Vietnam Armed Forces (VNAF) so they could effectively defend South Vietnam without armed assistance of the United States."[4] This report, published in November of 1971, came just four months before the North's Easter Offensive. The benefit of hindsight now shows that much of what was believed about the ability of South Vietnam to defend itself went out the window just a few months later.

The United States attempted the process of "Vietnamization" of the VNAF as surely as it did the ARVN forces, including doubling the size of the VNAF from twenty to forty squadrons, but this expansion and training mission lagged behind what the US ground forces were doing with their ARVN counterparts. By late 1969, the VNAF was "not yet capable of independently fighting the air war in South Vietnam."[5]

A CHECO report on the improvement and modernization of the VNAF noted that myriad problems existed for the VNAF: "a poor night operational capability, a combat assault capability which was less than optimum, inexperienced ALOs, ragged coordination between VNAF and ARVN, inadequate aerial support, and an overall lack of middle management." Despite all of this, the author of the report believed, perhaps quite falsely, that "time was proving to be on the side of the VNAF." This was simply not true.[6]

By March of 1971, despite a strong push for the VNAF to take over operations in South Vietnam, the VNAF were flying less than half of all strike sorties. Three months later their sortie rates had not improved. While the USAF could point to a vast improvement in VNAF capability, it was obvious to all involved that the VNAF was not big enough, trained enough, or equipped enough to take over air operations in South Vietnam. There also appeared to be another problem: USAF instructors seemed to be either unwilling or unable to fully turn over operations to the VNAF—what one report determined was the "disparity between American impetuosity and Asian patience."[7]

When North Vietnam invaded on March 30, 1972, Nixon's immediate actions included a massive deployment of American air power back to the region along an order of magnitude that the VNAF was simply incapable of copying. American air power flowed back into the region and successfully blunted the offensive, and then in turn went offensive in December of that year. Nixon pushed air power back into the region. Vietnamization took a backseat to the reintroduction of American arms, but this also proved that the Air Force of South Vietnam was never going to stand against an invasion by North Vietnam in the absence of American air support. President Nixon wrote in his daily diary and later, his memoirs, that

[o]f course, the weak link in our whole chain is the question as to whether the South Vietnamese have the will to fight. . . . The real problem is that the enemy is willing to sacrifice in order to win, while the South Vietnamese simply aren't willing to pay that much of a price in order to avoid losing. And, as Haig points out, all the air power in the world and strikes on Hanoi-Haiphong aren't

going to save South Vietnam if the South Vietnamese aren't able to hold on the ground.[8]

South Vietnam as a nation-state could not stand on its own without continued American involvement—something the United States was no longer willing to continue. American departure in 1973 meant South Vietnam's days were numbered; it was no longer a question of *if* South Vietnam would fall to North Vietnam, but *when*. That came in 1975 with the fall of Saigon.

Few members inside the US Air Force recognized that the war was truly lost in the early 1970s, refusing to even utter phrases that might be interpreted in that manner. Earl H. Tilford Jr., an intelligence officer who went on to become a noted historian of the air war in Vietnam, stated that "negative words, like *lost, ambushed, retreat*, although increasingly appropriate by 1971, were anathema."[9]

Colonel A. L. Gropman, in *War in the Third Dimension*, wrote: "Vietnam was a humiliating, exceptionally expensive, and probably unnecessary defeat. . . . America uselessly spilled its blood and squandered its treasure to fulfill an empty strategy."[10] Gropman echoes the sentiments felt by veterans of the conflict and those who have written on it since. The American involvement in Vietnam became an example of what not to do, but the lessons learned in that conflict were applied to the future. Each American military service—most notably the junior officers in each branch—went through a reckoning in Vietnam and applied those experiences to later training.

A report published by the US Senate's Committee on Foreign Relations in October of 1972, titled "Bombing as a Policy Tool in Vietnam," found that

> [o]f the five major goals set forth for the bombing, only one has been achieved. The bombing has succeeded in making North Vietnam pay a high price for her support of the war in the South. But the air war has not stopped the flow of supplies to the South, broken Hanoi's will, or forced the North Vietnamese to negotiate an end to the war.[11]

Even more damning, the report stated that "claims for strategic and interdiction bombing have consistently exceeded their accomplishments, and the extravagance of the rhetoric supporting the current air offensive against the North has a familiar ring."[12]

The US military spent the decade after the Vietnam War attempting to fix the mistakes made during that conflict. Each service underwent a fundamental transformation in organization, equipment, and training. Each of the services looked at the war from their unique perspective—air, land, and sea—and struggled to determine what went right and what went wrong. As mentioned, the US Navy's air arm created an Aggressor program and Fighter

Weapons School. The US Air Force created its own Aggressor squadrons and followed this by creating the world's largest and most comprehensive aerial realistic training exercise: Red Flag.

Although rarely explicitly stated, but implicitly understood and overtly hinted at, was this concern: If the Soviet Union's IADS system could significantly hinder the American war effort in Vietnam, what would the same system operated by Soviet soldiers do to American forces in a Western Europe scenario? American losses to the Soviet IADS system in Vietnam and similar losses suffered by the Israeli Air Force during the Yom Kippur War led the US Air Force chief of staff, General George S. Brown, to write the TAC commander in 1973: "I think it is apparent that surface-to-air missile defenses in the tremendous densities observed in this recent war do raise serious questions about the effectiveness of tactical air power. . . . [T]he price we would have to pay with the weaponry we have in hand doing our job against a well-equipped ground force would be unacceptably high." Another letter directed to General Brown noted the problems faced in Vietnam would be far worse against the Soviets. "Projecting the Southeast Asia kill ratios into a mid-intensity European conflict environment magnifies the problem of gaining and maintaining air superiority." The debacle in Vietnam was evidence of America's air forces not being well prepared for any modern air war, let alone that of a "limited conflict."[13]

Although modeled on a Soviet threat, the lessons from Vietnam found their way into this training environment. The US Army established the National Training Center (NTC) at Fort Irwin. All of these programs, courses, and exercises exist in 2020 and, though modified through trial, error, and experience, continue to train new generations of American soldiers, sailors, airmen, and marines in the American style of warfare. That being said, it is useful to take a brief look at the other participants in the "American War."

Vietnam

On April 21, 1975, Nguyen Van Thieu fled South Vietnam. Five days later, depending on the perspective of the individual, Saigon either *fell* or was *liberated*, and this cemented the defeat of American policy aims of limiting the spread of communism in the region. The day before the fall of the city, a photographer snapped a picture of an American UH-1 Huey on the roof of 22 Gia Long Street as long lines of evacuees attempted to climb aboard. Dozens of individuals stretched back down a staircase with no hope of leaving the city with the Americans. On board the aircraft carrier USS *Okinawa*, sailors pushed helicopters over the side of the ship to clear deck space for more arriving helicopters. Perhaps no better image represented the promise and failure of American air power in the war than these helicopters, the lifeblood of the army in the field, the most iconic of air power images during Vietnam, being dumped unceremoniously into the sea.

In 1995, the United States and Vietnam normalized diplomatic relations for the first time. By the early 2000s, American naval ships were once again docking at Da Nang and Cam Ranh Bay for the first time since America departed the region in 1975. President Barack Obama visited the country in 2016 and lifted the bans on the sale of US weapons to the country. With a rising China, Vietnam and the United States found a closer working relationship. There is also a growing industry of US veterans returning to the country to study the battlefields they once served on, like World War II veterans returning to Europe. In May of 2019, veterans returned and climbed Hamburger Hill. In 2012, the former chief of staff of the USAF, Merrill McPeak, traveled to and documented a visit to Laos and Vietnam in search of the remnants of the Ho Chi Minh Trail.[14]

Cambodia, Laos, and Thailand

In 1975 war broke out between Cambodia and Vietnam. Vietnam moved into the Khmer Rouge–controlled area of Kampuchea. Fighting continued from 1975 until 1979, when Vietnam invaded, occupied, and established a government in Cambodia: the People's Republic of Kampuchea. In 2020, the effects of American bombing continue to be felt in Laos, where less than 1 percent of un-exploded ordnance has been found. The country continues to hold the dubious honor of remaining the "most heavily bombed country in the world."[15]

Next to South Vietnam, Thailand supported the aims of the United States and housed the bulk of the US Air Force's assets at seven Royal Thai Air Force Bases. Over 80 percent of USAF strikes in North Vietnam flew out of a Royal Thai Air Force Base. A few years after the end of the war, the government of Thailand asked the US military to remove its entire presence from the country, and by June of 1976, no more US aircraft or personnel operated out of the country.

The Soviet Union

The Soviet Union, provider of surface-to-air missiles, air defense systems, and the Mikoyan-Gurevich Design Bureau aircraft to the North Vietnamese, learned its own hard lessons in the years after America left Southeast Asia.

In December 1979, Russia invaded Afghanistan and deposed its government with support from internal factions. The Soviet Union now embarked on its Vietnam and would, much like the Americans in Vietnam, lose 55,000 troops in Afghanistan fighting a war they were not tactically ready to fight. Into Afghanistan, the Soviet Union brought its superiority in numbers and technology against an unconventional foe. As Lester Grau noted in his translation of the Russian General Staff's report on the war, "The Soviet equipment was designed for a different war on different terrain. It failed to function optimally in the mountains and deserts of Afghanistan." This exact statement could be said of America's experience in Vietnam.[16]

A New Lost Cause

The US military did not operate two air forces during the Vietnam conflict, nor does it do so now. There was no "high-end" air force composed of fighters, fighter-bombers, and strategic bombers capable of peer-on-peer conflict with the Soviet Union and an equally sized "low-end" air force prepared for smaller conflicts. Sure, the USAF had these low-tech weapons, but moved beyond them in 1964 in a desire to ply their technological advancement against North Vietnam. The air force and the air arms of the other services used the same aircraft they would have used for war in Western Europe in the sky over the jungles, mountains, and deltas of Southeast Asia.

As mentioned in the introduction of this work, the statement—fervently believed by administration officials and senior military officers—"The dog we keep to lick the cat can lick the kittens too" proved to be incorrect, as the communist kittens, supported by the Soviet cat, demonstrated they were more than a match for American military strength abroad and political and public will at home. David Halberstam, author of *The Best and the Brightest*, noted that this was because of how America approached the war: "Their ability to calibrate this war was limited, their skills were tied to other wars in other places, and with very few exceptions they, like the French before them, tended to underestimate the bravery, strength, resilience, and the political dynamic which fed the indigenous force they were fighting."[17]

America lost Vietnam as surely as the Confederacy lost the Civil War, and just as happened back then, a Lost Cause ideology emerged among those who were defeated. The reason America lost, argued adherents to this ideology, was not found in a military defeat, but in political leadership that lacked the necessary will to do what needed to be done. It was noted that America never lost a large-scale battle during the entire conflict. As recently as 2011, then-president Barack Obama stated that the United States had "won every major battle" of the Vietnam War—"every single one." Perhaps most guilty in this regard were proponents of air power who, for the next generation, discussed what could have happened had the political leadership allowed it.

Stanley Karnow called the Vietnam conflict "a war that nobody won—a struggle between victims." The losses and damage that occurred in the United States, Cambodia, Laos, Thailand, and the now united Vietnam resonate today. Geographically, physically, and environmentally, the countries of Southeast Asia will continue to see and feel the effects of American air actions for generations to come.[18]

The losses suffered during the Vietnam War remain astounding. Beyond the 58,220 American service members killed in the conflict, there was also the cost of American machinery used to conduct the war. The USAF alone lost 2,257 aircraft in Southeast Asia between 1961 and 1973. These losses included 445 F-4 Phantom variants, enough for seventeen squadrons, as well as 397 F-105 Thunderchiefs. This represented 47 percent of the total F-105 fleet. So many F-105s were shot down that it led to the macabre joke, "Do you know what an optimist is? A Thud pilot who quits smoking."[19]

Furthermore, the bombing in South Vietnam was particularly ineffective. A 2016 study by Harvard, New York University, and the National Bureau of Economic Research took into account "discontinuities in quantitative ratings of hamlet security to identify the causal effects of bombing." This study concluded that "bombing increased the military and political activities of the communist insurgency, weakened local governance, and reduced noncommunist civic engagement. . . . A strategy emphasizing overwhelming firepower plausibly increased insurgent attacks and worsened attitudes towards the U.S. and South Vietnamese government." In other words, to the people of South Vietnam, the results could be summed up by the participant in an opening scene of the 1984 film *Ghostbusters*: "The effect? I'll tell you what the effect is; it's pissing me off."[20]

As recently as 2017, the idea of the failing of American bombing began to seep into the popular consciousness. Journalist Mark Bowden noted in a recent history of the Battle of Hue that "McNamara, the supreme quantifier, could no longer fight his own data. The numbers were in. Bombing had failed." It is beyond time for the American military—but those in the air arm, in particular—to reexamine what they believe about the Vietnam War and the efficacy of American bombing doctrine. A comforting explanation found its way into this new Lost Cause mentality—the invincibility of the American military on the field of battle. As one American military officer told a North Vietnamese counterpart, "You know . . . you never defeated us on the battlefield," to which the Communist officer replied, "That may be so, but it is also irrelevant."[21]

Appendix A: JCS 94-Target List

Target #	Target[1]
1	Na San airfield
2	Dien Bien Phu airfield
3	Hanoi/Gia Lam airfield [limited jet-capable] (plus petroleum, oil, lubricants [POL] storage 1965)
4	Dong Hoi airfield [limited jet-capable] (airfield closest to South Vietnam)
5	Vinh airfield [limited jet-capable]
6	Phuc Yen airfield [jet-capable] (plus NNE POL storage 1966)
7	Hanoi/Bac Mai airfield [limited jet-capable]
8	Haiphong/Cat Bi airfield [jet-capable] (plus POL storage 1965)
9	Haiphong/Kien An airfield [limited jet-capable] (plus POL storage 1965)
10	Ninh Binh railroad/highway bridge
11	Hai Duong railroad/highway bridge
12	Hanoi railroad/highway bridge (Red River)
13	Hanoi railroad/highway bridge (canal)
14	Thanh Hoa railroad/highway bridge
15	Viet Tri railroad/highway bridge (on Route 2: Hanoi—Lao Cai—Kunming, China)
16	Dap Cau railroad/highway bridge (on route from Hanoi to Chinese border)
17	Haiphong highway bridge (on Route 10: Haiphong to NE DRV and China)

Target #	Target[1]
18	Lang Son railroad/highway bridge
19	Yen Vien railroad yard
20	Hanoi railroad repair shops (Gia Lam)
21	Hanoi railroad yard/shops
22	Xuan Mai barracks SSW
23	Xuan Mai barracks NNW and headquarters
24	Chanh Hoa barracks SE and division headquarters
25	Son La barracks/supply depot/military region headquarters NW
26	Dien Bien Phu barracks
27	Unnamed barracks[2]
28	Ban Xom Lom barracks
29	Quang Suoi barracks NE
30	Hanoi military headquarters; North Vietnam air defense headquarters
31	Ha Dong barracks/supply depot
32	Vu Con barracks and supply depot
33	Dong Hoi barracks WNW (probable division headquarters)
34	Vinh Yen barracks/training area N
35	Son Tay barracks SW and supply depot
36	Vit Thu Lu barracks/storage area (guerrilla staging area)
37	Moc Chau barracks
38	Vinh barracks and headquarters military region IV
39	Chap Le barracks NW
40	Phu Qui ammunition depot SW
41	Phu Van ammunition depot E (major depot)
42	Phu Van POL storage and ammunition depot NE
43	Qui Hau ammunition depot W
44	Yen Bai ordnance depot
45	Haiphong ammunition depot SW (Kien An)
46	Ban Phieng Hay ammunition depot
47	Yen Son ordnance and ammunition depot
48	Haiphong POL storage (largest POL storage facility in North Vietnam)
49	Hanoi POL storage
50	Vinh POL storage
51	Nguyen Khe POL storage (Thach Loi)
52	Vinh supply depot E

Target #	Target[1]
53	Phu Van supply depot SE
54	Thien Linh Dong supply depot S
55	Vinh Son supply depot SW/SE
56	Phu Qui barracks/supply depot
57	Hanoi Ministry of National Defense/MZ Headquarters
58	Hanoi supply depot S/barracks
59	Hanoi supply depot N/barracks
60	Thai Nguyen supply depot N
61	Xom Chang barracks S
62	Van Dien supply depot/barracks
63	Thuan Chau barracks/supply depot
64	Xom Bang ammunition depot (supports Pathet Lao in Laotian panhandle)
65	Hanoi SAM support facility[3]
66	Hanoi international radio communications transmitter facility
67	Hanoi international radio communications receiver facility
68	Cam Pha Port (mine laying and bombing targets)
69	Hon Gai Port (mine laying and bombing targets)
70	Haiphong Port (mine laying and bombing targets)
71	Ben Thuy port facilities/transshipment center (mine laying and bombing targets)
72	Port Wallut naval base (mine laying and bombing targets)
73	Hanoi port facilities/Red River (mine laying and bombing targets)
74	Quang Khe Port approaches (mine laying area)
75	Viet Tri chemical plant (explosives)
76	Thai Nguyen iron and steel complex
77	Hanoi machine tool and engineering equipment plant
78	Haiphong phosphatic fertilizer plant (explosives)
79	Bac Giang chemical fertilizer plant (explosives)
80	Haiphong West thermal power plant
81	Hanoi thermal power plant
82	Uong Bi thermal power plant
83	Road/Rail Route 1 (Hamrong to Hanoi)
84	Road/Rail Route 1 (Hamrong to Hanoi)
85	Road/Rail Route 1 (Vinh to Hamrong)
86	Road/Rail Route 1 (Vinh to Hamrong)

Target #	Target[1]
87	Road/Rail Route 5 (Hanoi to Haiphong)
88	Road/Rail Route 5 (Hanoi to Haiphong)
89	Route 7 (Laos/North Vietnam border)
90	Route 8 (vicinity Nape, Laos to Roa Qua) (main supply route to Central Laos)
91	Route 12 (Laos/North Vietnam border to Xom Ma Na) (main supply route into southern Laos and South Vietnam)
92	Route 19
93	Route 6
94	Route Alternate to Route 6

Appendix B:
List of Project CHECO Reports

Report #	Title	Publication Date
1	CHECO–Abstract–History: War in Vietnam, 1961–1963	31-May-64
2	CHECO–Part I–Summary, Oct 1961–Dec 1963	31-May-64
3	CHECO–Part II–The Threat, Oct 1961–Dec 1963	31-May-64
4	CHECO–Part III–Political/Policy Influences, Oct 1961–Dec 1963	31-May-64
5	CHECO–Part IV–Command Structure/Relationships, Oct 1961–Dec 1963	31-May-64
6	CHECO–Part V–Air Operations, Oct 1961–Dec 1963	31-May-64
7	CHECO–Part VI–Support Activities, Oct 1961–Dec 1963	31-May-64
8	Southeast Asia Studies and Interviews by Joseph W. Grainger and Others	6-Jun-64
9	Expository Paper #1–Punitive Air Strikes	11-Mar-65
10	Expository Paper #2–Possible Communist Counter to Punitive Air Strikes	21-Apr-65
11	Expository Paper #3–CAS	18-May-65
12	First SAC B-52 Saturation Bombing in South Vietnam	29-Jun-65
13	BARREL ROLL 7	3-Jul-65
14	Escalation of the War in SEA, Jul–Dec 1964	15-Jul-65
15	First Test and Combat Use of the AC-47	8-Dec-65
16	Nguyen Cao Ky	14-Dec-65

Report #	Title	Publication Date
17	The Battle of Binh Gia, 27 Dec 1964–1 Jan 1965	27-Dec-65
18	The Siege of Plei Me, 19–29 Oct 1965	24-Feb-66
19	SILVER BAYONET, 9–28 Nov 1965	28-Feb-66
20	Operation HARVEST MOON, 8–18 Dec 1965	3-Mar-66
21	YANKEE TEAM, May 1964–Jun 1965	8-Mar-66
22	ROLLING THUNDER, Mar–Jun 1965	28-Mar-66
23	The Fall of A Shau	18-Apr-66
24	The Defense of Attopeu, 4–5 Mar 1966	16-May-66
25	The Defense of Lima Site 36, 17–19 Feb 1966	25-May-66
26	Operation BIRMINGHAM, 24 Apr–15 May 1966	29-Jun-66
27	Attack Against Tan Son Nhut, 13 Apr 1966	8-Jul-66
28	USAF Operations from Thailand, 1964–1965	10-Aug-66
29	US MiG Credits in Vietnam, Feb 1965–Aug 1966	18-Aug-66
30	TIGER HOUND	6-Sep-66
31	Operation HAWTHORNE, 2–21 Jun 1966	8-Sep-66
32	Night Interdiction in SEA	9-Sep-66
33	Operation MASHER and WHITE WING, 24 Jan–6 Mar 1966	9-Sep-66
34	Evolution of the ROE for Southeast Asia, 1960–1965	30-Sep-66
35	ARC LIGHT B-52 Strikes, Jun–Dec 1965	9-Oct-66
36	USAF Search and Rescue in SEA, 1961–1966	24-Oct-66
37	USAF Reconnaissance in SEA, 1961–1966	25-Oct-66
38	Operation TALLY HO	21-Nov-66
39	Operation EL PASO	30-Nov-66
40	Ammunition Problems in SEA, 1966	1-Dec-66
41	Command and Control, 1965	15-Dec-66
42	The War in Vietnam, 1965	25-Jan-67
43	Air Operations in the DMZ Area, 1966	15-Feb-67
44	Assault Airlift Operations	23-Feb-67
45	Air Tactics Against North Vietnamese Air/Ground Defenses	27-Feb-67
46	Tactical Airlift, Jul–Dec 1966	28-Feb-67
47	Control of Air Strikes in SEA, 1961–1966	1-Mar-67
48	Night Close Air Support in RVN, 1961–1966	15-Mar-67
49	Operation ATTLEBORO, 14 Sep–26 Nov 1966	14-Apr-67
50	Second Defense of Lima Site 36, 6–7 Jan 1967	28-Apr-67

Report #	Title	Publication Date
51	Operations THAYER and IRVING, 8 Sep 1966–12 Feb 1967	12-May-67
52	Operation ENTERPRISE, The Battle of Doi Ma Creek	24-May-67
53	Interdiction in SEA, 1965–1966	25-May-67
54	LUCKY TIGER Special Air Warfare Operations	31-May-67
55	LUCKY TIGER Combat Operations	15-Jun-67
56	ROLLING THUNDER, Jul 1965–Dec 1966	15-Jul-67
57	Operation HICKORY	24-Jul-67
58	Operation PAUL REVERE and SAM HOUSTON, 10 May 1965–5 Apr 1967	27-Jul-67
59	COMBAT SKYSPOT	9-Aug-67
60	USAF Posture in Thailand, 1966	28-Aug-67
61	ARC LIGHT, 1965–1966	15-Sep-67
62	Short Rounds, 1965–May 1967	28-Sep-67
63	Herbicide Operations in Southeast Asia, Jul 1961–Jun 1967	11-Oct-67
64	The War in Vietnam, 1966	23-Oct-67
65	USAF Operations from Thailand, Air Operations, 1966	31-Oct-67
66	Counterinsurgency in Thailand, 1966	8-Nov-67
67	Operation JUNCTION CITY, 22 Feb–14 May 1967	17-Nov-67
68	ROLLING THUNDER	17-Nov-67
69	Air-to-Air Encounters over North Vietnam, Jan–Jun 1967	30-Nov-67
70	Air Operations in the Delta, 1962–1967	8-Dec-67
71	Ambush at XT686576, 17 Oct 1967	29-Dec-67
72	Operation NEUTRALIZE, 12 Sep–31 Oct 1967	5-Jan-68
73	USAF Search and Rescue, Jul 1966–Nov 1967	19-Jan-68
74	CHECO Digest, Jan 1968	31-Jan-68
75	CHECO Digest, Feb 1968	27-Feb-68
76	ARC LIGHT, Jan–Jun 1967	22-Mar-68
77	CHECO Digest, Mar 1968	31-Mar-68
78	USAF Civic Action in the Republic of Vietnam, 1966–1967	1-Apr-68
79	The Pueblo Incident	15-Apr-68
80	The War in Vietnam, Jan–Jun 1967	29-Apr-68
81	The Pueblo Incident, 22 Jan–29 Feb 1968	15-May-68
82	Viet Cong Offensive in III Corps, Oct–Dec 1967	15-May-68
83	Air War in the DMZ, Jan–Aug 1967	20-May-68

Report #	Title	Publication Date
84	Battle for Dak To, 2–3 Nov 1967	21-Jun-68
85	Single Manager for Air in South Vietnam, Jan 1967–Apr 1968	1-Jul-68
86	Kham Duc, 10–14 May 1968	8-Jul-68
87	IGLOO WHITE, Initial Phase	31-Jul-68
88	Riverine Operations in the Delta, Feb 1966–Jun 1968	1-Aug-68
89	The Fall of Site 85	9-Aug-68
90	Air Response to the Tet Offensive, 30 Jan–29 Feb 1968	12-Aug-68
91	Short Rounds, Jun 1967–Jun 1968	23-Aug-68
92	Operation DELAWARE, 19 Apr–17 May 1968	2-Sep-68
93	Khe Sanh (Operation NIAGARA), 22 Jan–31 Mar 1968	13-Sep-68
94	Psychological Operations by USAF/VNAF in SVN, Jan 1965–Jun 1968	16-Sep-68
95	The EC-47 in SEA, May 1966–Jun 1968	20-Sep-68
96	Visual Reconnaissance in I Corps, Jan–Aug 1968	30-Sep-68
97	Organization, Mission, and Growth of the Vietnamese Air Force, 1949–1968	8-Oct-68
98	7 AF Tactical Air Control Center Operations, Nov 1967–May 1968	15-Oct-68
99	COLLEGE EYE, 4 Apr 1965–30 Jun 1968	1-Nov-68
100	USAF Operations from Thailand, Jan 1967–Jul 1968	20-Nov-68
101	EB-66 Operations in SEA, Jan–Dec 1967	26-Nov-68
102	The War in Vietnam, Jul–Dec 1967	29-Nov-68
103	The USAF Helicopter in SEA, 1961–1968	4-Dec-68
104	ECM and USAF Penetrations of NVN Air/Ground Defenses, 1966–1968	7-Dec-68
105	TRUSCOTT WHITE, Apr–Jun 1968	11-Dec-68
106	The Defense of Saigon, Nov 1967–Aug 1968	14-Dec-68
107	Attack on Udorn, 26 Jul 1968	27-Dec-68
108	The ABCCC in Southeast Asia, 2 Jan 1964–Oct 1968	15-Jan-69
109	Strike Control and Reconnaissance in SEA, 1962–1968	22-Jan-69
110	Operation THOR, 1–7 Jul 1968	24-Jan-69
111	VNAF FAC Operations in SVN, Sep 1961–Jul 1968	28-Jan-69
112	FAC Operations in Close Air Support Role in SVN, 1965–1968	31-Jan-69
113	Tactical Electronic Warfare Operations in SEA, 1962–1968	10-Feb-69

Report #	Title	Publication Date
114	Air Traffic Control in SEA, 1955–1969	14-Feb-69
115	Tactical Recon Photography Request/Distribution, 1966–1968	15-Feb-69
116	Impact of Darkness and Weather on Air Operations in SEA, 1965–1968	10-Mar-69
117	USAF Support of Special Forces in SEA, Nov 1961–Feb 1969	10-Mar-69
118	Enemy Capture/Release of USAF Personnel in SEA	15-Mar-69
119	USAF Civic Action in the Republic of Vietnam, 1968	17-Mar-69
120	Single Manager for Air in South Vietnam, May–Dec 1968	18-Mar-69
121	USAF Civic Action in Thailand, 1964–1968	22-Mar-69
122	USAF Posture in Thailand, 1967	25-Mar-69
123	COIN in Thailand, Jan 1967–Dec 1968	26-Mar-69
124	Control of Air Strikes, 1967–1968	30-Jun-69
125	Interdiction in Route Package One, 1968	30-Jun-69
126	Interdiction in SEA, Nov 1966–Oct 1968	30-Jun-69
127	Tactical Airlift Operations, Jan 1967–Dec 1968	30-Jun-69
128	7 AF Local Base Defense Operations, Jul 1965–Dec 1968	1-Jul-69
129	Air Response to Immediate Air Requests in SVN	15-Jul-69
130	Reconnaissance in SEA, Jul 1966–Jun 1969	15-Jul-69
131	USAF Search and Rescue, Nov 1967–Jun 1969	30-Jul-69
132	Air War in the DMZ, Sep 1967–Jun 1969	1-Aug-69
133	Command and Control, 1966–1968	1-Aug-69
134	III DASC Operations, Jul 1965–Dec 1968	1-Aug-69
135	IV DASC Operations, 1965–1969	1-Aug-69
136	USAF Support of Counterinsurgency in BARREL ROLL Area	1-Aug-69
137	ARC LIGHT, Jun 1967–Dec 1968	15-Aug-69
138	Short Rounds, Jun 1968–May 1969	15-Aug-69
139	TACC Fragging Procedures	15-Aug-69
140	Post-Pueblo USAF Actions–Korea/Japan, Jan 1968–Jan 1969	25-Aug-69
141	Air Tactics Against North Vietnamese Air/Ground Defenses, Dec 1966–Nov 68	30-Aug-69
142	Air to Air Encounters over North Vietnam, Jul 1967–Dec 1968	30-Aug-69
143	The Role of USAF Gunships in SEA, 1967–1969	30-Aug-69
144	Defense of Da Nang, Oct 1968–Apr 1969	31-Aug-69
145	Direct Air Support Centers in I Corps, Jul 1965–Jan 1969	31-Aug-69

Report #	Title	Publication Date
146	Interdiction in III Corps, CTZ, Project DART	31-Aug-69
147	Riverine Operations in the Delta, May 1968–Jun 1969	31-Aug-69
148	Rules of Engagement, Jan 1966–Nov 1969	31-Aug-69
149	The DASCs in II Corps Tactical Zone, Jul 1965–Jun 1967	31-Aug-69
150	Project RED HORSE, Sep 1965–Jun 1969	1-Sep-69
151	OV-10 Operations in SEA, Jul 1968–Jun 1969	15-Sep-69
152	ROLLING THUNDER, Jan 1967–Nov 1968	1-Oct-69
153	The Fourth Offensive, 23 Feb–3 Apr 1969	1-Oct-69
154	The Siege of Ben Het, May–Jun 1969	1-Oct-69
155	A Shau Valley Campaign, Dec 1968–May 1969	15-Oct-69
156	Jet Forward Air Controllers in SEA, 1967–1969	15-Oct-69
157	Tactical Control Squadron Operations in SEA, 1962–1969	15-Oct-69
158	Air Support of Counterinsurgency in Laos, Jul 1968–Nov 1969	10-Nov-69
159	Air Munitions in SEA, 1965–1969	15-Nov-69
160	USAF SAC Operations in Support of SEA	17-Dec-69
161	IGLOO WHITE, Jul 1968–Dec 1969	10-Jan-70
162	SEA Glossary, 1961–1970	1-Feb-70
163	USAF Posture in Thailand, 1968	1-Feb-70
164	USAF Posture in Thailand, COIN in Thailand, 1969	1-Feb-70
165	VNAF Improvement and Modernization Program, 1968–Apr 1970	5-Feb-70
166	Rescue at Ban Phanop, 5–7 Dec 1969	15-Feb-70
167	Air Support in Quang Ngai Province	25-Feb-70
168	The EC-121 Incident, 15 Apr 1969	15-Mar-70
169	The Air War in Vietnam, 1968–1969	1-Apr-70
170	Air Operations in Northern Laos, 1 Nov 1969–1 Apr 1970	5-May-70
171	Impact of Geography on Air Operations in SEA	11-Jun-70
172	Forward Airfields for Tactical Airlift in SEA	15-Jun-70
173	Army Aviation in RVN, A Case Study	11-Jul-70
174	USAF Aerial Port Operations	5-Aug-70
175	Tactical Air in Support of Ground Forces in Vietnam	1-Sep-70
176	The Cambodian Campaign, 29 Apr–30 Jun 1970	1-Sep-70
177	Second Generation Weaponry in SEA, 1966–1970	10-Sep-70
178	The EC-47 in SEA, Apr 1968–Jul 1970	12-Sep-70

Report #	Title	Publication Date
179	The Royal Laotian Air Force, 1954–1970	15-Sep-70
180	USAF Tactics Against Air & Ground Defenses in SEA, Nov 1968–May 1970	25-Sep-70
181	The RAAF in SEA, 1964–1970	30-Sep-70
182	COMMANDO VAULT	12-Oct-70
183	The Employment of Air by the Thais and Koreans in Southeast Asia, 1964–1970	30-Oct-70
184	Interdiction in Waterways and POL Pipelines	11-Dec-70
185	The Cambodian Campaign, Jul–Oct 1970	31-Dec-70
186	Air Operations in Northern Laos, 1 Apr–1 Nov 1970	15-Jan-71
187	Interdiction at Ban Bak, 19 Dec 1970–5 Jan 1971	26-Jan-71
188	Short Rounds and Related Incidents, Jun 1969–Dec 1970	15-Feb-71
189	The Defense of Dak Seang, 1 Apr–9 May 1970	15-Feb-71
190	Lam Son 719, The South Vietnamese Incursion in Laos, 30 Jan–24 Mar 1971	24-Mar-71
191	USAF Search and Rescue in SEA, Jul 1969–Dec 1970	23-Apr-71
192	Air Operations in Northern Laos, 1 Nov 1970–1 Apr 1971	3-May-71
193	Aerial Refueling in Southeast Asia, 1964–1970	15-Jun-71
194	USAF Civic Action in the Republic of Vietnam, Jan 1969–31 Mar 1971	19-Jun-71
195	COIN in Thailand, Jan 1969–Dec 1970	1-Jul-71
196	RANCH HAND Herbicide Operations in SEA, 1967–1971	13-Jul-71
197	The Royal Thai Air Force, 1911–1971	3-Sep-71
198	Local Base Defense in RVN, Jan 1969–Jun 1971	14-Sep-71
199	CHECO Report Summaries	15-Sep-71
200	Aerial Protection of Mekong River Convoys	1-Oct-71
201	Vietnamization of the Air War, 1970–1971	8-Oct-71
202	IGLOO WHITE, Jan 1970–Sep 1971	1-Nov-71
203	Psychological Operations: Air Support in SEA, Jun 1968–May 1971	1-Nov-71
204	The VNAF Air Divisions, Reports on Improvement and Modernization, Jan 1970–Jul 1971	23-Nov-71
205	USAF Tactical Reconnaissance in SEA, Jul 1969–Jun 1971	23-Nov-71
206	Fixed Wing Gunships in SEA, Jul 1969–Jul 1971	30-Nov-71
207	Attack on Cam Ranh, 25 Aug 1971	15-Dec-71
208	SEA Glossary, 1961–1971	1-Feb-72

Report #	Title	Publication Date
209	Evasion and Escape in SEA, 1964–1971	4-Feb-72
210	Tactical Airlift in SEA, Jan 1969–Nov 1971	15-Feb-72
211	Khmer Air Operations, Nov 1970–Nov 1971	15-Jun-72
212	COMMANDO HUNT VI, 15 May–31 Oct 1971	7-Jul-72
213	Short Rounds, 1971	15-Jul-72
214	USAF Control of Air Strikes in Support of Indigenous Lao Ground Forces	19-Jul-72
215	PROUD DEEP ALPHA	20-Jul-72
216	OV-1/AC-119 Hunter-Killer Team, Apr 1970–Nov 1971	10-Oct-72
217	The USAF Response to the Spring 1972 NVN Offensive: Situation and Redeployment, Mar–July 1972	10-Oct-72
218	Search and Rescue Operations in SEA, Jan 1971–Mar 1972	17-Oct-72
219	Kontum: Battle for the Central Highlands, 30 Mar–10 Jun 1972	27-Oct-72
220	PAVE MACE/COMBAT RENDEZVOUS, 1967–1972	26-Dec-72
221	Air Defense in Southeast Asia, 1945–1971	17-Jan-73
222	The Battle for An Loc, 5 Apr–26 Jun 1972	31-Jan-73
223	Base Defense in Thailand, 1968–1972	18-Feb-73
224	The 1972 Invasion of Military Region I: Fall of Quang Tri and Defense of Hue	15-Mar-73
225	Rules of Engagement, Nov 1969–Sep 1972	1-May-73
226	Air War in Northern Laos, 1 Apr–30 Nov 1971	22-Jun-73
227	MAP Aid to Laos, 1959–1972	25-Jun-73
228	BUFFALO HUNTER, 1970–1972	24-Jul-73
229	PAVE AEGIS Weapons System (AC-130E Gunship)	30-Jul-73
230	INK Development and Employment	24-Sep-73
231	LINEBACKER: Overview of the First 120 Days	27-Sep-73
232	Guided Bomb Operations in SEA: The Weather Dimension, 1 Feb–31 Dec 1972	1-Oct-73
233	Airlift to Besieged Areas, 7 Apr–31 Aug 1972	7-Dec-73
234	The F-111 in SEA, Sep 1972–Jan 1973	21-Feb-74
235	Air Operations in the Khmer Republic, 1 Dec 1971–15 Aug 1973	15-Apr-74
236	COMBAT SNAP (AIM-9J SEA Introduction)	24-Apr-74
237	The Bolovens Campaign, 28 Jul–28 Dec 1971	8-May-74

Report #	Title	Publication Date
238	Psychological Operations Against North Vietnam, Jul 1972–Jan 1973	24-May-74
239	USAF Quick Reaction Forces	20-Jun-74
240	Vietnamization of the Tactical Air Control System	23-Sep-74
241	The Air War in Laos, 1 Jan 1972–22 Feb 1973	15-Oct-74
242	Search and Rescue Operations in SEA, Apr 1972–Jun 1973	27-Nov-74
243	An Overview of Insurgency and Counterinsurgency in Thailand Through 1973, A Background Survey for Perspective and a Guide to the Literature	1-Jan-75
244	Drug Abuse in SEA	1-Jan-75
245	Southeast Asia Tactical Data Systems Interface	1-Jan-75
246	VNAF Improvement and Modernization Program, Jul 1971–Dec 1973	1-Jan-75
247	Joint Personnel Recovery in SEA	1-Sep-76
248	Rules of Engagement, Oct 1972–Aug 1973	1-Mar-77
249	Short Rounds, Jan 1972–Aug 1973	1-Nov-77
250	LINEBACKER Operations, Sep–Dec 1972	31-Dec-78
251	USAAG/7 AF in Thailand, Policy Changes and the Military Role, 1973–1975	27-Jan-79

Sources: AFHRA, Research Guide to the Contemporary Historical Examination of Current Operations (CHECO) Reports of Southeast Asia (1961–1975); Daniel S. Hoadley, "What Just Happened? A Historical Evaluation of Project CHECO," Thesis, School of Advanced Air and Space Studies, Air University, June 2013.

Note: I have included the complete list as an appendix for one reason: With the digitization of media, a large number of these reports can now be accessed online with a simple Internet search (although a handful remain classified and not as available), and as such, instant gratification might be available to those who choose to pursue further research.

Appendix C: List of Named Aerial Operations during the Vietnam War

Named Operation	Purpose	Location	Applicable Dates
Arc Light	B-52 CAS missions	Aircraft stationed at Guam and Thailand; bombing conducted in South Vietnam	1965–1973
Farm Gate	Advisory mission; early training of South Vietnam's Air Force	South Vietnam	1962–1965
Pierce Arrow	Retaliatory strikes after Gulf of Tonkin incident	North Vietnam	1964
Flaming Dart	Retaliatory strikes after attack at Camp Holloway	North Vietnam	1965
Rolling Thunder	Gradual bombing campaign to disrupt war-making effort and discourage North Vietnam aggression[1]	North Vietnam	1965–1968
Barrel Roll	Interdiction campaign along country border with South Vietnam	Laos	1964–1973
Steel Tiger	Interdiction campaign along country border with South Vietnam	Laos	1965–1968

Named Operation	Purpose	Location	Applicable Dates
Commando Hunt	Interdiction campaign along country border with South Vietnam	Laos	1968–1972
Menu (Breakfast, Lunch, Snack, Dinner, Dessert, and Supper)	B-52 operations in Cambodia against NVA	Cambodia	March 17, 1969– May 26, 1970
Patio	Fighter-bomber TACAIR operations	Cambodia	April–May 1970
Freedom Deal	Fighter-bomber TACAIR	Cambodia	May 1970 to August 1973
Igloo White	Sensor operation to detect movement along Ho Chi Minh Trail	North Vietnam, Laos, South Vietnam	1968–1973
Ranch Hand	Herbicide Operations	South Vietnam	1962–1971
Linebacker I	Strategic Bombing Campaign[2]	North Vietnam	May 9, 1972– October 23, 1972
Linebacker II	Strategic Bombing Campaign[3]	North Vietnam: Hanoi and Haiphong	December 18–29, 1972

Archival Collections[1]

US National Archives and Records Administration (NARA), Washington, DC

Logbooks of US Navy Ships and Stations, 1941–1983. Deck logs consist of chronological entries documenting the daily activities of a commissioned navy ship, unit, station, or other command. Information contained in the logs was often generated from the quartermaster's notebook, https://www.archives.gov/research/military/logbooks/navy-online. Including:

- USS *Forrestal*
- USS *Maddox*
- Pentagon Papers, "Report of the Office of the Secretary of Defense Vietnam Task Force," https://www.archives.gov/research/pentagon-papers

Richard Nixon Presidential Library

- Presidential Daily Diary
- H. R. Haldeman Diaries
- National Security Memoranda

Air Force Historical Research Agency (AFHRA), Maxwell Air Force Base, Alabama

The Air Force Historical Research Agency is the repository for US Air Force historical documents. The collection, begun in Washington, DC, during World

War II, moved in 1949 to Maxwell Air Force Base, the site of Air University, to provide research facilities for professional military education students, the faculty, visiting scholars, and the general public. It consists today of over 70 million pages devoted to the history of the service, and represents the world's largest and most valuable organized collection of documents on US military aviation.

- Aerial Victory Credits
- Project Trigger Files

Air Force Historical Support Division, Washington, DC, at Joint Base Anacostia-Bolling

The Air Force Historical Support Division (AFHSD) is part of the Air Force History and Museums Program. AFHSD is primarily the historical research and book writing element of the Air Force History program. Historians at AFHSD also provide historical information, analysis, and perspective to air force leaders and their staffs to support planning, policy development, and decision making. Although this office (formerly known as the Air Force Historical Studies Office [AFHSO]), has published numerous books, they also published fifty-five special studies, which were researched and written by historians working at the AFHSD during the 1960s and 1970s. The AFHSD was then known as the USAF Historical Division Liaison Office, and later, as the Office of Air Force History. The focus of twenty-six of these special studies and the impetus for the organization's creation was the air war in Southeast Asia, http://www.afhistory.af.mil.

Air Force Special Operations Command, Office of History

The Barksdale Global Air Power Museum, Barksdale AFB, Louisiana

Department of State (DOS), Office of Historian, Washington, DC

Foreign Relations of the United States (FRUS), the official documentary historical record of major US foreign policy decisions: FRUS, 1964–1968, Vietnam, Volumes I–VII.

National Museum of the US Air Force, Wright-Patterson Air Force Base, Ohio

Naval History and Heritage Command (NHHC)

Red Baron Reports (RBR)

US Air Force Academy, Clark Special Collections Branch, Colorado

Project CHECO Report Files (see appendix B).

US Navy History and Heritage Command, Washington, DC

US Navy's "Vietnam Command File, 1959–1973."

US Army Center of Military History, Washington, DC

Virtual Vietnam Archive, Vietnam Center and Archive, Texas Tech University[2]

By their own account, the Virtual Vietnam Archive currently "contains over 4 million pages of scanned materials. Types of material include documents, photographs, slides, negatives, oral histories, artifacts, moving images, sound recordings, maps, and collection finding aids. All non-copyrighted and digitized materials are available for users to download." All of their sources are on a by-nation basis, which is even more impressive given the size of their collection.

University of California at Riverside, Center for Bibliographical Studies and Research

University of Washington Southeast Asia Center

Vietnamese Sources

Bien phong, paper of the Vietnam Border Defense Force, "Introduction of the Book: The Aerial Battles in the Skies of Vietnam (1965–1975) Seen from Both Sides," http://www.bienphong.com.vn/gioi-thieu-cuon-sach-nhung-tran-khong-chien-tren-bau-troi-viet-nam-1965-1975-nhin-tu-hai-phia.

Vietnam State Records and Archives Department, Books

Nguyen Huu Oanh. *Dien Bien Phu Tren Khong: Suy Ngam Qua Chuyen Ke Cua Nhuoi Trong Cuoc*

Publications commemorating the victory of "Dien Bien Phu in the Air" (*Công bố các ấn phẩm kỷ niệm Chiến thắng "Điện Biên Phủ trên không"*), https://luutru.gov.vn/tin-tong-hop/cong-bo-cac-an-pham-ky-niem-chien-thang-%E2%80%9Cdien-bien-phu-tren-khong%E2%80%9D-1726-vtlt.htm.

Book launch: "The Aerial Battles in the Skies of Vietnam (1965–1975) Seen from Both Sides," https://luutru.gov.vn/tin-tong-hop/ra-mat-cuon-sach-%E2%80%9Cnhung-tran-khong-chien-tren-bau-troi-viet-nam-(1965-1975)-%E2%80%93-nhin-tu-hai-phia%E2%80%9D—2038-vtlt.htm.

Opening of the exhibition, "Defeating B-52s," https://luutru.gov.vn/tin-noi-bat/mo-cua-trien-lam-%E2%80%9Cdanh-thang-b-52%E2%80%9D.htm.

Notes

Introduction

1. Thomas C. Thayer, *War Without Fronts: The American Experience in Vietnam* (Boulder, CO: Westview Press, 1985), xxi; Sam Kinison, *Back to School*, film directed by Alan Metter (Los Angeles, CA: Orion Pictures, 1986).

2. The decision to break the air wars of Southeast Asia into six separate air wars is my own interpretation. A colleague of mine at the Smithsonian noted that they believe enough distinction exists for three separate air wars. Historian Mark Clodfelter places his count at four: In-Country, Out-Country (Laos, Cambodia, and North Vietnam), Strategic Air War against the North, and Nixon's Air War of 1972. I believe air power was executed in so disjointed a manner that the correct number is six. That is the author's story, and he's sticking to it.

3. Stanley Karnow, *Vietnam: A History* (New York: Penguin Books, 1997), 450; Clifford J. Rogers and Ty Seidule, senior editors, *The West Point History of Warfare*, vol. 7, http://www.westpointhistoryofwarfare.com/, USAFA H100-Introduction to Military History, Gregory A. Daddis, "American Escalation in Vietnam 1965–1967," chapter 29.6.

4. The two most famous works on the conflict in Vietnam are undoubtedly Neil Sheehan's *A Bright Shining Lie* (New York: Vintage Books, 1989) and Stanley Karnow's *Vietnam: A History*, the former using one man's experiences (John Paul Vann) to explain the conflict, the latter, the entirety of the conflict itself. For works focusing on the air war, begin with the Air Force History and Museums Programs books, including Earl H. Tilford's *Setup: What the Air Force Did in Vietnam and Why*, Jacob Van Staaveren's *Gradual Failure: The Air War over North Vietnam 1965–1966*, Bernard Nalty's *Air War Over South Vietnam, 1968–1975*, and Wayne Thompson's *To Hanoi and Back: The USAF and North Vietnam, 1966–1973*. The most famous

academic work on air power in Vietnam is Mark Clodfelter's *The Limits of Air Power: The American Bombing of North Vietnam* (Lincoln, NE: Bison Books, 2006).

5. For the US Navy's operations during Vietnam there is *Launch the Intruders: A Naval Attack Squadron in the Vietnam War, 1972* by Carol Reardon; John Darrell Sherwood's *Afterburner: Naval Aviators in the Vietnam War*; and *Rampant Raider: An A-4 Skyhawk Pilot in Vietnam* by Stephen Roberts Gray. Sherwood also produced the US Navy's official history: *Nixon's Trident Naval Power in Southeast Asia, 1968–1972*. For more popular books telling the USAF side of events, see *Bury Us Upside Down*, *Thud Ridge*, *Palace Cobra*, *When Thunder Rolled*, and *Vietnam above the Treetops*. Perhaps the most popular in recent years is the aptly named autobiography of Robin Olds, *Fighter Pilot*. Marshall Michel's *Clashes: Air Combat Over North Vietnam, 1965–1972* remains the quintessential read on the air-to-air war, and includes both navy and air force actions. There is also Randy "Duke" Cunningham's *Fox Two: The Story of America's First Ace in Vietnam*. Other books published in recent years include *The Phantom Vietnam War*, *Phantom in the Sky: A Marine's Backseat View of the Vietnam War*, and *Sherman Lead: Flying the F-4D Phantom II in Vietnam*.

6. One such book that makes this claim is *MiG Aces of the Vietnam War* by Hungarian Air Force officer Istvan Toperczer. Another is Stephen Coonts and Barrett Tillman's *Dragon's Jaw: An Epic Story of Courage and Tenacity in Vietnam*, which supposedly used "untapped Vietnamese sources." However, it's important to note that footnotes in both of these books do not indicate specific sources from any Vietnamese archives. Richard Boniface's *MiGs Over North Vietnam* relies on interviews conducted by the author, but as of publication of this work, there remains no comprehensive study of the air war from the perspective of North Vietnam. Marshall L. Michel's *The 11 Days of Christmas* does provide some Vietnamese sources, including newspapers and manuscripts, but there is no way to track down the latter.

7. Luu Trong Lan, *The Christmas Bombing—Dien Bien Phu in the Air: A Triumph of Vietnamese Will and Intelligence* (Hanoi, Vietnam: Gioi Publishers, 2004); this endnote serves as a plea for an academic interested in air power and the Vietnam War to undertake the study of Vietnamese. Merle Pribbenow, *Victory in Vietnam: The Official History of the People's Army of Vietnam, 1954–1975* (Lawrence: University Press of Kansas, 2002), xvii–xviii. Merle Pribbenow's *Victory in Vietnam* was originally published as *History of the People's Army of Vietnam, Vol. II: The Maturation of the People's Army of Vietnam during the Resistance War against the Americans to Save the Nation* (*Lich su Quan doi Nhan dan Viet Nam, Tap II: Thoi Ky Truong Thanhcua Quan Doi Nhan Dan Viet Nam trong cuoc Khang Chien Chong My, Cuu Nuoc* 1954–1975) by the Military History Institute of Vietnam, Ministry of Defense, People's Army Publishing House.

8. David W. Blight, *Race and Reunion: The Civil War in American Memory* (Cambridge, MA: Belknap Press/Harvard University Press, 2002), 258, 261.

9. Gary W. Gallagher and Alan T. Nolan, eds., *The Myth of the Lost Cause and Civil War History* (Bloomington: Indiana University Press, 2000), 1.

10. Marshall L. Michel, *The 11 Days of Christmas: America's Last Vietnam Battle* (New York: Encounter Books, 2001), 234. In addition to being a noted historian on

Vietnam, Michel also flew over three hundred combat missions in the F-4 Phantom during the Vietnam War.

11. Edward Kaplan, *To Kill Nations: American Strategy in the Air–Atomic Age and the Rise of Mutually Assured Destruction* (Ithaca, NY: Cornell University Press, 2015), 137.

Chapter 1: Getting Involved

1. The South Vietnam Air Force (VNAF) was, in Vietnamese, the *Không lực Việt Nam Cộng hòa* (KLVNCH). For the sake of simplicity, I have used "VNAF" for South Vietnam Air Force and "NVAF" for North Vietnam Air Force. It was not until unification in 1975 that both air forces became the *Không quân Nhân dân Việt Nam*, or Vietnam People's Air Force (VPAF).

2. "Agreement on the Cessation of Hostilities in Viet-Nam," July 20, 1954, Article 17, paragraph (a), retrieved from https://www.mtholyoke.edu/acad/intrel/genevacc .htm on April 8, 2020; Frank Futrell, *The United States Air Force in Southeast Asia: The Advisory Years to 1965* (Washington, DC: Office of Air Force History, 1981), 79–80. The air force also used modified T-28s and C-47s.

3. Robin Williams, *Good Morning, Vietnam*, film directed by Barry Levinson (Los Angeles, CA: Touchstone Pictures, 1987). For clarity's sake I have chosen to use the more-familiar "VC" rather than "NLF."

4. Project CHECO, Southeast Asia Report, #58, "The Threat: October 1961–December 1963," May 1964, 1–3, 9; Sheehan, *A Bright Shining Lie*.

5. Daniel S. Hoadley, "What Just Happened? A Historical Evaluation of Project CHECO," School of Advanced Air and Space Studies, 2013; Project CHECO, Southeast Asia Report, #241, "The VNAF Air Division's Reports on Improvement and Modernization," November 23, 1971, ii; AFHRA, "Research Guide to Contemporary Historical Examination of Current Operations (CHECO)," Reports of Southeast Asia (1961–1965). Because these reports remain the single greatest original source documents on the various air wars and operations, they are quoted extensively throughout this work. A complete list of all reports can be found in appendix B.

6. Project CHECO, Southeast Asia Report, #58, 1–3, 9.

7. Futrell, *The United States Air Force in Southeast Asia: The Advisory Years to 1965*, 79.

8. Project CHECO, Southeast Asia Report, #58, 1–3; McNamara made these statements at an SECDEF conference held at Pacific Command on December 16, 1961.

9. Project CHECO, Southeast Asia Report, #78, "Control of Air Strikes in SEA, 1961–1966," March 1967, 4.

10. Project CHECO, Southeast Asia Report, #187, "Evolution of the Rules of Engagement for Southeast Asia," September 1966, 1; A. J. C. Lavalle, ed., USAF Southeast Monograph Series, Vol. III, Monographs 4 and 5; A. J. C. Lavalle, *The Vietnamese Air Force, 1951–1975: An Analysis of Its Role in Combat and Fourteen Hours at Koh*

Tang (Washington, DC: Office of Air Force History, 1985), 8; Project CHECO, Southeast Asia Report, #79, "Control of Air Strikes in SEA 1961–1968," March 1, 1967, 8.

11. Project CHECO, Southeast Asia Report, #187, 3–5.

12. Project CHECO, Southeast Asia Report, #78, 6.

13. Project CHECO, Southeast Asia Report, #78, 10; Lavalle, *The Vietnamese Air Force, 1951–1975*, 4–5.

14. Project CHECO, Southeast Asia Report, #187, 8.

15. Lyndon Johnson Oral History Collection at the Miller Center for Public Affairs, University of Virginia, General Curtis LeMay, June 28, 1971, 26–27.

16. Lyndon Johnson Oral History Collection at the Miller Center for Public Affairs, University of Virginia, General Joseph McConnell, August 28, 1969, 16.

17. Leon Goure, "Southeast Asia Trip Report, Part I: The Impact of Air Power in South Vietnam" (Santa Monica, CA: RAND, December 1964), RM–4400–PR (Part 1). The RAND (Research and Development) Corporation is an American think tank which provides research studies to the US military.

18. Goure, "Southeast Asia Trip Report, Part I," v–vi.

19. Sheehan, *A Bright Shining Lie*, 94.

20. William A. Buckingham, *Operation Ranch Hand: The Air Force and Herbicides in Southeast Asia, 1961–1971* (Washington, DC: Office of Air Force History, 1982), 199–201.

21. Project CHECO, Southeast Asia Report, #187, 16.

22. Air force units fell under the Commander in Chief, Pacific Air Forces (CINCPACAF), headquartered in Hawaii, which included the 13th Air Force and the newly established 2nd ADVON (Advanced Echelon), which later became the 2nd Air Division, reporting directly to the commander of MACV. The 2nd Air Division served two masters, the commander of MACV and CINCPACAF, and remained the senior air force organization in-theater until April of 1966 and the establishment of the 7th Air Force. For simplicity's sake, I have only mentioned the more-familiar 7th Air Force above. Futrell, *The United States Air Force in Southeast Asia: The Advisory Years to 1965*, 99.

23. Mark Moyar, *Triumph Forsaken: The Vietnam War, 1954–1965* (New York: Cambridge University Press, 2006), 276.

24. Department of State (DOS), Foreign Relations of the United States (FRUS), Vietnam, Vol. I, #278, 611.

25. DOS, FRUS, Vietnam, Vol. I, #388, 848.

26. DOS, FRUS, Vietnam, Vol. I, #393, 873; #396, 876.

27. AFHSO, USAF Statistical Review, 1965, https://www.afhistory.af.mil/USAF -STATISTICS, 35, 39.

28. According to the research guide compiled by the Air Force Historical Research Agency, the CHECO acronym initially stood for Contemporary Historical Evaluation of Counterinsurgency Operations. It was later changed to Contemporary Historical Evaluation of Combat Operations, and finally, changed again to Contemporary Historical Examination of Current Operations.

29. Project CHECO Reports, Box 2, letter from Harris to McConnell, March 12, 1965, letter attached to first report.

30. Ibid.

31. Project CHECO, Southeast Asia Report, #9, "Expository Paper #1: Punitive Air Strikes," March 11, 1965, 1.

32. Project CHECO #169, "Possible Communist Counter to Punitive Air Strikes," April 1965, 7.

33. Lieutenant Colonel Dallas K. Stephens Sr., audio recording of letter, in author's collection. "Tie Me Kangaroo Down, Sport" by Rolf Harris had become a hit in Australia, the UK, and the United States in the early 1960s.

34. Stephens, audio recording, in author's collection.

35. Ibid.

36. Ibid.; "Norman Dale Eaton," Arlington Cemetery, http://www.arlington cemetery.net/ndeaton.htm, accessed September 20, 2019. Eaton's remains were located in 2007, returned to the United States, and interred at Arlington National Cemetery.

37. C. R. Anderegg, interview with author, October 5, 2016; 11210101001, Richard Hamilton Collection, Vietnam Center and Archive, Texas Tech University, 19, 41.

38. C. R. Anderegg interview, October 5, 2016; Terry L. Thorsen, *Phantom in the Sky: A Marine's Back Seat View of the Vietnam War* (Denton: University of North Texas Press, 2019), 174.

39. 11210101001, Richard Hamilton Collection, 43.

40. NARA, Pentagon Papers, 5890508, "Evolution of the War: Air War in the North: 1965–1968," Vol. I, 1.

41. NARA, Pentagon Papers, 5890508, 2.

42. Project CHECO, Southeast Asia Report, #9, 12.

43. Naval History and Heritage Command (NHHC), "Bombing as a Policy Tool in Vietnam: A Staff Study Based on the Pentagon Papers," Committee on Foreign Relations, US Senate, October 12, 1972, https://www.history.navy.mil/research/library/online-reading-room/title-list-alphabetically/b/bombing-as-policy-tool-vietnam.html, accessed June 26, 2017.

Chapter 2: The War in the South: Buildup

1. Karnow, *Vietnam: A History*, 416.

2. This "dual-hatted" MACV deputy for air operations was initially also the commander of the 2nd Air Division. This lasted until 1966, when the air division was inactivated and 7th Air Force activated. Thus, Moore became the first commander of 7th Air Force, but also the last commander of the 2nd Air Division.

3. Carl Berger, ed., *The United States Air Force in Southeast Asia, 1961–1973: An Illustrated Account* (Washington, DC: Office of Air Force History, 1984), 80, 342.

4. John Andreas Olsen, ed., *Air Commanders* (Washington, DC: Potomac Books, 2012), 225; William W. Momyer, *Airpower in Three Wars (WWII, Korea, Vietnam)* (Maxwell AFB, AL: Air University Press, 2003), 73; "General William Wallace Momyer," Official US Air Force biography, http://www.af.mil/AboutUs/Biographies/Display/tabid/225/Article/106156/general-william-wallace-momyer.aspx, retrieved on February 2, 2017; Buckingham, *Operation Ranch Hand*, 206.

5. Olsen, *Air Commanders*, 238–39; Gregory A. Daddis, *Westmoreland's War: Reassessing American Strategy in Vietnam* (New York: Oxford University Press, 2014), 96. SAC's control of aircraft also extended to KC-135 refueling aircraft.

6. Mrozek, Donald J. *Air Power and the Ground War in Vietnam* (Maxwell AFB, AL: Air University Press, 1988), 23.

7. Ian Horwood, *Interservice Rivalry and Airpower in the Vietnam War* (Fort Leavenworth, KS: Combat Studies Institute Press), 4.

8. As far back as 1942–1943, US Army publications indicated that air power was "co-equal" with the ground component. FM–100–20.

9. Peter B. Mersky, *U.S. Marine Corps Aviation Since 1912* (Annapolis, MD: Naval Institute Press, 2009), 201.

10. One of the most confusing aspects of command and control of aircraft during the Vietnam War was the relationship between the 7th and 13th Air Force. The deputy to the commanders of both 7th and 13th was the same individual throughout the Vietnam War. At the outset of the conflict, 13th AF was the senior organization, but as forces flowed into the country and 7th Air Force grew in size, it became the dominant organization. The 13th AF wings were stationed in Thailand and the 7th AF in South Vietnam. Since 7th AF was responsible for control of tactical air strikes, this book principally discusses the commander of 7th AF. John T. Cornell, editor of *Air Force* magazine, noted that "[w]hen US fighters from bases in Thailand were in the air, they belonged to 7th Air Force in Saigon. When they were on the ground, they belonged to 13th Air Force in the Philippines." John T. Correll, "Disunity of Command," *Air Force* magazine, January 1, 2005, https://www.airforcemag.com/article/0105disunity, retrieved July 2, 2020.

11. During Vietnam the HU-1A became the UH-1A, a designation employed by US Army rotary-wing assets today. Dozens of variants of the UH-1 saw service during the Vietnam conflict.

12. William Mitchell, *Winged Defense* (Mineola, NY: Dover Publications, 2006) xii.

13. John T. Tolson, *Airmobility: 1961–1971* (Washington, DC: Department of the Army, US Government Printing Office, 1999), 15; Warren A. Trest, *Air Force: Roles and Missions* (Washington, DC: Air Force History and Museums Program, 1998), 195.

14. Tolson, *Airmobility: 1961–1971*, 20, 24.

15. George L. MacGarrigle, *Combat Operations: Taking the Offensive, October 1966–October 1967* (The United States Army in Vietnam) (Washington, DC: US Army Center for Military History, 1998), 11.

16. Tolson, *Airmobility: 1961–1971*, 26–27.

17. Ibid., 253.

18. Berger, ed., *The United States Air Force in Southeast Asia, 1961–1973*, 40; 673 Air Base Wing, Office of History, "A Brief History of the 3rd Wing," no date, retrieved from https://www.jber.jb.mil/Portals/144/units/3wg/PDF/3wg-lineage.pdf, March 1, 2020.

19. AFA, "The US Air Force in the Vietnam War," 18.

20. Marcelle S. Knaack, *Encyclopedia of US Air Force Aircraft and Missile Systems, Volume I: Post–World War II Fighters* (Washington, DC: Office of Air Force History, 1978), 168.

21. Ibid., 176–78.

22. AFA, "The US Air Force in the Vietnam War," 11.

23. John Schlight, *Help from Above: Air Force Close Air Support of the Army 1946–1973* (Washington, DC: Air Force History and Museums Program, 2003), 324; Mark Clodfelter, *Fifty Shades of Friction: Combat Climate, B-52 Crews, and the Vietnam War* (Washington, DC: National Defense University Press, 2016), 6.

24. Schlight, *Help from Above*, 325–26.

25. Momyer, *Airpower in Three Wars*, 116.

26. Clodfelter, *Fifty Shades of Friction*, 7; John Schlight, *The War in South Vietnam* (Washington, DC: Air Force History and Museums Program, 1999), 52.

27. Schlight, *Help from Above*, 324.

28. Clodfelter, *Fifty Shades of Friction*, 7.

29. Ibid., 11.

30. Ibid., 11; Air Combat Command, Tactical Air Command Histories, 1965, Vol. 1, 793–94, 804; Brian Laslie, *The Air Force Way of War* (Lexington: University Press of Kentucky, 2015), 3.

31. AFA, "The US Air Force in the Vietnam War," 9–10.

Chapter 3: The War in the South: Close Air Support

1. 168300010685, Bud Harton Collection, Vietnam Center and Archive, Texas Tech University; 04111144008, Central Intelligence Agency Collection, Vietnam Center and Archive, Texas Tech University.

2. Clodfelter, *The Limits of Air Power*, 58.

3. Although the most well-known of the landing zones that day, X-Ray was one of five LZs for the American Cavalry and ARVN units, and was the farthest south. Moving north there was Columbus and Albany, both along the front of the Massif, and north of the Ia Drang River there was Gulf and Crook.

4. William Head, "A Re-Assessment of the Battle of Ia Drang Valley, 1965: The Role of Airpower, Heroic Soldiers, and the Wrong Lessons," *Virginia Review of Asian Studies*, Vol. 16 (2014), 30.

5. The US Army's G3 General Staff of the US I Field Force journal itself is held in the US National Archives and Records Administration (NARA) holdings, but copies can also be found at http://www.generalhieu.com/, retrieved August 19, 2019. Nguyen Van Hieu was an ARVN general stationed on the G3 staff at the time of the Ia Drang battle; the website is dedicated in his memory.

6. Nguyen Van Tin, "The Use of B-52 Strike in Ia Drang Campaign General Westmoreland's Best Kept Military Secret," February 19, 2016, retrieved from http://www.generalhieu.com/iadrang_westmoreland_best_kept_secret-2.htm on August 20, 2019.

7. Westmoreland quoted in Nguyen Van Tin, "The Use of B-52 Strike in Ia Drang Campaign."

8. Head, "A Re-Assessment of the Battle of Ia Drang Valley, 1965," 35; Project CHECO, Southeast Asia Report, #19, "Silver Bayonet," February 28, 1966, 2.

9. Project CHECO, Southeast Asia Report, #19, 4.

10. Ibid., 6.

11. Ibid., 10.

12. 16900101001, Merle Pribbenow Collection, Vietnam Center and Archive, Texas Tech University.

13. Head, "A Re-Assessment of the Battle of Ia Drang Valley, 1965," 51.

14. Thorsen, *Phantom in the Sky*, 174; Project CHECO, Southeast Asia Report, #23, "The Fall of A Shau," April 18, 1966, 1; "After Action Report: The Battle for A Shau," 1070309025, Glenn Helm Collection, Vietnam Center and Archive, Texas Tech University. The Nung Chinese originally lived in the North and closer to the border with China, but fled south after the 1954 Accords.

15. "After Action Report: The Battle for A Shau."

16. Project CHECO, Southeast Asia Report, #67, "Operation Junction City," November 17, 1967, viii–ix.

17. Project CHECO, Southeast Asia Report, #67, viii; MacGarrigle, *Combat Operations: Taking the Offensive*, 101.

18. Project CHECO, Southeast Asia Report, #67, v–vi, 3.

19. Ibid., 6.

20. Ibid., 7.

21. MacGarrigle, *Combat Operations: Taking the Offensive*, 133.

22. MacGarrigle, *Combat Operations: Taking the Offensive*, 73; Project CHECO, Southeast Asia Report, #93, "Khe Sanh"; Mrozek, *Air Power and the Ground War in Vietnam*, 78; Bernard C. Nalty, *Air Power and the Fight for Khe Sanh* (Washington, DC: Office of Air Force History, 1986), 19.

23. Project CHECO, Southeast Asia Report, #93, 2, 7.

24. Ibid., 5.

25. Ibid., 5, 23.

26. Ibid., 24.

27. National Museum of the United States Air Force (NMUSAF), "OPERATION NIAGARA: A Waterfall of Bombs at Khe Sanh," retrieved from https://www.nationalmuseum.af.mil/Visit/Museum-Exhibits/Fact-Sheets/Display/Article/195674/operation-niagara-a-waterfall-of-bombs-at-khe-sanh on August 23, 2019.

28. Project CHECO, Southeast Asia Report, #93, 24; AFHSO, Jacob Van Staaveren, "The Air Force in Southeast Asia: Toward a Bombing Halt," 1968, 11.

29. Project CHECO, Southeast Asia Report, #93, 12.

30. AFHSO, Van Staaveren, "The Air Force in Southeast Asia," 9.

31. Ibid., 13.

32. Project CHECO, Southeast Asia Report, #90, "Air Response to the Tet Offensive," August 12, 1968, 2.

33. Nalty, *Air War Over South Vietnam*, 13; Project CHECO, Southeast Asia Report, #90, 9; Peter B. Mersky, *U.S. Marine Corps Aviation Since 1912*, 232; William Momyer, Airpower in Three Wars, 351, 354

34. Project CHECO, Southeast Asia Report, #90, 9; Bernard C. Nalty, *Air War Over South Vietnam, 1968–1975* (Washington, DC: Air Force History and Museums Program, 2000), 19.

35. Mersky, *U.S. Marine Corps Aviation Since 1912*, 226; Schlight, *The War in South Vietnam*, 282; Nalty, *Air War Over South Vietnam*, 13; Project CHECO, Southeast Asia Report, #90, 33.

36. Nalty, *Air War Over South Vietnam*, 24.

37. John Schlight, *A War Too Long: The History of the USAF in Southeast Asia, 1961–1975* (Washington, DC: Air Force History and Museums Program, 1996), 43.

38. Berger, ed., *The United States Air Force in Southeast Asia, 1961–1973*, 56.

39. Schlight, *A War Too Long*, 43; Project CHECO, Southeast Asia Report, #90, 10, 28, 59.

40. Berger, ed., *The United States Air Force in Southeast Asia, 1961–1973*, 56.

41. Project CHECO, Southeast Asia Report, #86, "Kham Duc," July 8, 1968, 3, 16; Alan L. Gropman, *Airpower and the Airlift Evacuation of Kham Duc* (Washington, DC: Office of Air Force History, 1985), 4.

42. "Excerpts from Sitreps Pertaining to Action at Kham Duc," Support Document from Project CHECO Report #129, No Date, Folder 1037, Box 0004, Vietnam Archive Collection, Vietnam Center and Archive, Texas Tech University, accessed May 17, 2017, http://www.vietnam.ttu.edu/virtualarchive/items.php?item=F0311000 41037.

43. Gropman, *Airpower and the Airlift Evacuation of Kham Duc*, 6.

44. Project CHECO, Southeast Asia Report, #86, 5; "Excerpts from Sitreps Pertaining to Action at Kham Duc"; Mrozek, *Air Power and the Ground War in Vietnam*, 141–42; Gropman, *Airpower and the Airlift Evacuation of Kham Duc*, 9.

45. "Excerpts from Sitreps Pertaining to Action at Kham Duc."

46. Gropman, *Airpower and the Airlift Evacuation of Kham Duc*, 25; Nalty, *Air War Over South Vietnam, 1968–1975*, 106.

47. Project CHECO, Southeast Asia Report, #86, 13–14.

48. Ibid., 17.

49. Gropman, *Airpower and the Airlift Evacuation of Kham Duc*, 53.

50. There is a discrepancy about when the CCT team arrived at Kham Duc. An official USAF history, *Airpower and the Airlift Evacuation of Kham Duc*, indicated they arrived on the 10th, but the CHECO report, written in the immediate aftermath of the battle, said they disembarked the final C-130. I have chosen to go with that source. Project CHECO, Southeast Asia Report, #86, 19–20.

51. Fred Smith, interview with author, April 21, 2017.

52. Project CHECO, Southeast Asia Report, #86, 7.

53. Ibid., vi.

54. Mrozek, *Air Power and the Ground War in Vietnam*, 142.

55. Nalty, *Air War Over South Vietnam*, 141.

56. Nalty, *Air War Over South Vietnam*, 333–34; Rebecca Grant, "Linebacker I," *Air Force Magazine*, June 2012, 72.

57. Nalty, *Air War Over South Vietnam*, 358.

58. Daddis, *Westmoreland's War*, 97.

59. Richard Hallion, "America as a Military Aerospace Nation," in John Andreas Olsen, ed., *Airpower Applied* (Annapolis, MD: Naval Institute Press, 2017), 63; AFHRA, General John D. Ryan files, 168.7085, folder 61.

Chapter 4: "To Deter Hanoi . . .": The War in the North

1. James N. Eastman Jr., et al., *Aces and Aerial Victories 1965–1973* (Washington, DC: Office of Air Force History, 1976), 19.

2. NHHC, "Bombing as a Policy Tool in Vietnam"; AFHRA, Air War College Report No. 3634, "Target Selection Process: Categories and Decision Levels," by Lt. Col. William E. Long, April of 1968, IRIS 01103665, 3. The NVAF and Vietnam People's Air Force (VPAF) are often used interchangeably. Since most American documents use NVAF, I have chosen to use those initials throughout.

3. Ed Rasimus, *When Thunder Rolled: An F–105 Pilot over North Vietnam* (Washington, DC: Smithsonian Books, 2003), 26–27.

4. This is maximum takeoff weight for an F-4; empty weight was 30,328 pounds. See Knaack, *Encyclopedia of US Air Force Aircraft and Missile Systems, Vol. 1: Post–World War II Fighters*.

5. 11210101001, Richard Hamilton Collection, 37.

6. AMC Office of History, "Vietnam: The First Tanker War," retrieved from https://www.amc.af.mil/News/Article-Display/Article/147242/vietnam-the-first-tanker-war on August 30, 2019.

7. Rasimus, *When Thunder Rolled*, 59.

8. NARA, Pentagon Papers, 5890508, 34.

9. The 94 targets were first presented in JCSM 729–64 Appendix A, and discussed in FRUS, Vietnam, Vol. I, 719, note 7; Charles Tustin Kamps, "The JCS 94-Target List: A Vietnam Myth that Distorts Military Thought," *Aerospace Power Journal* (Spring 2001), 71.

10. AFHRA, Air War College Report No. 3634, 14; Kamps, "The JCS 94-Target List," 71.

11. DOS, FRUS 1964–1968, Vol. II, Vietnam, January–June 1965, #9, 18–19.

12. DOS, FRUS 1964–1968, Vol. II, Vietnam, January–June 1965, #306, 670–71, 765.

13. DOS, FRUS 1964–1968, Vol. III, Vietnam, January–June 1965, #100, 670–71, 280.

14. Rostow quoted in Ben R. Rich and Leo Janos, *Skunk Works* (New York: Little, Brown and Company, 1994), 244–45. Rostow refers directly to the SR-71 Blackbird, although initially these reconnaissance flights were carried out by the CIA's A-12, until 1968, when the USAF's SR-71 took over these missions. The aircraft are often (if incorrectly) used interchangeably.

15. Graham A. Cosmas, *The Joint Chiefs of Staff and the War in Vietnam 1960–1968, Part 3* (Washington, DC: Office of Joint History, 2009), 3.

16. Perhaps apocryphal, the Johnson quote appears in William Westmoreland, *A Soldier Reports* (New York: Doubleday, 1976), 119; Admiral James L. Holloway III, USN (Ret.), "Tactical Command and Control of Carrier Operations," given at the Colloquium on Contemporary History, January 23, 1991, No. 4.

17. Momyer, *Airpower in Three Wars*, 188, 231, 233.

18. DOS, FRUS 1964–1968, Vol. III, Vietnam. January–June 1965, #100, 670–71; 281.

19. NARA, Pentagon Papers, 5890508, 36, 48–49.

20. Project CHECO, Southeast Asia Report, #231, "Linebacker: Overview of the First 120 Days," September 27, 1973, 2.

21. Ibid., 3.

22. Project CHECO, 1966 report quoted in Southeast Asia Report, #231, 3–4.

23. NARA, Pentagon Papers, 5890508, 42.

24. Rasimus, *When Thunder Rolled*, 57.

25. AFHRA, Richard S. Ritchie OHI, K239.0512–630, 71.

26. Jacob Van Staaveren, *Gradual Failure: The Air War over North Vietnam 1965–1966* (Washington, DC: Air Force History and Museums Program, 2002), 199–200.

27. AFA, "The US Air Force in the Vietnam War," 26.

28. NARA, Pentagon Papers, 5890508, 79; DOS, FRUS, 1964–168, Vol. IV, #41, 129.

29. NARA, Pentagon Papers, 5890508, 79.

30. NARA, Pentagon Papers, 5890508, 53–54.

31. DOS, FRUS, 1964–1968, Vol. V, Vietnam, #439, 1967, 1116.

32. McConnell quoted in AFHRA, Air War College Report No. 3634, 24.

33. E. L. Rabben and C. L. Beckel, "WSEG Staff Study 124: A Method for Finding Targets on the Ho Chi Minh Trail," Defense Documentation Center, June 1966, 2.

34. Ibid., 2, 11. An LOC is a line of communication that can include communication, transportation, and supply routes.

35. Don Shepperd, ed., *Misty: First-Person Stories of the F-100 Fast FACs in the Vietnam War* (1st Books Library, 2002), 3. The Misty FACs also proved to be notable for their members' later careers, including Bud Day, Merrill McPeak, Ronald Fogleman, and more; Merrill McPeak, *Hangar Flying* (Lake Oswego, OR: Lost Wingman Press, 2012), 278; CHECO #215, "Jet Forward Air Controllers in SEAsia," October 15, 1969, 1; Air Force Association (AFA), Misty Fast-FAC Panel, 2011; transcription in author's collection.

36. Shepperd, ed., *Misty: First-Person Stories*, 22–23; Project CHECO, Southeast Asia Report, #156, "Jet Forward Air Controllers in SEAsia," October 15, 1969, 1; AFA, Misty Fast-FAC Panel, 2011.

37. Interview with General Merrill McPeak, USAF (Ret.), September 30, 2016. Notes in author's collection.

38. AFA, Misty Fast-FAC Panel, 2011; Interview with General Merrill McPeak.

39. Aircraft needed at least one air-to-air refueling, but typically two refuelings over the trail during the day.

40. Rasimus, *When Thunder Rolled*, 71.

41. Rick Newman and Don Shepperd, *Bury Us Upside Down: The Misty Pilots and the Secret Battle for the Ho Chi Minh Trail* (New York: Presidio Press, 2007), 41–42, 303–04; George E. Day, *Return with Honor* (Mesa, AZ: Champlin Fighter Museum Press, 1989), 1, 35–36.

42. Project CHECO, Southeast Asia Report, #156, 8–9, 14.

43. 11210101001, Richard Hamilton Collection, 37–38; Rasimus, *When Thunder Rolled*, 40.

44. E-mail from "sparkies" to The CASBar, re: Where we came from before Wild Weasel, November 12, 1998, Folder 01, Box 03, Jan Churchill Collection, Vietnam Center and Archive, Texas Tech University, accessed June 9, 2017, https://www.vietnam.ttu.edu/virtualarchive/items.php?item=13550301065.

45. E-mail from "sparkies" to The CASBar, re: Where we came from before Wild Weasel.

46. Project CHECO, Southeast Asia Report, #69, "Air-to-Air Encounters Over North Vietnam, January 1–June 30, 1967," November 30, 1967, 5.

47. DOS, FRUS, 1964–1968, Vol. II, #318, 693–94.

48. Momyer, *Airpower in Three Wars*, 133.

49. DOS, FRUS, 1964–1968, Vol. III, #87, 240–43.

50. DOS, FRUS, 1964–1968, Vol III, #90, 253–57; Laslie, *Air Force Way of War*, 6; Van Staaveren, *Gradual Failure*, 165.

51. AFHSO Special Studies/Blue Books, Bernard C. Nalty, "Tactics and Techniques of Electronic Warfare: Electronic Countermeasures in the Air War Against North Vietnam, 1965–1973," 1977, 31–32.

52. 11210101001, Richard Hamilton Collection, 38; AFHSO, Nalty, "Tactics and Techniques of Electronic Warfare," 32–33.

53. Brief Report, Re: In-Country Clearance for Wild Weasel Aircraft [Best Quality], Support Document from Project CHECO Report #228, March 10, 1966, Folder 1109, Box 0012, Vietnam Archive Collection, Vietnam Center and Archive, Texas Tech University, accessed June 14, 2017, https://www.vietnam.ttu.edu/virtualarchive/items.php?item=F031100121109.

54. NHHC, COLL/20, FLAG PLOT/Vietnam, Box 123, Folder 2, "Wild Weasel."

55. AFHSO, Nalty, "Tactics and Techniques of Electronic Warfare," 40.

56. Message, Re: Wild Weasel/Iron Hand Tactics [Best Quality], Support Document from Project CHECO Report #228, 09 December 1966, Folder 1142, Box 0012, Vietnam Archive Collection, Vietnam Center and Archive, Texas Tech University, accessed June 14, 2017, https://www.vietnam.ttu.edu/virtualarchive/items.php?item=F031100121142.

57. Van Staaveren, *Gradual Failure*, 196–97.

58. NHHC, COLL/20, FLAG PLOT/Vietnam, Box 123, Folder 2, "AGM–45 SHRIKE Missiles."

59. AFHSO, Nalty, "Tactics and Techniques of Electronic Warfare," 44.

60. Muir S. Fairchild Research and Information Center (MSFRIC), Fairchild Documents, "SEA Tactics Review Brochure, Vol. I," 1.

61. DOS, FRUS, Vol. III, #142, 389; #148, 404.

62. DOS, FRUS, Vol. III, #142, 408.

63. Air University Library, "SEAsia Tactics Review Brochure," April 1973, 1.

64. Ibid., 3.

65. AFHRA, Air War College Report No. 3634, 2, 4.

66. Ibid., 4.

67. Project CHECO, Southeast Asia Report, #231, 6.

68. John D. Sherwood, *Nixon's Trident: Naval Power in Southeast Asia, 1968–1972* (Washington, DC: Naval History and Heritage Command, 2009), 23.

69. Interview with Colonel C. R. Anderegg, October 5, 2016; ACC, TAC Files, "SEA Tactics Review Brochure," Vol. I, 1973, 4.

70. Project CHECO, Southeast Asia Report, #231, 9.

71. Ibid., 19–22.

72. Knaack, *Encyclopedia of US Air Force Aircraft and Missile Systems, Vol. 1: Post–World War II Fighters*, 229, 232; Project CHECO, Southeast Asia Report, #250, "Linebacker Operations: September–December 1972," December 31, 1978, 38. Although the F-111 was known widely as the Aardvark (possibly for its snout-like nose), the USAF did not officially give it the name Aardvark until its retirement.

73. Project CHECO, Southeast Asia Report, #250, 36.

74. Project CHECO, Southeast Asia Report, #250, 35; Colonel Coltman's and Captain Brett's remains were positively identified and interred at Arlington on April 3, 2002, and August 1, 2002, respectively.

75. TTU, Project CHECO Report #234, "The F-111 in Southeast Asia, September 1972–January 1973," February 21, 1974, 27.

76. Project CHECO, Southeast Asia Report, #250, 36.

77. Ibid., 37.

78. Shepperd, ed., *Misty: First-Person Stories*, 453.

79. Everett Alvarez Jr. and Anthony S. Pitch, *Chained Eagle: The True Heroic Story of Eight and One-Half Years as a POW by the First American Shot Down over North Vietnam* (New York: Donald I. Fine, Inc., 1989), 23–24; Karnow, *Vietnam: A History*, 388–89.

80. Interview with Fred Smith, April 21, 2017.

81. Ibid.

82. News 5 Cleveland, "How News of the *Apollo 11* Mission Made It to the POWs in the Hanoi Hilton," https://www.youtube.com/watch?v=gbObXyfFhJ4, retrieved on September 2, 2019.

83. John McCain, "John McCain: How Neil Armstrong Inspired a POW," *Washington Post*, September 13, 2012, https://www.washingtonpost.com/opinions/john-mccain-how-neil-armstrong-inspired-a-pow/2012/09/13/5bd707e2-fdc0-11e1-b153-218509a954e1_story.html, retrieved on September 27, 2019.

84. Alexander Zuyev, *Fulcrum* (New York: Warner Books, 1992), 211–12; Doyle McManus and Stephanie Grace, "Some Vietnam POWs May Be Alive in Russia," *Los Angeles Times*, June 16, 1992, retrieved on May 8, 2018, http://articles.latimes.com/1992-06-16/news/mn-472_1_vietnam-war.

85. DOS, FRUS, 1964–1968, Vol. V, Vietnam, 1967, 1117.

86. Ulysses S. G. Sharp, *Strategy for Defeat: Vietnam in Retrospect* (Novato, CA: Presidio Press, 1998), 270.

87. Antulio J. Echevarria II, *Reconsidering the American Way of War: US Military Practice from the Revolution to Afghanistan* (Washington, DC: Georgetown University Press, 2014), 142.

Chapter 5: The US Navy's Air War: An Attack Pilot's War

1. Stephen Howarth, *To Shining Sea: A History of the United States Navy, 1775–1991* (New York: Random House, 1991), 517.

2. Ibid., 516.

3. Ed Beakley, interview with author, February 15, 2017; Carol Reardon, *Launch the Intruders: A Naval Attack Squadron in the Vietnam War, 1972* (Lawrence: University Press of Kansas, 2005), xiv; Mersky, *U.S. Marine Corps Aviation Since 1912*, 221.

4. Reardon, *Launch the Intruders*, 305.

5. For USAF development and acceptance of F-4, see Knaack, *Encyclopedia of US Air Force Aircraft and Missile Systems*, 265; Rasimus*, When Thunder Rolled*, 57.

6. National Archives, Logbooks of US Navy Ships and Stations, 1941–1983, USS *Maddox*, July 1964.

7. James Stockdale quoted in Karnow, *Vietnam: A History*, 386.

8. Naval History and Heritage Command (NHHC), Tonkin Gulf Crisis, publicly released information, retrieved on June 23, 2017, List of Targets in North Vietnam Under Attack by Carrier Aircraft, August 4, 1964, https://www.history.navy.mil/research/library/online-reading-room/title-list-alphabetically/t/tonkin-gulf-crisis/publicly-released-information.html.

9. Ibid.

10. Thorsen, *Phantom in the Sky*, vii–viii.

11. NHHC, COLL/20, FLAG PLOT/VIETNAM, Box 13, Folder 1, "I1/6–PHUC YEN/MIGS STRIKES BY SAC."

12. NHHC, COLL/20, FLAG PLOT/Vietnam, Box 116, JCS to CINCPAC, April 13, 1965.

13. NHHC, COLL/20, FLAG PLOT/Vietnam, Box 123, SAM Sites Folder, "Message to CINPACFLT," August 28, 1967; Box 115, Folder 2.

14. NHHC, COLL/20, FLAG PLOT/VIETNAM, Box 123, SAM Sites Folder, CNO Message, August 31, 1966.

15. NHHC, COLL/20, FLAG PLOT/Vietnam, Box 115, Folder 2.

16. NHHC, COLL/20, FLAG PLOT/VIETNAM, Box 123, SAM Sites Folder, "Anti-SAM Tactics," September 27, 1967; "CNO to CINCPACFLT," September 5, 1967.

17. NHHC, COLL/20, FLAG PLOT/VIETNAM, Box 123, SAM Sites Folder, CINCPACFLT message, November 15, 1967.

18. NHHC, COLL/20, FLAG PLOT/Vietnam, Box 116, "Aircraft Loss Messages," May 23, 1967.

19. Ibid.

20. NHHC, COLL/20, FLAG PLOT/Vietnam, Box 115, "RT 55" folder, "Analysis of Air Operations in NVN."

21. NHHC, COLL/20, FLAG PLOT/VIETNAM, Box 123, SAM Sites Folder, "Estimate of SAM Resupply Rate," March 29, 1967.

22. NHHC, COLL/20, FLAG PLOT/Vietnam, Box 123, SAM Sites Folder, "Captured Material," May 30, 1967.

23. NHHC, COLL/20, FLAG PLOT/VIETNAM, Box 119, Phuc Yen Folder, "PAC-FLT INTSUM 93–67," September 30, 1967.

24. UCR, CBSR, "American Warplanes Drop Bombs on North Vietnam's Largest MiG Field," *Medera Tribune*, Vol. 76, No. 112, October 24, 1976, https://cdnc.ucr .edu/?a=d&d=MT19671024.2.8&e=————-en—20—1—txt-txIN————1, retrieved on June 24, 2019; NHHC, COLL/20, FLAG PLOT/VIETNAM, Box 119, Phuc Yen Folder, "SECRET/LIMDIS" message with no title; Rene J. Francillon, *Tonkin Gulf Yacht Club: US Carrier Operations off Vietnam* (Annapolis, MD: Naval Institute Press, 1988), 101–02.

25. Francillon, *Tonkin Gulf Yacht Club*, 35; AFHRA, "Aerial Victory Tables WWI, WWII, Korea, Vietnam, Database." The AFHRA is the official keeper of the USAF's Aerial Victory credits beginning in World War I through the last official air-to-air kill during Operation Allied Force in 1999.

26. NHHC, COLL/20, FLAG PLOT/VIETNAM, Box 201, MiG Engagements, lesson learned folder, May 9–10, 1968.

27. Ibid.

28. NHHC, COLL/20, FLAG PLOT/VIETNAM, Box 201, MiG Engagements, lesson learned folder, July 10, 1968; Edward J. Marolda, *By Sea, Air, and Land: An Illustrated History of the US Navy and the War in Southeast Asia* (Washington, DC: Naval Historical Center, 1994), 392; also available at https://www.history.navy .mil/research/library/online-reading-room/title-list-alphabetically/b/by-sea-air-land -marolda/enemy-aircraft-shot-down-by-naval-aviators-in-southeast-asia.html.

29. NHHC, COLL/20, FLAG PLOT/VIETNAM, Box 119, "A6 CHICOM Border Violation Folder," Memo for SECDEF.

30. NHHC, COLL/20, FLAG PLOT/VIETNAM, Box 119; Francillon, *Tonkin Gulf Yacht Club*, 125.

31. NHHC, COLL/20, FLAG PLOT/VIETNAM, Box 119, "A6 CHICOM Border Violation Folder," Naval Message transcript of Peking International Service news release.

32. National Archives, Logbooks of US Navy Ships and Stations, RG 24, NA ID: 594258, "USS *Forrestal* (CVA–59) July 7, 1967," retrieved on June 23, 2017, https:// catalog.archives.gov/search?q=%22Forrestal%20(CVA–59)%22&f.oldScope=online &f.level=fileunit&f.ancestorNaIds=594258&sort=naIdSort%20asc.

33. Francillon, *Tonkin Gulf Yacht Club*, 136. The fire aboard the USS *Enterprise* occurred while not "on-station" and instead began near Pearl Harbor in the lead-up to a TF-77 deployment.

34. Stephen R. Gray, *Rampant Raider: An A-4 Skyhawk Pilot in the Vietnam War* (Annapolis, MD: Naval Institute Press, 2017), 201.

35. Reardon, *Launch the Intruders*, xiv–xv.

36. NHHC, Histories, Naval Aviation Histories, "Report of the Air-to-Air Missile System Capability Review, July–November 1968 (aka, The Ault Report)," sections 1–4, 1, 8, retrieved on June 30, 2019, https://www.history.navy.mil/research/histories/naval-aviation-history/ault-report.html.

37. Ibid., 1.

38. Ibid., 2.

39. Ibid., 21. The USAF eventually solved this problem with the implantation of the "Designed Operational Capability (DOC) Statements" which assigned a primary and secondary mission set to each squadron and ensured that an air-to-air squadron comprised of F-4s would indeed be proficient at their primary mission.

40. NHHC, "Report of the Air-to-Air Missile System Capability Review," 21.

41. Ibid., 35.

42. Ibid., 37.

43. Dan Pedersen, *Top Gun: An American Story* (New York: Hachette Books, 2019), 144.

44. Rick Llinares and Chuck Lloyd, *Warfighters: The Story of the USAF Weapons School and the 57th Wing* (Atglen, PA: Schiffer Publishing, 1996), 141.

45. Pedersen, *Top Gun*, 162.

46. John Darrell Sherwood, *Nixon's Trident: Naval Power in Southeast Asia, 1968–1972*, Washington, DC: Naval History and Heritage Command, 2009, 77; Pedersen, *Top Gun*, 4–5. Dan Pedersen uses the number "644" for all naval aviators killed, wounded, or captured.

Chapter 6: Strategic Air Power at Bay?

1. Raymond W. Leonard, "Learning from History: Linebacker II and U.S. Air Force Doctrine," *Journal of Military History* 58 (April 1994), 275.

2. US Department of Veterans Affairs, Military Health History Pocket Card, retrieved on August 1, 2019, https://www.va.gov/OAA/pocketcard/m-vietnam.asp.

3. "Constant" was a headquarters USAF Code Word, supposedly named for the call sign of Major General Hoyt S. "Sandy" Vandenberg. Vandenberg was the son of the World War II general and second chief of staff of the USAF. Gaillard R. Peck Jr., *America's Secret MiG Squadron: The Red Eagles of Project CONSTANT PEG* (Oxford, UK: Osprey Publishing, 2012), 59; Grant, "Linebacker I," *Air Force Magazine*.

4. Earl H. Tilford Jr., *Setup: What the Air Force Did in Vietnam and Why* (Maxwell AFB, AL: Air University Press, 1991), 228.

5. Project CHECO, Southeast Asia Report, #231, 9.

6. Ibid., 10.

7. Tilford Jr., *Setup*, 235.

8. Project CHECO, Southeast Asia Report, #231, 9.

9. Grant, "Linebacker I," *Air Force Magazine*.

10. Pribbenow, *Victory in Vietnam*, 317.

11. W. Hays Parks, "Linebacker and the Law of War," *Air University Review*, January–February 1983, http://www.airpower.maxwell.af.mil/airchronicles/aureview/1983/jan-feb/parks.html, retrieved on April 11, 2017; Project CHECO, Southeast Asia Report, #231, 58.

12. Brig. Gen. James R. McCarthy and Lt. Col. Robert E. Rayfield, "Linebacker II: A View from the Rock," *USAF Southeast Asia Monograph Series*, Vol. VI, Monograph 8 (Washington, DC: Office of Air Force History, 1985), 40; William F. Andrews, "To Fly and Fight: The Experience of American Airmen in Southeast Asia" (PhD dissertation, George Mason University, 2011), 324–25; quoted from Mark Clodfelter, "Fifty Shades of Friction," 13.

13. Robert O. Harder, *Flying from the Black Hole: The B-52 Navigator-Bombardiers of Vietnam* (Annapolis, MD: Naval Institute Press, 2013), 11; Michel, *The 11 Days of Christmas*, 67, 83.

14. Harder, *Flying from the Black Hole*, 11.

15. McCarthy and Rayfield, "Linebacker II: A View from the Rock," 47. Although the B-52's official name is the Stratofortress, it is more commonly called the BUFF, for Big Ugly Fat Fucker.

16. "B-52 Raid on Hanoi with Combat Livemap, 12/26/1972," retrieved May 12, 2020, https://youtu.be/60ihI7VU2OY. This particular recording from B-52 "Lilac 01," flying during Linebacker II, contains internal crew communications, Red Crown warnings, and snippets of other B-52 communications. It was recorded on the night of December 26, 1972. The gunner was the only enlisted man on the B-52 crew and was far removed from the rest of the crew, but his position in the rear of the aircraft provided a unique vantage point, and the information he relayed was critical.

17. McCarthy and Rayfield, "Linebacker II: A View from the Rock," 61; Michel, *The 11 Days of Christmas*, 139

18. McCarthy and Rayfield, "Linebacker II: A View from the Rock," 83, 85, 86.

19. Dana Drenkowski and Lester W. Grau, "Patterns and Predictability: The Soviet Evaluation of Operation Linebacker II," *Journal of Slavic Military Studies*, Vol. 20 (2007), 3, 39; Michel, *The 11 Days of Christmas*, 239.

20. Harder, *Flying from the Black Hole*, 14.

21. Michel, *The 11 Days of Christmas*, 33; also MIT web seminar, delivered by Marshall Michel, October 2, 2002, http://web.mit.edu/SSP/seminars/wed_archives02fall/michel.htm.

22. Harder, *Flying from the Black Hole*, 15; Drenkowski and Grau, "Patterns and Predictability," 6.

23. Air Operations Report 73/3, "An Analysis of USAF Combat Damage and Losses in SEA," iii.

24. Richard H. Kohn, *Strategic Air Warfare: An Interview with Generals Curtis E. LeMay, Leon W. Johnson, David A. Burchinal, and Jack J. Catton*, USAF Warrior Studies (Washington DC: Office of Air Force History, 1988), 125.

25. Clodfelter, *The Limits of Air Power*, 203–10.

26. Drenkowski and Grau, "Patterns and Predictability," 1, 11.

27. John D. Sherwood, *Afterburner: Naval Aviators and the Vietnam War* (New York: New York University Press, 2004), 291; Thomas C. Hone, "Strategic

Bombardment Constrained: Korea and Vietnam" in R. Cargill Hall, ed., *Case Studies in Strategic Bombardment* (Washington, DC: Air Force History and Museums Program, 1998), 516. The Vietnamese National Archives published several books on what is considered one of the greatest victories of the "American War," including Nguyen Huu Oanh, *Dien Bien Phu Tren Khong*.

28. Michel, *The 11 Days of Christmas*, 233; TS. LE HUY VINH, "Air Defense Campaign at the End of 1972: A Special Feature of Vietnamese Air Defense Command," *Quoc phong toan dan*, retrieved on May 14, 2020, http://tapchiqptd.vn/vi/su-kien -lich-su/chien-dich-phong-khong-cuoi-nam-1972-net-dac-sac-cua-nghe-thuat-tac -chien-phong-khong-viet-nam/11024.html; Pribbenow, *Victory in Vietnam*, 327.

29. Project CHECO, Southeast Asia Report, #231, 72; McCarthy and Rayfield, "Linebacker II: A View from the Rock," 173.

30. Mersky, *U.S. Marine Corps Aviation Since 1912*, 248; McCarthy and Rayfield, "Linebacker II: A View from the Rock," 175.

31. Clodfelter, "Fifty Shades of Friction," 12.

Chapter 7: Laos, Cambodia, and the War against the Ho Chi Minh Trail

1. Rasimus, *When Thunder Rolled*, 68.

2. Ben Kiernan and Taylor Owen, "Making More Enemies than We Kill? Calculating U.S. Bomb Tonnages Dropped on Laos and Cambodia, and Weighing Their Implications," *Asia-Pacific Journal*, Vol. 13, Issue 16, No. 3 (April 27, 2015), 1–2.

3. Tilford, *Setup*, 195.

4. Ibid., 194.

5. Interview with General Merrill McPeak.

6. Ibid.

7. Ibid.

8. Project CHECO, Southeast Asia Report, #87, "Igloo White (Initial Phase)," July 31, 1968, vi, 1; Project CHECO, Southeast Asia Report, #161, "Igloo White (July 1968–December 1969)," January 10, 1970, 38. Although Igloo White remains the most recognized name of the operation, in its early concepts it was also known as Practice Nine, Illinois City, Dye Marker, and Muscle Shoals.

9. Bernard C. Nalty, *The War Against Trucks: Aerial Interdiction in Southern Laos, 1968–1972* (Washington, DC: Air Force History and Museums Program, 2005), 19; Project CHECO, "IGLOO WHITE (initial Phase)," vi, 4.

10. Project CHECO, Southeast Asia Report, #87, vi, 21–23.

11. Ibid., vi, 19.

12. Ibid., vi, 30–31.

13. Project CHECO, Southeast Asia Report, #202, "Igloo White (January 1970– September 1971)," November 1, 1971, 9.

14. 7th Air Force Report quoted in Project CHECO, Southeast Asia Report, #202, 100.

15. Nalty, *The War Against Trucks*, 296.

16. Project CHECO, Southeast Asia Report, #50, "Second Defense of Lima Site 36 (January 6–7, 1967)," April 28, 1967, 1–2.

17. Matt Proietti, *At All Costs: The True Story of Vietnam War Hero Chief Master Sgt. Dick Etchberger*, Chief Master Sergeant Richard Etchberger Foundation, Kay Press, 2015, 75–79.

18. 3671308017, George J. Veith Collection, Vietnam Center and Archive, Texas Tech University, 7; 11272519010, Garnett Bell Collection, Vietnam Center and Archive, Texas Tech University, 7.

19. Peter Baker, "Nixon Tried to Spoil Johnson's Vietnam Peace Talks in '68, Notes Show," *New York Times*, January 2, 2017; Jason Daley, "Notes Indicate Nixon Interfered with 1968 Peace Talks," *Smithsonian Magazine*, January 2, 2017.

20. Nalty, *Air War Over South Vietnam, 1968–1975*, 127, 129; Nixon Foundation, Kissinger memorandum to the President, March 16, 1969; Karnow, *Vietnam: A History*, 607.

21. Nalty, *Air War Over South Vietnam, 1968–1975*, 133; Tang quoted in Nalty, *The War against Trucks*, 137; 3671215034, George J. Veith Collection, Vietnam Center and Sam Johnson Vietnam Archive, Texas Tech University.

22. 3671215034, George J. Veith Collection, Vietnam Center and Sam Johnson Vietnam Archive, Texas Tech University.

23. Nalty, *Air War Over South Vietnam, 1968–1975*, 133; Nalty, *The War against Trucks*, 137.

24. 3671215034, George J. Veith Collection; "DOD Report on Selected Air and Ground Operations in Cambodia and Laos"; Nalty, *Air War Over South Vietnam, 1968–1975*, 185–86.

25. "Report, Joint Chiefs of Staff–Sensitive Operations in Southeast Asia, 1964–1973," 1071313002, Glenn Helm Collection, Vietnam Center and Sam Johnson Vietnam Archive, Texas Tech University.

26. Project CHECO, Southeast Asia Report, #176, "The Cambodian Campaign, April 29–June 30, 1970," September 1, 1970, xv; Project CHECO, Southeast Asia Report, #185, "The Cambodian Campaign, July–October 1970," December 31, 1970, 50.

27. "Report, Joint Chiefs of Staff–Sensitive Operations in Southeast Asia, 1964–1973"; 3671215034, George J. Veith Collection.

28. Nalty, *The War Against Trucks*, 151; Karnow, *Vietnam: A History*, 629; Mersky, *U.S. Marine Corps Aviation Since 1912*, 239.

29. Kiernan and Owen, "Making More Enemies than We Kill?," 2, 6.

30. Ibid., 6.

31. Thayer, *War without Fronts*, 84; Nalty, *The War Against Trucks*, 299.

Chapter 8: The Air-to-Air War

1. Air Force Historical Research Agency (AFHRA), Richard S. Ritchie OHI, K239.0512–630, 6.

2. Red Baron Reports (RBR), Vol. IV, 19.

3. Project CHECO, Southeast Asia Report, #69, "Air-to-Air Encounters over North Vietnam, January 1–June 30, 1967," November 30, 1967, 3.

4. James N. Eastman Jr., et al., *Aces and Aerial Victories 1965–1973* (Washington, DC: Office of Air Force History, 1976), 117–25; AFHRA, Aerial Victory Credits (contact AFHRA directly to obtain a copy of the database: https://www.afhra.af.mil/Contact-Us/).

5. John Stillion and John Perdue, "Air Combat Past, Present, Future," RAND Report for Project Air Force, August 2008, https://www.defenseindustrydaily.com/files/2008_RAND_Pacific_View_Air_Combat_Briefing.pdf. Since Desert Storm, twenty of sixty-one kills were BVR due in large part to the AIM-120 AMRAAM. Despite this prolific increase in BVR kills, other factors demonstrate that BVR employment is not as certain as sometimes stated. The US Air Force has recorded ten AIM-120 kills, and four of those were not BVR. Furthermore, of those cited, two were non-maneuvering fleeing aircraft, and none of the ten were actively employing electronic countermeasures. In each of these situations the United States had a numerical advantage and none of the enemy aircraft were equipped with a BVR weapon.

6. RBR, Vol. IV, 32–33.

7. Steven A. Fino, *Tiger Check: Automating the US Air Force Fighter Pilot in Air-to-Air Combat, 1950–1980* (Baltimore, MD: Johns Hopkins University Press, 2017), 164, 166.

8. Fino, *Tiger Check*, 171.

9. AFHRA, OHI, F. C. Bleese, K.2390512–1077, 59.

10. Momyer quoted in Steven A. Fino, "Breaking the Trance: The Perils of Technological Exuberance in the U.S. Air Force Entering Vietnam," *Journal of Military History* 77 (April 2013), 632. Momyer did not address his implied disdain for guns on modern fighter aircraft in his autobiography, *Airpower in Three Wars*.

11. Fino, "Breaking the Trance," 637, 644.

12. Ritchie, quoted in Michael Hankins, "The Teaball Solution: The Evolution of Air Combat Technology in Vietnam, 1968–1972," *Air Power History* (Fall 2016), 13; also in AFHRA, Captain Richard S. Ritchie OHI, K239.0512–630, 37; Interview with Colonel C. R. Anderegg.

13. Hankins, "The Teaball Solution," 9.

14. Sherwood, *Nixon's Trident*, 25.

15. Project CHECO, Southeast Asia Report, #69, vi.

16. Project CHECO, Southeast Asia Report, #69, 10; Robin Olds et al., *Fighter Pilot: The Memoirs of Legendary Ace Robin Olds*, 274.

17. For Operation Bolo, see: James R. McGovern, *Black Eagle: General Daniel "Chappie" James* (Tuscaloosa: University of Alabama Press, 2002), 89–92; Robin Olds, *Fighter Pilot: The Memoirs of Legendary Ace Robin Olds* (New York: St. Martin's Griffin Press, 2010), 274, 280–282; Project CHECO, Southeast Asia Report, #69, 50.

18. Momyer quoted in Project CHECO, Southeast Asia Report, #142, "Air-to-Air Encounters Over North Vietnam, July 1967–December 1968," August 30, 1969, 4, 9–10.

19. NHHC, COLL/20, FLAG PLOT/Vietnam, Box 123, Folder 2, "Sparrow and Sidewinder Minimum Range"; Project CHECO, Southeast Asia Report, #142, 5.

20. Project CHECO, Southeast Asia Report, #142, 32.

21. Todd P. Harmer and C. R. Anderegg, "Report of the Project Trigger Study Team: The Shootdown of Trigger 4," Headquarters USAF, April 2001, 3.

22. Laslie, *The Air Force Way of War*, 14; John Stillion, "Trends in Air-to-Air Combat: Implications for Future Air Superiority," Center for Strategic and Budgetary Assessments, 2015, 18; Hankins, "The Teaball Solution," 17–18; C. R. Anderegg, *Sierra Hotel: Flying Air Force Fighters in the Decade after Vietnam* (Washington, DC: Air Force History and Museums Program, 2001), 33.

23. Randy Cunningham, "Naval Intelligence Debriefing of 10 May 1972, MiG Engagement by VF 96," May 1972, 6.

24. Ibid., 8.

25. Drenkowski and Grau, "Patterns and Predictability," 26; Pribbenow, *Victory in Vietnam*, 315.

26. Cunningham, "Naval Intelligence Debriefing of 10 May 1972," 6.

27. Judith Henchy, "Preservation and Archives in Vietnam," February 1998, https://www.clir.org/pubs/reports/henchy/pub70, retrieved on May 1, 2020. According to one researcher, in order to do archival research in Vietnam, "requests for documents must be approved by the director of the archive, the central government agency overlooking the archives (in Hanoi), and then by the storage staff" (http://archivesmadeeasy.pbworks.com/w/page/24662285/Vietnamese%20National%20Archives%20III), retrieved on May 1, 2020. These two authors are Roger Boniface and Istvan Toperczer, neither of whom is American.

28. Istvan Toperczer, *MiG Aces of the Vietnam War* (Atglen, PA: Schiffer Military History Publishing, 2015), 230.

29. Western literature is sparse when it comes to how many aces the VPAF actually had, and the claims of the VPAF do not always match reported losses by the United States. For more detailed information, see Toperczer, *MiG Aces of the Vietnam War*, 230; "North Vietnamese Aces," Acepilots.com, http://acepilots.com/vietnam/viet_aces.html, retrieved on July 19, 2019; Roger Boniface, *MiGs Over North Vietnam: The Vietnam People's Air Force in Combat, 1965–1975* (Mechanicsburg, PA: Stackpole Books, 2008), 215–18.

30. Project CHECO, Southeast Asia Report, #69, 25–26; RBR, Vol. IV, 12; Marshall Michel, *Clashes: Air Combat Over North Vietnam 1965–1972* (Annapolis, MD: Naval Institute Press, 1997), 16.

31. ACC, TAC Files, "SEA Tactics Review Brochure," Vol. I, 1973, 11.

32. RBR, Vol. IV, 14; ACC, TAC Files, "SEA Tactics Review Brochure," 11; AFHRA, OHI, Richard S. Ritchie OHI, K239.0512–630, 16.

33. RBR, Vol. IV, 14; ACC, TAC Files, "SEA Tactics Review Brochure," 11; AFHRA, OHI, Richard S. Ritchie OHI, K239.0512–630, 18–19.

34. ACC, TAC Files, "SEA Tactics Review Brochure," 11.

35. Wayne Thompson, *To Hanoi and Back: The USAF and North Vietnam, 1966–1973* (Washington DC: Air Force History and Museums Program, 2000), 255–56; Michel, *The 11 Days of Christmas*, 244–45. Museums in Hanoi do have displays dedicated to heroic pilots who either shot down a B-52 or used their MiGs to crash into a B-52.

36. Michel, *Clashes: Air Combat over North Vietnam*, 4.

37. RBR, Vol. IV, 2.

38. RBR, Vol. I, 15, 33–34.

39. RBR, Vol. I, 79.

40. RBR, Vol. I, 55, 59.

41. RBR, Vol. I, 59–60.

42. RBR, Vol. I, 59; Fino, *Tiger Check*, 166.

43. RBR, Vol. IV, 1.

44. Ibid.

45. Ibid.

46. RBR, Vol. IV, 5.

47. RBR, Vol. IV, 2.

48. RBR, Vol. IV, 3.

49. AFHRA, Trigger 4 files, K143.044–90, Transcripts and Cockpit Recordings; Harmer and Anderegg, "Report of the Project Trigger Study Team."

50. Harmer and Anderegg, "Report of the Project Trigger Study Team," 9.

51. Ibid., 24.

Denouement and Conclusion

1. Project CHECO, Southeast Asia Report, #9, "Expository Paper #1: Punitive Air Strikes," March 11, 1965, 4.

2. Thayer, *War Without Fronts*, 79.

3. John D. Sherwood, *Afterburner*, 1; Rasimus, *When Thunder Rolled*, 249.

4. Project CHECO, Southeast Asia Report, #204, "The VNAF Air Divisions, Reports on Improvement and Modernization, January 1970–July 1971," November 23, 1971, 2.

5. Project CHECO, Southeast Asia Report, #201, "Vietnamization of the Air War 1970–1971," October 8, 1971, 3.

6. Project CHECO, Southeast Asia Report, #204, 119.

7. Project CHECO, Southeast Asia Report, #201, 21, 29, 73.

8. Richard M. Nixon, *The Memoirs of Richard Nixon* (New York: Grosset & Dunlap, 1978), 587.

9. Tilford, *Setup*, xv.

10. R. A. Mason, ed. *War in the Third Dimension: Essays in Contemporary Air Power* (London: Brassey's Defence Publishers, 1986), 33.

11. NHHC, "Bombing as a Policy Tool in Vietnam."

12. Ibid.

13. AFHRA, George S. Brown Files, 168.7121, folder 19; Air Combat Command, Tactical Air Command Files, box labeled "1973," 1:227; also Laslie, *The Air Force Way of War*, 38.

14. ABC News, "US Completely Lifts Ban on Weapons Sale to Vietnam, Barack Obama Says," May 23, 2016, https://www.abc.net.au/news/2016-05-23/us-completely -lifts-ban-on-weapons-sale-to-vietnam,obama-says/7438794, retrieved on September

1, 2019; Paul Schemm, "Climbing Hamburger Hill 50 Years after the Vietnam War's Brutal, Haunting Battle," *Washington Post*, May 10, 2019, https://www.washington post.com/history/2019/05/10/climbing-hamburger-hill-years-after-vietnam-wars -brutal-haunting-battle, retrieved on September 1, 2019.

15. Ben Kiernan and Taylor Owen, "Making More Enemies than We Kill? Cal-culating US Bomb Tonnages Dropped on Laos and Cambodia, and Weighing Their Implications," *Asia-Pacific Journal*, Vol. 13, Issue 16, No. 3 (April 27, 2015), 1, 6.

16. Lester W. Grau, ed. *The Soviet-Afghan War: How a Superpower Fought and Lost* (Lawrence: University Press of Kansas, 2002), 312.

17. David Halberstam, *The Best and the Brightest* (New York: Ballantine Books [1969] 1992), ix.

18. Karnow, *Vietnam: A History*, 11

19. USAF, Southeast Asia Review, Final Issue, February 28, 1984, 24; Air Force Association, *The Air Force in the Vietnam War*, 25. The USAF procured a total of 833 F-105s in all variants: Knaack, *Encyclopedia of US Air Force Aircraft and Missile Systems, Vol. I, Post–World War II Fighters*, 204.

20. Melissa Dell and Pablo Querubin, "Nation Building through Foreign Inter-vention: Evidence from Discontinuities in Military Strategies" (Harvard and NBER, NYU, June 2016); Bill Murray et al., *Ghostbusters* (Burbank, CA: RCA/Columbia Pictures Home Video, 1984).

21. Mark Bowden, *Hue 1968: A Turning Point in the American War in Vietnam* (New York: Atlantic Monthly Press, 2017), 27; Karnow, *Vietnam, A History*, 19.

Appendix A: JCS 94-Target List

1. AFHRA, K717-0423-28, Rolling Thunder, March 28, 1966, Headquarters PACAF Tac Eval Center, 14–15; Charles Tustin Kamps, "The JCS 94-Target List," *Aerospace Power Journal*, Spring 2001, 73–76.

2. Kamps notes in "The JCS 94-Target List," "Although in the 'barracks' group, a target numbered 27 did not appear in any sources consulted."

3. Kamps notes in "The JCS 94-Target List," "Although in the 'depot' group, a target numbered 65 did not appear in any sources consulted. In a later edition of the list, the number 65.8 was reserved for the Hanoi SAM support facility."

Appendix C: List of Named Aerial Operations during the Vietnam War

1. Stated purpose of Rolling Thunder was to "provide a morale boost to South Vietnamese forces, interdict the flow of supplies going south, and discourage North Vietnamese aggression."

2. In answer to the Easter Offensive.

3. To induce North Vietnam to return to the peace table and bring an end to American involvement in the conflict.

Archival Collections

1. Writing about Vietnam proved to be the most difficult project this author has ever taken on. Much like the air wars of Vietnam themselves, the archives are vast and located in scattered locations across the country, from Washington, DC, to Montgomery, Alabama, to Lubbock, Texas. The air wars crossed all branches of the services as well as diplomatic and political lines. Aerial conflict was strategic, operational, and tactical, often more than one of these at a time. Linking the aerial conflict across years, country borders, and operations was as difficult as locating the sources to tell the story in the first place.

2. Between the Vietnam Center and Archive at Texas Tech University and the Clark Special Collections Branch at the US Air Force Academy, I was able to locate and use the Contemporary Historical Examination of Current Operations (CHECO) Reports of Southeast Asia (1961–1975) (see appendix B). To save space I simply noted a particular Project CHECO Report rather than include which archive they came from. A list of the Project CHECO Reports available from Texas Tech's online database can be found here: http://www.vietnam.ttu.edu/virtualarchive/items .php?item=F031100430004 (No Date, Box 0043, Folder 0004, Sam Johnson Vietnam Archive Collection, The Vietnam Center and Archive, Texas Tech University, accessed May 17, 2017).

Bibliography

Books

Alvarez, Everett, Jr. and Anthony S. Pitch. *Chained Eagle: The True Heroic Story of Eight and One-Half Years as a POW by the First American Shot Down over North Vietnam.* New York: Donald I. Fine, Inc., 1989.

Anderegg, C. R. *Sierra Hotel: Flying Air Force Fighters in the Decade after Vietnam.* Washington, DC: Air Force History and Museums Program, 2001.

Ballard, Jack S. *The United States Air Force in Southeast Asia, Development and Employment of Fixed-Wing Gunships, 1962–1972.* Washington, DC: Office of Air Force History, 1982.

Berger, Carl, Ed. *The United States Air Force in Southeast Asia, 1961–1973: An Illustrated Account.* Washington, DC: Office of Air Force History, 1984.

Blight, David W. *Race and Reunion: The Civil War in American Memory.* Cambridge, MA: Belknap Press/Harvard University Press, 2002.

Boniface, Roger. *MiGs Over North Vietnam: The Vietnam People's Air Force in Combat, 1965–1975.* Mechanicsburg, PA: Stackpole Books, 2008.

Bowden, Mark. *Hue 1968: A Turning Point in the American War in Vietnam.* New York: Atlantic Monthly Press, 2017.

Bowers, Ray L. *The United States Air Force in Southeast Asia: Tactical Airlift.* Washington, DC: Office of Air Force History, 1983.

Buckingham, William A. *Operation Ranch Hand: The Air Force and Herbicides in Southeast Asia, 1961–1971.* Washington, DC: Office of Air Force History, 1982.

Castle, Timothy N. *One Day Too Long: TOP SECRET Site 85 and the Bombing of North Vietnam.* New York: Columbia University Press, 1999.

Clodfelter, Mark. *The Limits of Air Power: The American Bombing of North Vietnam.* New York: Free Press, 1989.

——. *Violating Reality: The Lavelle Affair, Nixon, and the Parsing of Truth*. Washington, DC: National Defense University Press, March 2016.

——. *Fifty Shades of Friction: Combat Climate, B-52 Crews, and the Vietnam War*. Washington, DC: National Defense University Press, September 2016.

Coonts, Stephen. *Flight of the Intruder*. Annapolis, MD: Naval Institute Press, 1986.

Coonts, Stephen, and Barrett Tilman. *Dragon's Jaw: An Epic Story of Courage and Tenacity in Vietnam*. New York: Da Capo Press, 2019.

Cosmas, Graham A. *The Joint Chiefs of Staff and the War in Vietnam 1960–1968, Part 2*. Washington, DC: Office of Joint History, 2009–2012.

——. *The Joint Chiefs of Staff and the War in Vietnam 1960–1968, Part 3*. Washington, DC: Office of Joint History, 2009–2012.

Crane, Conrad C. *American Air Power Strategy in Korea, 1950–1953*. Lawrence: University of Kansas Press, 2000.

Cunningham, Randy. *Fox Two: The Story of America's First Ace in Vietnam*. Mesa, AZ: Champlin Fighter Museum, 1984.

Daddis, Gregory A. *Westmoreland's War: Reassessing American Strategy in Vietnam*. New York: Oxford University Press, 2014.

Day, George E. *Return with Honor*. Mesa, AZ: Champlin Fighter Museum Press, 1989.

Dildy, Douglas C., and Tom Cooper. *F-15C Eagle vs. MiG-23/25: Iraq 1991*. Oxford, UK: Osprey Publishing, 2016.

Eastman, James N. Jr., Walter Hanak, and Lawrence Paszek, eds. *Aces and Aerial Victories 1965–1973*. Washington, DC: Office of Air Force History, 1976.

Echevarria, Antulio J., II. *Reconsidering the American Way of War: US Military Practice from the Revolution to Afghanistan*. Washington, DC: Georgetown University Press, 2014.

Engelman, Larry. *Tears Before the Rain: An Oral History of the Fall of South Vietnam*. New York: Oxford University Press, 1990.

Fino, Steven A. *Tiger Check: Automating the US Air Force Fighter Pilot in Air-to-Air Combat, 1950–1980*. Baltimore, MD: Johns Hopkins University Press, 2017.

Flanagan, John F. *Vietnam Above the Treetops: A Forward Air Controller Reports*. New York: Praeger Publishers, 2003.

Francillon, Rene J. *Tonkin Gulf Yacht Club: US Carrier Operations off Vietnam*. Annapolis, MD: Naval Institute Press, 1988.

Frankum, Ronald B. *Like Rolling Thunder: The Air War in Vietnam 1964–1972*. Boulder, CO: Rowman & Littlefield, 2005.

Futrell, Frank. *The United States Air Force in Southeast Asia: The Advisory Years to 1965*. Washington, DC: Office of Air Force History, 1981.

——. *Ideas, Concepts, Doctrine: Basic Thinking in the United States Air Force 1907–1960*. Maxwell Air Force Base, AL: Air University Press, [1971], 1989.

——. *Ideas, Concepts, Doctrine: Basic Thinking in the United States Air Force 1961–1984*. Maxwell Air Force Base, AL: Air University Press, 1989.

Gallagher Gary W., and Alan T. Nolan, eds. *The Myth of the Lost Cause and Civil War History*. Bloomington: Indiana University Press, 2000.

Grant, Zalin. *Over the Beach*. New York: W. W. Norton, 1986.

Grau, Lester W., ed. *The Soviet-Afghan War: How a Superpower Fought and Lost.* Lawrence: University Press of Kansas, 2002.

Gray, Stephen R. *Rampant Raider: An A-4 Skyhawk Pilot in the Vietnam War.* Annapolis, MD: Naval Institute Press, 2007.

Gropman, Alan L. *Airpower and the Airlift Evacuation of Kham Duc.* Maxwell Air Force Base, AL: Airpower Research Institute, 1979.

Halberstam, David. *The Best and the Brightest.* New York: Ballantine Books, [1969] 1992.

Hall, R. Cargill. *Case Studies in Strategic Bombardment.* Washington, DC: Air Force History and Museums Program, 1998.

Hannah, Craig C. *Striving for Air Superiority: The Tactical Air Command in Vietnam.* College Station, TX: Texas A&M University Press, 2002.

Harder, Robert O. *Flying from the Black Hole: The B-52 Navigator-Bombardiers of Vietnam.* Annapolis, MD: Naval Institute Press, 2009.

Higham, Robin. *Air Power: A Concise History.* Manhattan, KS: Sunflower University Press, 1984.

Higham, Robin, and Stephen J. Harris, eds. *Why Air Forces Fail: The Anatomy of Defeat.* Lexington: The University Press of Kentucky, 2006.

Higham, Robin, and Carol Williams. *Flying Combat Aircraft of the USAAF-USAF* (Vol. 2). Manhattan, KS: Sunflower University Press, 1978.

Horwood, Ian. *Interservice Rivalry and Airpower in the Vietnam War.* Leavenworth, KS: Combat Studies Institute Press, 2006.

Howarth, Stephen. *To Shining Sea: A History of the United States Navy, 1775–1991.* New York: Random House, 1991.

Hughes, Thomas P. *Human Built World: How to Think about Technology and Culture.* Chicago: University of Chicago Press, 2004.

Kaplan, Edward. *To Kill Nations: American Strategy in the Air—Atomic Age and the Rise of Mutually Assured Destruction.* Ithaca, NY: Cornell University Press, 2015.

Kitfield, James. *Prodigal Soldiers: How the Generation of Officers Born of Vietnam Revolutionized the American Style of War.* Washington, DC: Brassey's Publishing, 1995.

Knaack, Marcelle Size. *Encyclopedia of US Air Force Aircraft and Missile Systems, Volume 1: Post–World War II Fighters.* Washington, DC: Air Force Office of History, 1978.

———. *Encyclopedia of US Air Force Aircraft and Missile Systems, Volume 2: Post–World War II Bombers.* Washington, DC: Air Force Office of History, 1988.

Kohn, Richard H. *Strategic Air Warfare: An Interview with Generals Curtis E. LeMay, Leon W. Johnson, David A. Burchinal, and Jack J. Catton* (USAF Warrior Studies). Washington DC: Office of Air Force History, 1988.

Laslie, Brian D. *The Air Force Way of War: U.S. Tactics and Training after Vietnam.* Lexington: University Press of Kentucky, 2015.

Lavelle, A. J. C., ed. *USAF Southeast Asia Monograph Series. Volumes I–V.* Washington, DC: Office of Air Force History, 1985.

———. *The Vietnamese Air Force, 1951–1975: An Analysis of its Role in Combat and Fourteen Hours at Koh Tang.* Washington, DC: Office of Air Force History, 1985.

Linn, Brian McAllister. *The Echo of Battle: The Army's Way of* War. Cambridge, MA: Harvard University Press, 2007.

Llinares, Rick, and Chuck Lloyd. *Warfighters: The Story of the USAF Weapons School and the 57th Wing.* Atglen, PA: Schiffer Military Press, 1996.

Luu Trong Lan. *The Christmas Bombing—Dien Bien Phu in the Air: A Triumph of Vietnamese Will and Intelligence.* Hanoi, Vietnam: Gioi Publishers, 2004.

MacGarrigle, George L. *Combat Operations: Taking the Offensive, October 1966– October 1967* (The United States Army in Vietnam). Washington, DC: US Army Center for Military History, 1998.

Marolda, Edward J. *By Sea, Air, and Land: An Illustrated History of the US Navy and the War in Southeast Asia.* Washington, DC: Naval Historical Center, 1994.

Mason, R. A., ed. *War in the Third Dimension: Essays in Contemporary Air Power.* London, UK: Brassey's Defence Publishers, 1986.

McCarthy, Brig. Gen. James R. and Lt. Col. Robert E. Rayfield. "Linebacker II: A View from the Rock." *USAF Southeast Asia Monograph Series,* Vol. VI, Monograph 8. Washington, DC: Office of Air Force History, 1985.

McGovern, James R. *Black Eagle: General Daniel "Chappie" James, Jr.* Tuscaloosa: University Press of Alabama, 1985.

McNamara, Robert S., James G. Blight, and Robert K. Brigham. Robert K. *Argument without End: In Search of Answers to the Vietnam Tragedy.* New York: PublicAffairs, 1999.

McPeak, Merrill. *Hangar Flying.* Lake Oswego, OR: Lost Wingman Press, 2012.

Mersky, Peter B. *U.S. Marine Corps Aviation Since 1912* (4th ed.). Annapolis, MD: Naval Institute Press, 2009.

Mersky, Peter B., and Norman Polmar. *The Naval Air War in Vietnam.* Baltimore, MD: Nautical and Aviation Publishing Company of America, 1986.

Michel, Marshall. *Clashes: Air Combat Over North Vietnam, 1965–1972.* Annapolis, MD: Naval Institute Press, 1997.

———. *The 11 Days of Christmas: America's Last Vietnam Battle.* New York: Encounter Books, 2001.

Millett, Allan R., and Peter Maslowski. *For the Common Defense: A Military History of the United States of America.* New York: Free Press, 1984.

Mitchell, William. *Winged Defense.* Mineola, NY: Dover Publications, 2006.

Momyer, William W. *Airpower in Three Wars (WWII, Korea, Vietnam).* Maxwell Air Force Base, AL: Air University Press, 2003.

Moyar, Mark. *Triumph Forsaken: The Vietnam War, 1954–1965.* New York: Cambridge University Press, 2006.

Mrozek, Donald J. *Air Power and the Ground War in Vietnam: Ideas and Actions.* Maxwell Air Force Base, AL: Air University Press, 1988.

———. *The US Air Force after Vietnam: Postwar Challenges and Potential for Responses.* Maxwell Air Force Base, AL: Air University Press, 1988.

Nalty, Bernard C. *Air Power and the Fight for Khe Sanh.* Washington, DC: Office of Air Force History, 1986.

———. *Air War Over South Vietnam, 1968–1975.* Washington, DC: Air Force History and Museums Program, 2000.

———. *The War Against Trucks: Aerial Interdiction in Southern Laos, 1968–1972.* Washington, DC: Air Force History and Museums Program, 2005.

Newman, Rick, and Don Shepperd. *Bury Us Upside Down: The Misty Pilots and the Secret Battle for the Ho Chi Minh Trail.* New York: Presidio Press, 2007.

Nichols, John B., and Barrett Tillman. *On Yankee Station: The Naval Air War Over Vietnam.* Annapolis, MD: Naval Institute Press, 1987.

Nixon, Richard M. *The Memoirs of Richard Nixon.* New York: Grosset & Dunlap, 1978.

Olds, Robin, Christina Olds, and Ed Rasimus. *Fighter Pilot: The Memoirs of Legendary Ace Robin Olds.* New York: St. Martin's Griffin Press, 2010.

Olsen, John Andreas, ed. *A History of Air Warfare.* Washington, DC: Potomac Books, 2010.

———. *Air Commanders.* Washington, DC: Potomac Books, 2012.

Pape, Robert A. *Bombing to Win: Air Power and Coercion in War.* Ithaca, NY: Cornell University Press, 1996.

Peck, Gaillard R. Jr. *America's Secret MiG Squadron: The Red Eagles of Project CONSTANT PEG.* Oxford, UK: Osprey Publishing, 2012.

Pedersen, Dan. *Top Gun: An American Story.* New York: Hachette Books, 2019.

Prados, John. Vietnam: The History of an Unwinnable War, 1945-1975. Lawrence, KS: University Press of Kansas, 2009.

Pribbenow, Merle L. *Victory in Vietnam: The Official History of the People's Army of Vietnam, 1954–1975,* trans. Lawrence: University Press of Kansas, 2002.

Proietti, Matt. *At All Costs: The True Story of Vietnam War Hero Chief Master Sgt. Dick Etchberger.* Chief Master Sergeant Richard Etchberger Foundation, Kay Press, 2015.

Rasimus, Ed. *When Thunder Rolled: An F-105 Pilot over North Vietnam.* Washington, DC: Smithsonian Press, 2003.

———. *Palace Cobra: A Fighter Pilot in the Vietnam Air War.* New York: St. Martin's Press, 2006.

Reardon, Carol. *Launch the Intruders: A Naval Attack Squadron in the Vietnam War, 1972.* Lawrence: University Press of Kansas, 2005.

Rich, Ben, and Leo Janos. *Skunk Works.* New York: Little, Brown and Company, 1994.

Robbins, Christopher. *The Ravens: Pilots of the Secret War of Laos.* Bangkok, Thailand: Asia Books, 2000.

Rochester, Stuart I. *The Battle Behind Bars: Navy and Marine POWs in the Vietnam War.* Washington, DC: Naval History and Heritage Command, 2010.

Salter, James. *The Hunters.* New York: Vintage International Press, 1999.

Schlight, John. *A War Too Long: The History of the USAF in Southeast Asia, 1961–1975.* Washington, DC: Air Force History and Museums Program, 1996.

———. *The War in South Vietnam: The Years of the Offensive, 1965–1968.* Washington, DC: Air Force History and Museums Program, 1999.

———. *Help from Above: Air Force Close Air Support of the Army, 1946–1973.* Washington, DC: Air Force History and Museums Program, 2003.

Schulimson, Jack. *The Joint Chiefs of Staff and the War in Vietnam, 1960–1968, Part 1.* Washington, DC: Office of Joint History, 2011.

Sharp, Ulysses S. G. *Strategy for Defeat: Vietnam in Retrospect.* Novato, CA: Presidio Press, 1998.

Sheehan, Neil. *A Bright Shining Lie: John Paul Vann and America in Vietnam.* New York: Random House, 1988.

Shepperd, Don, ed. *Misty: First-Person Stories of the F-100 Fast-FACs in the Vietnam War.* 1st Books Library, 2002.

Sherwood, John D. *Afterburner: Naval Aviators and the Vietnam War.* New York: New York University Press, 2004.

———. *Nixon's Trident: Naval Power in Southeast Asia, 1968–1972.* Washington, DC: Naval History and Heritage Command, 2009.

Slife, James C. *Creech Blue: General Bill Creech and the Reformation of the Tactical Air Forces.* Maxwell Air Force Base, AL: Air University Press, 2008.

Thayer, Thomas C. *War Without Fronts: The American Experience in Vietnam.* Boulder, CO: Westview Press, 1985.

Thompson, Wayne. *To Hanoi and Back: The USAF and North Vietnam, 1966–1973.* Washington, DC: Air Force History and Museums Program, 2000.

Thorsen, Terry L. *Phantom in the Sky: A Marine's Back Seat View of the Vietnam War.* Denton: University of North Texas Press, 2019.

Tilford, Earl H. Jr. *Setup: What the Air Force Did in Vietnam and Why.* Maxwell Air Force Base, AL: Air University Press, 1991.

———. *The USAF Search and Rescue in Southeast Asia.* Washington, DC: Center for Air Force History, 1992.

Tolson, John T. *Airmobility: 1961–1971.* Washington, DC: Department of the Army, US Government Printing Office, 1999.

Toperczer, Istvan. *MiG Aces of the Vietnam War.* Atglen, PA: Schiffer Military History Publishing, 2015.

Trest, Warren A. *Air Force: Roles and Missions.* Washington, DC: Air Force History and Museums Program, 1998.

———. *Air Commando One: Heinie Aderholt and America's Secret Air Wars.* Washington, DC: Smithsonian Institute Press, 2000.

Van Creveld, Martin. *The Age of Airpower.* New York: PublicAffairs, 2011.

Van Staaveren, Jacob. *Interdiction in Southern Laos, 1960–1968.* Washington, DC: Center for Air Force History, 1993.

———. *Gradual Failure: The Air War over North Vietnam, 1965–1966.* Washington, DC: Air Force History and Museums Program, 2002.

Webb, William J. *The Joint Chiefs of Staff and the War in Vietnam, 1969–1970.* Washington, DC: Office of Joint History, 2002.

Webb, William J., and Walter S. Poole. *The Joint Chiefs of Staff and the War in Vietnam 1971–1973.* Washington, DC: Office of Joint History, 2007.

Weigley, Russell F. *The American Way of War: A History of the United States Military Strategy and Policy.* Bloomington: Indiana University Press, 1973.

Werrell, Kenneth P. *Chasing the Silver Bullet: U.S. Air Force Weapons Development from Vietnam to Desert Storm.* Washington, DC: Smithsonian Press, 2003.

Westmoreland, William. *A Soldier Reports.* New York: Doubleday, 1976.

White, William D. *U.S. Tactical Air Power: Missions, Forces, and Costs*. Washington, DC: The Brookings Institute, 1974.

Worden, Mike. *Rise of the Fighter Generals: The Problem of Air Force Leadership, 1945–1982*. Maxwell Air Force Base, AL: Air University Press, 1998.

Zuyev, Alexander. *Fulcrum: A Top Gun Pilot's Escape from the Soviet Empire*. New York: Warner Books, 1992.

Articles

Baker, Peter. "Nixon Tried to Spoil Johnson's Vietnam Peace Talks in '68, Notes Show," *New York Times*, January 2, 2017.

Correll, John T. "Disunity of Command," *Air Force* magazine, January 1, 2005, https://www.airforcemag.com/article/0105disunity, retrieved July 2, 2020.

Daley, Jason. "Notes Indicate Nixon Interfered with 1968 Peace Talks," *Smithsonian Magazine*, January 2, 2017.

Drenkowski, Dana, and Lester W. Grau. "Patterns and Predictability: The Soviet Evaluation of Operation Linebacker II," *Journal of Slavic Military Studies*, Vol. 20 (2007).

Fino, Steven A. "Breaking the Trance: The Perils of Technological Exuberance in the U.S. Air Force Entering Vietnam," *Journal of Military History*, 77, April 2013, 625–55.

Goure, Leon. "Southeast Asia Trip Report, Part I: The Impact of Air Power in South Vietnam." Santa Monica, CA: RAND, December 1964, RM-4400-PR (Part 1).

Grant, Rebecca. "Linebacker I," *Air Force Magazine*, June 2012.

Hallion, Richard. "America as a Military Aerospace Nation," in John Andreas Olsen, ed., *Airpower Applied*. Annapolis, MD: Naval Institute Press, 2017.

Hankins, Michael W. "The Teaball Solution: The Evolution of Air Combat Technology in Vietnam, 1968–1972," *Air Power History* (Fall 2016).

Head, William. "A Re-Assessment of the Battle of Ia Drang Valley, 1965: The Role of Airpower, Heroic Soldiers, and the Wrong Lessons," *Virginia Review of Asian Studies*, Vol. 16 (2014).

Kamps, Charles Tustin. "The JCS 94-Target List: A Vietnam Myth that Distorts Military Thought," *Aerospace Power Journal* (Spring 2001).

Kiernan, Ben, and Taylor Owen. "Making More Enemies than We Kill? Calculating US Bomb Tonnages Dropped on Laos and Cambodia, and Weighing Their Implications," *Asia-Pacific Journal*, Vol. 13, Issue 16, No. 3 (April 27, 2015).

Leonard, Raymond W. "Learning from History: Linebacker II and U.S. Air Force Doctrine," *Journal of Military History* 58 (April 1994), 267–303.

Linder, James C. "The War in Laos: The Fall of Lima Site 85 in March 1968," *Studies in Intelligence*, Vol. 59, No. 2015, 1120.

McCain, John. "John McCain: How Neil Armstrong Inspired a POW," *Washington Post*, September 13, 2012, https://www.washingtonpost.com/opinions/john-mccain-how-neil-armstrong-inspired-a-pow/2012/09/13/5bd707e2-fdc0-11e1-b153-218509a954e1_story.html, retrieved on September 27, 2019.

McManus, Doyle, and Stephanie Grace. "Some Vietnam POWs May Be Alive in Russia," *Los Angeles Times*, June 16, 1992, retrieved on May 8, 2018, http://articles .latimes.com/1992-06-16/news/mn-472_1_vietnam-war.

Parks, W. Hays. "Linebacker and the Law of War," *Air University Review*, January–February 1983, http://www.airpower.maxwell.af.mil/airchronicles/aureview/1983/jan-feb/parks.html.

Schemm, Paul. "Climbing Hamburger Hill 50 Years after the Vietnam War's Brutal, Haunting Battle," *Washington Post*, May 10, 2019, https://www.washingtonpost .com/history/2019/05/10/climbing-hamburger-hill-years-after-vietnam-wars -brutal-haunting-battle, retrieved on September 1, 2019.

UCR, CBSR. "American Warplanes Drop Bombs on North Vietnam's Largest MiG Field," *Medera Tribune*, Vol. 76, No. 112, October 24, 1976, https://cdnc.ucr .edu/?a=d&d=MT19671024.2.8&e=-------en--20--1--txt-txIN--------1, retrieved on June 24, 2019.

Werrell, Kenneth P. "Linebacker II: The Decisive Use of Airpower?" *Air University Review*, January–March 1987, retrieved from http://www.airpower.maxwell.af.mil/airchronicles/aureview/1987/werrell.html.

Military Documents

"After Action Report: The Battle for A Shau," 1070309025, Glenn Helm Collection, Vietnam Center and Archive, Texas Tech University.

"Agreement on the Cessation of Hostilities in Viet-Nam," July 20, 1954, Article 17, paragraph (a), retrieved from https://www.mtholyoke.edu/acad/intrel/genevacc .htm on April 8, 2020.

Air Base Wing, Office of History. "A Brief History of the 3rd Wing," no date, retrieved from https://www.jber.jb.mil/Portals/144/units/3wg/PDF/3wg-lineage.pdf, March 1, 2020.

Air Combat Command (ACC). Tactical Air Command Files, "1965," Vol. 1.

——. Tactical Air Command Files, "1973," 1:227.

——. Tactical Air Command Files. "SEA Tactics Review Brochure," Vol. I, 1973.

Air Force Association (AFA). Misty Fast-FAC Panel, 2011; transcription in author's collection.

——. "The US Air Force in the Vietnam War."

Air Force Historical Research Agency (AFHRA), "Aerial Victory Credits/Tables WWI, WWII, Korea, Vietnam, Database." (Contact AFHRA directly to obtain a copy of the database: https://www.afhra.af.mil/Contact-Us.)

——. Air War College Report No. 3634, "Target Selection Process: Categories and Decision Levels," by Lt. Col. William E. Long, April of 1968, IRIS 01103665.

——. General John D. Ryan files, 168.7085, folder 61.

——. George S. Brown Files, 168.7121, folder 19.

——. K717-0423-28, Rolling Thunder, March 28, 1966, Headquarters PACAF Tac Eval Center.

——. OHI, F. C. Bleese, K.2390512–1077.

———. OHI, Lt. Col. Billie Keeler.

———. OHI, Richard S. Ritchie, K239.0512–630.

———. Research Guide to the Contemporary Historical Examination of Current Operations (CHECO) Reports of Southeast Asia (1961–1975).

———. Trigger 4 files, K143.044–90, Transcripts and Cockpit Recordings.

Air Mobility Command (AMC), Office of History, "Vietnam: The First Tanker War," retrieved from https://www.amc.af.mil/News/Article-Display/Article/147242/vietnam-the-first-tanker-war, on August 30, 2019.

Air Operations Report 73/3, "An Analysis of USAF Combat Damage and Losses in SEA."

Air University Library, "SEAsia Tactics Review Brochure," April 1973.

"BREVITY Multiservice Brevity Codes," headquarters TRADOC, 2002.

"A Brief History of the 3rd Wing," 673 Air Base Wing, Office of History, no date, retrieved from Joint Base Elmendorf-Richardson Alaska, https://www.jber.jb.mil/Portals/144/units/3wg/PDF/3wg-lineage.pdf, March 1, 2020.

Brief Report, Re: In-Country Clearance for Wild Weasel Aircraft [Best Quality], Support Document from Project CHECO Report #228, 10 March 1966, Folder 1109, Box 0012, Vietnam Archive Collection, Vietnam Center and Archive, Texas Tech University, accessed June 14, 2017, https://www.vietnam.ttu.edu/virtualarchive/items.php?item=F031100121109.

Bud Harton Collection. Vietnam Center and Archive, Texas Tech University.

Central Intelligence Agency Collection. Vietnam Center and Archive, Texas Tech University.

Cunningham, Randy. "Naval Intelligence Debriefing of 10 May 1972, MiG Engagement by VF 96," May 1972.

"DOD Report on Selected Air and Ground Operations in Cambodia and Laos." Library of Congress, https://tile.loc.gov/storage-services/service/frd/pwmia/364/112650.pdf, September 10, 1973.

Douglas Pike Collection, Unit 03–Technology, Vietnam Center and Archive, Texas Tech University, https://vva.vietnam.ttu.edu/repositories/2/resources/984.

E-mail from "sparkies" to The CASBar, re: Where we came from before Wild Weasel, November 12, 1998, Folder 01, Box 03, Jan Churchill Collection, Vietnam Center and Archive, Texas Tech University, accessed June 9, 2017, https://www.vietnam.ttu.edu/virtualarchive/items.php?item=13550301065.

"Excerpts from Sitreps Pertaining to Action at Kham Duc." Support Document from Project CHECO Report #129, No Date, Folder 1037, Box 0004, Vietnam Archive Collection, Vietnam Center and Archive, Texas Tech University, accessed May 17, 2017, http://www.vietnam.ttu.edu/virtualarchive/items.php?item=F031100041037.

Garnett Bell Collection. Vietnam Center and Archive, Texas Tech University.

"General William Wallace Momyer." Official US Air Force biography, http://www.af.mil/AboutUs/Biographies/Display/tabid/225/Article/106156/general-william-wallace-momyer.aspx, retrieved February 2, 2017.

George J. Veith Collection. Vietnam Center and Archive, Texas Tech University.

Harmer, Todd P., and C. R. Anderegg. "Report of the Project Trigger Study Team: The Shootdown of Trigger 4," Headquarters USAF, April 2001.

Holloway III, Admiral James L., USN (Ret.). "Tactical Command and Control of Carrier Operations," given at the Colloquium on Contemporary History, January 23, 1991, No. 4.

Merle Pribbenow Collection. Vietnam Center and Archive, Texas Tech University.

Message, Re: Wild Weasel/Iron Hand Tactics [Best Quality], Support Document from Project CHECO Report #228, 09 December 1966, Folder 1142, Box 0012, Vietnam Archive Collection, Vietnam Center and Archive, Texas Tech University, accessed June 14, 2017, https://www.vietnam.ttu.edu/virtualarchive/items.php?item=F031100121142.

Muir S. Fairchild Research and Information Center (MSFRIC). Fairchild Documents, "SEA Tactics Review Brochure, Vol. I."

National Museum of the United States Air Force (NMUSAF). "OPERATION NIAGARA: A Waterfall of Bombs at Khe Sanh," retrieved from https://www.nationalmuseum.af.mil/Visit/Museum-Exhibits/Fact-Sheets/Display/Article/195674/operation-niagara-a-waterfall-of-bombs-at-khe-sanh on August 23, 2019.

Rabben, E. L., and C. L. Beckel. "WSEG Staff Study 124: A Method for Finding Targets on the Ho Chi Minh Trail," Defense Documentation Center, June 1966.

"Report, Joint Chiefs of Staff–Sensitive Operations in Southeast Asia, 1964–1973," 1071313002, Glenn Helm Collection, Vietnam Center and Sam Johnson Vietnam Archive, Texas Tech University.

Richard Hamilton Collection, Vietnam Center and Archive, Texas Tech University. https://vva.vietnam.ttu.edu/repositories/2/digital_objects/121249.

US Department of Veterans Affairs, Military Health History Pocket Card, retrieved on August 1, 2019, https://www.va.gov/OAA/pocketcard/m-vietnam.asp.

AFHSO Special Studies/Blue Books

Nalty, Bernard C. "Tactics and Techniques of Electronic Warfare: Electronic Countermeasures in the Air War Against North Vietnam, 1965–1973," 1977.

Pfau, Richard A., and William H. Greenhalgh Jr. "The B-57G–Tropic Moon III, 1967–1972."

Rowley, Ralph A. "Tactics and Techniques of Close Air Support Operations, 1961–1973," 1976.

USAF Statistical Review, 1965, https://www.afhistory.af.mil/USAF-STATISTICS/.

Van Staaveren, Jacob. "USAF Deployment Planning for Southeast Asia," 1967.

———. "The Air Force in Southeast Asia: Toward a Bombing Halt," 1968.

———. "USAF Plans and Operations: The Air Campaign Against North Vietnam, 1966," 1968.

Miscellaneous

ABC News. "US Completely Lifts Ban on Weapons Sale to Vietnam, Barack Obama Says," May 23, 2016, https://www.abc.net.au/news/2016-05-23/us-completely-lifts

-ban-on-weapons-sale-to-vietnam,obama-says/7438794, retrieved on September 1, 2019.

Back to School. Film directed by Alan Metter. Los Angeles, CA: Orion Pictures, 1986.

Dell, Melissa, and Pablo Querubin. "Nation Building through Foreign Intervention: Evidence from Discontinuities in Military Strategies," Harvard and NBER, NYU, June 2016.

Ghostbusters. Burbank, CA: RCA/Columbia Pictures Home Video, 1984.

Good Morning, Vietnam. Film directed by Barry Levinson. Los Angeles, CA: Touchstone Pictures, 1987.

Henchy, Judith. "Preservation and Archives in Vietnam." Council on Library and Information Resources, February 1998, https://www.clir.org/pubs/reports/henchy/pub70, retrieved on May 1, 2020.

Lyndon Johnson Oral History Collection at the Miller Center for Public Affairs, University of Virginia, General Joseph McConnell, August 28, 1969.

———. University of Virginia, General Curtis LeMay, June 28, 1971.

Michel, Marshall. MIT web seminar, delivered October 2, 2002, http://web.mit.edu/SSP/seminars/wed_archives02fall/michel.htm.

News 5 Cleveland. "How News of the *Apollo 11* Mission Made It to the POWs in the Hanoi Hilton," https://www.youtube.com/watch?v=gbObXyfFhJ4, retrieved on September 2, 2019.

Nixon Foundation. Kissinger memorandum to the President, March 16, 1969.

"Norman Dale Eaton." Arlington Cemetery, http://www.arlingtoncemetery.net/ndeaton.htm, accessed September 20, 2019.

"North Vietnamese Aces." Acepilots.com, http://acepilots.com/vietnam/viet_aces.html, retrieved on July 19, 2019.

Rogers, Clifford J., and Ty Seidule, senior editors. *The West Point History of Warfare*, vol. 7, http://www.westpointhistoryofwarfare.com, USAFA H100-Introduction to Military History, Gregory A. Daddis, "American Escalation in Vietnam 1965–1967," chapter 29.6.

Stephens Sr., Lieutenant Colonel Dallas K. Audio recording of letter, in author's collection.

Stillion, John. "Trends in Air-to-Air Combat: Implications for Future Air Superiority," Center for Strategic and Budgetary Assessments, 2015.

Stillion, John, and John Perdue. "Air Combat Past, Present, Future," RAND Report for Project Air Force, August 2008, https://www.defenseindustrydaily.com/files/2008_RAND_Pacific_View_Air_Combat_Briefing.pdf.

TS. LE HUY VINH, "Air Defense Campaign at the End of 1972: A Special Feature of Vietnamese Air Defense Command," *Quoc phong toan dan*, retrieved on May 14, 2020, http://tapchiqptd.vn/vi/su-kien-lich-su/chien-dich-phong-khong-cuoi-nam-1972-net-dac-sac-cua-nghe-thuat-tac-chien-phong-khong-viet-nam/11024.html.

Van Tin, Nguyen. "The Use of B-52 Strike in Ia Drang Campaign General Westmoreland's Best Kept Military Secret," February 19, 2016, retrieved from http://www.generalhieu.com/iadrang_westmoreland_best_kept_secret-2.htm on August 20, 2019.

Theses and Dissertations

Andrews, William F. "To Fly and Fight: The Experience of American Airmen in Southeast Asia," PhD dissertation, George Mason University, 2011.

Dong Nguyen Ha. "The Ho Chi Minh Trail and Operation Commando Hunt: The Failure of an Aerial Interdiction Campaign," University of North Texas, 2020.

Fino, Steven A. "'All the Missiles Work': Technological Dislocations and Military Innovation: A Case Study on US Air Force Air-to-Air Armament Post–World War II through Operation Rolling Thunder," School of Advanced Air and Space Studies, Drew Papers #12, 2015.

Hoadley, Daniel S. "What Just Happened? A Historical Evaluation of Project CHECO," School of Advanced Air and Space Studies, Air University, 2013.

Thompson, Robert John III. "More Sieve than Shield: The U.S. Army and CORDS in the Pacification of Phu Yen Province, Republic of Vietnam, 1965–1972," University of Southern Mississippi, 2016.

Interviews

Anderegg, C. R. Interview with author, October 5, 2016.

Beakley, Ed. Interview with author, February 15, 2017.

McPeak, General Merrill, USAF (Ret.). Interview with author, September 30, 2016.

Smith, Fred. Interview with author, April 21, 2017.

Index

About the Author

Brian D. Laslie is deputy command historian at the North American Aerospace Defense Command (NORAD) and United States Northern Command (USNORTHCOM) as well as an adjunct professor at both the US Air Force Academy and The Citadel. A 2001 graduate of The Citadel, he received his PhD from Kansas State University. He is the author of *The Air Force Way of War: U.S. Tactics and Training After Vietnam*, which was selected for the 2016 Chief of Staff of the Air Force reading list and the 2017 Chief of the Royal Air Force reading list, and *Architect of Air Power: General Laurence S. Kuter and the Birth of the United States Air Force*. He can be reached at https://www.brianlaslie.com.

War and Society

Series Editors: Michael B. Barrett and Kyle Sinisi

The study of military history has evolved greatly over the past fifty years, and the "War and Society" series captures these changes with the publication of books on all aspects of war. The series not only examines traditional military history with its attention to battles and leaders, but also explores the broader impact of war upon the military and society. Affecting culture, politics, economies, and state power, wars have transformed societies since the ancient world. With books that cut across all time periods and geographical areas, this series reveals the history of both the conduct of war and its societal consequences.

Gabriel Baker, *Spare No One: Mass Violence in Roman Warfare*

Marc Gallicchio, *The Scramble for Asia: U.S. Military Power in the Aftermath of the Pacific War*

Brian D. Laslie, *Air Power's Lost Cause: The American Air Wars of Vietnam*

Geoffrey Megargee, *War of Annihilation: Combat and Genocide on the Eastern Front, 1941*

Lawrence Sondhaus, *German Submarine Warfare in World War I: The Onset of Total War at Sea*

Haruo Tohmatsu and H. P. Willmott, *A Gathering Darkness: The Coming of War to the Far East and the Pacific, 1921–1942*

Alan Warren, *Slaughter and Stalemate in 1917: British Offensives from Messines Ridge to Cambrai*

H. P. Willmott, *The War with Japan: The Period of Balance, May 1942–October 1943*

Thomas W. Zeiler, *Unconditional Defeat: Japan, America, and the End of World War II*

Milton Keynes UK
Ingram Content Group UK Ltd.
UKHW021410031023
429866UK00034B/611